The

A

The Pentathlon of the Ancient World

FRANK ZARNOWSKI

McFarland & Company, Inc., Publishers
Jefferson, North Carolina, and London

ISBN 978-0-7864-6783-9
softcover : acid free paper ∞

LIBRARY OF CONGRESS CATALOGUING DATA ARE AVAILABLE

BRITISH LIBRARY CATALOGUING DATA ARE AVAILABLE

On the cover: Interior of an Attic red-figure kylix,
ca. 510–500 BCE (Campana Gallery, Louvre Museum)

Manufactured in the United States of America

*McFarland & Company, Inc., Publishers
Box 611, Jefferson, North Carolina 28640
www.mcfarlandpub.com*

For Sarah, Rachel
and the Boyers

Table of Contents

Preface

Each spring I spend a week in the Austrian Alps with the world's most knowledgeable people on track and field's decathlon and heptathlon, what are encapsulated in the world of athletics as "combined events." One, Rooney Magnusson, is a retired university mathematician from Stockholm. The other is an engineer, Konrad Lerch, who directs the famous Hypo-Bank combined-events meeting in Götzis, Austria, an annual gathering that attracts the genre's best athletes.

I travel to this village in the Alps to officiate, report, advise, referee, and shout approval for the world's most versatile athletes. But mostly I go to talk with Magnusson and Lerch, men who are the modern brain trust of an athletic concept that stretches back three millennia.

That concept of athletic versatility no doubt began in the Peloponnese either in the late 8th or early 7th century B.C. The Greeks selected five events as their test of all-around excellence and called it "pentathlon" (five struggles). The modern secretariat uses ten and today the track and field test of versatility—encompassing basic skills of speed, strength, spring and endurance—is called decathlon. The event is utilized to determine the holder of the title "world's greatest athlete." More than any other place that appellation is bestowed in Götzis. The world record has been set here on three occasions.[1]

My first decathlon book, a history, included a chapter on the ancient pentathlon, simply assuming, like everyone else, that my subject had its roots in its archaic Greek counterpart.[2] Like most modern track and field writers, I was more fan than scholar, and this supposition, it seemed, was a no-brainer. The truth, however, is much more complicated.

A second book uncovered a wholly contemporary and different story on how the decathlon (and its subsequent gender and indoor spin-offs) began.[3] The ancient Greek pentathlon played no more than a minor role in the development of its modern relative. Nonetheless, my interest in the ancient pentathlon provided the welcome opportunity to write this book, the third in a reverse trilogy, which completes the history of combined events.

I surmised that, because of its close association with the ancient Olympic Games, much information about the pentathlon would be readily available. What I found was a quagmire of explanations, descriptions and opinions on the pentathlon's conduct and significance. Specifically, there seemed no consensus on the order of events, how the winners were determined, and, more importantly, whether anyone cared outside a small group of classical scholars. Much of what I found was unreliable, or worse, simply false. I felt like I was doing research on the Internet and did not know what to believe. Much of the unreliability can be explained because some of the ancient texts were undependable. And modern scholars simply picked up and reported these misconceptions as the truth. As a result, much of what I found about the pentathlon, from overviews to technical material, was flawed.

The appeal to me was that the ancient pentathlon had all of the trappings of its modern equivalent but without the numbers. Gone were scores, recorded times in minutes, tenths or hundredths of seconds, and measurements in meters, feet, inches. And no points, no scoring tables. But the basic idea, to conceive a test of all-around athletic ability, remained. I dove into research knowing that there was no great need for a book like this except among classical scholars and for the dedicated enthusiasts who pack the stands or line the fields in places like Götzis, or Talence, France, or Eugene, Oregon, or Bernhausen, Germany, or Des Moines, Iowa, or DeSanzano, Italy, trying to get a glimpse of the world's best athletes.

What I brought to the investigation was half a century of experience of competing in, organizing, coaching, promoting, conducting and reporting combined events. My training as an economist helped. Many aspects of combined events are universal and do not apply just to the modern era of sport. They apply just as fittingly to ancient Greece. The amount of misinformation about the ancient pentathlon, due to a lack of understanding of athletics in general and combined events in particular, has been truly Olympic. I compiled a library of everything on the subject: 200 journal articles, books, unpublished manuscripts and videos. I visited dozens of museums and took two trips to Greece. A few of my conclusions differ from those of some classical scholars and may disquiet some historians and sports fans—yet I feel that I have answered most of the basic pentathlon questions which have been debated for many decades; specifically, the order of events, how the pentathlon was contested, how the winner was determined, and how the winner was received. The process resulted in the present history of the event.

My approach was to consider the surviving archeological, artistic and literary evidence as well as its interpretation from more than 180 years of scholarship and apply it within a modern combined events context. For example, bio-mechanics helped judge how some of the sub-events were conducted; organizational concepts and modern combined events rules were applied to ascertain how the ancient pentathlon was managed; probability theory was employed to determine the likelihood of a fourth or fifth event; modern record keeping procedures led to a pentathlon record book. All the while I looked for historical parallels to modern combined events. Piecing these together and viewing the ancient pentathlon as single contest and not a hodgepodge of independent events, allows a much clearer picture of the ancient pentathlon than has heretofore been presented.

Misinformation about the ancient pentathlon has plagued scholarship for years. A single example will suffice. In 1907 classical scholar E.N. Gardiner penned a description of the ancient Greek discus throw. At ancient Olympia, the discus was only ever contested as part of the pentathlon. In effect, all ancient discus throwers were pentathletes. I had read Gardiner's description several times but until recently, never carefully. Using Myron's *Discobolos* as a starting point he, in excruciating detail, describes how the Greeks threw the discus. And for half a century his explanation remained. In fact, Gardiner had it backward and had his athlete throwing the discus in the opposite direction! Why did no one catch this obvious biomechanical error? Track and field coaches and classical scholars may well be discrete groups, neither reading the other's literature. Gardiner was probably unfamiliar with how modern events are conducted, but believed he had a handle on how the ancient events were performed.[4]

Part One of the present work includes a discussion of the nature of the pentathlon, a chapter on how the pentathlon was likely conducted and a description of how the victor was determined. The five chapters of Part Two describe each of the pentathlon's sub-events, in the order in which they were contested.

Part Three offers a chapter on the history of the ancient pentathlon and what is known of its champions, as much as can be pieced together. Part Four presents a handful of chapters describing the recognition and reward of ancient pentathletes, including estimates of the contemporary value of their prizes. At the last minute I decided to start this part with a "record book." It was initially slated for a place in the appendix, but the material grew so voluminously that I felt it deserved a chapter by itself. It was important to include the Greek names in this record yet the sources I used sometimes disagreed about the spelling of Greek names in Greek. I have chosen the most likely spellings and am responsible for any errors.

The final part describes the return (and death) of the ancient pentathlon in modern times. Its modern Olympic history lasted just 18 years. A final chapter examines the influence of the ancient pentathlon on its modern counterpart. The reader is encouraged to review the endnotes carefully, for much technical and historical information is used to support conclusions. Illustrations, appendices, a historical time line, maps, a glossary and bibliography fill out the book.

I would like to thank the staffs at Baker-Berry Library at Dartmouth College and Mount St. Mary's College/University for their assistance in obtaining much of my research materials. I am indebted to Jennie Knox for her photographic expertise and to Don and Sharon Boyer, whose frequent trips to Olympia and photographs were inspirational. This book would not have been possible without the computer assistance of Denton Kreitz of Thurmont, Maryland, and Kory Hirak of Dartmouth College, who continually saved the files from persistent computer crashes. My work builds on decades of ardent scholarship, much of it insightful, some of it useful and all of it motivating. Doubtless there are errors and omissions remaining in my own work and I would be grateful to be informed of them in care of the publisher.

In the course of completing the Pentathlon Record book in Chapter 10, I was immensely aided by several wonderful individuals in the Classics Department of Dartmouth College, Hanover, New Hampshire. In particular Professor Paul Christesen, and his student, Lea Schroeder, who checked and verified the spelling of all of the Greek names in the alphabetical register of the chapter. I was fortunate that they were so generous with their time.

Much of what I have to say is not new. What is new is that all the appropriate information is now in one place, making this, in effect, a reference volume on an ancient sport. This cannot be the end of the pentathlon story; there may be future archeological or literary discoveries. But I am for the present satisfied. The details will give us more to talk about in the Austrian Alps.

Historical Timeline: Important Dates in Ancient Greek Athletic History

Many dates are approximate

B.C.
776   Olympic Games begin (Hippias date)

Archaic Period

ca. 750	Iliad of Homer
ca. 725	Odyssey of Homer
708	Lampis wins lst pentathlon at Olympia
668	Philombrotos of Sparta wins last of 3 pentathlons at Olympia
628	only boys' pentathlon at Olympia
586/82	Pythian Games begin
582	Isthmian Games begin
573	Nemean Games begin
566	Greater Pamathenaea Games begin
560	earliest evidence of Gymnasium
ca. 550	Panathenaea amphorae appear
544	lst victory statues dedicated at Olympia
548–32	Pythokritos of Sicyon plays flute at 6 Olympic Pentathlons
500	Akmatidas of Sparta wins at Olympia akoniti
ca. 490	Ainetos of Amyklai dies during pentathlon victory ceremony
490–480	Persians invade Greek mainland
484–480	Theopompos of Heraia wins and repeats as Olympic champion

Classical Period

ca. 468	Three Hellanodikai officiate pentathlon
464	Xenophon of Corinth wins stade and pentathlon and Pindar writes Olympian Ode #13 to him
ca. 460	Sogenes of Aegina wins boys' pentathlon and Pindar writes Nemean #7 Ode to him

The pentathlon of antiquity has engendered many modern questions but was never controversial to the ancient Greeks. The event was conducted in a simple, straightforward manner. This black figured amphora shows three runners (given the angle of the knee lift they are likely sprinters) on one side and Athena on the obverse. Musee Vivenel, Compiegne, France (Erich Lessing/Art Resource, New York).

460–50	Myron completes Discobolus
450	Stadium III at Olympia
ca. 450	Automedes win and Bacchylides writes Nemean Ode # 9 to him
435	statue of Zeus dedicated at Olympia
431	Peloponnesian War begins
404	Peloponnesian War ends
5th c	Nicolades of Corinth wins 8 major pentathlon crowns
400	Hippias of Elis compiles Olympic victor list
399	Socrates executed
380	Plato writes *Republic*
364	Arcadians and Eleans wage war at Olympia
356	Philip of Macedonia controls Greece
350	Plato writes *Laws*
333	Alexander the Great begins campaign to conquer the known world
332	Kallippos of Athens bribes way to Olympic pentathlon crown, city pays fine
330	Aristotle writes *Politics*
323	Alexander the Great dies
322	Aristotle dies

Hellenistic Period

3rd c	Gorgos of Elis wins record 4 pentathlons at Olympia (speculative dates)
200	Timon of Elis wins at Olympia and comes close to periodonken but is banned from Corinth
146	Corinth burned, Greek becomes Roman colony
86	consul Sulla loots Treasuries at Olympia
78	Julius Caesar begins political career
50	athletic guilds begin
44	Julius Caesar dies

Imperial Period

27	Augustus becomes first Roman emperor and Virgil writes *Aeneid*
4	Tiberius becomes Roman emperor
lst c	King Herod of Judea becomes president of Games at Olympia

A.D.

67–66	Nero competes in Greece
86	Capitoline games of Rome begin
137	Aelius Granianus of Sikyon wins pentathlon, *diaulos* and race in armor, repeats pentathlon win in 141
ca. 140	new stadium built at Olympia
2nd c	popularity of Greek festivals peaks
175	Pausanias identifies pentathlon statues at Olympia
220	Sextus Julius Africanus compiles Olympic victor list
229–33	Demetrios of Salamis wins pentathlon and stadion
267	Goths plunder Olympia
365	Pankratios of Athens last known Olympic pentathlon winner
385	last known Olympic winner
393	Theodosius I bans pagan festivals
426	Theodosius II orders all pagan temples destroyed
476	Western Roman Empire falls
521	final isolympic games at Antioch
6th c	earthquakes destroy much of Olympia

Introduction

This book is about an ancient Greek sport, the pentathlon, a principal feature of a vast number of athletic festivals lasting no less than twelve centuries. Two main and interrelated issues are examined: the longstanding questions about the conduct of the event and its extant record.

Today, to chronicle a history of a sport, we would use record books, films, biographies, interviews, news accounts and rulebooks. Yet none of this is available for the ancient pentathlon. The evidence we have to work with—archaeological, artistic and literary—is meager and has to be patched together since only pieces are available. Piecing together a description of an event (like the ancient pentathlon) is like trying to understand the American Revolutionary War from plaques on park statues; it's tricky, possible, but unreliable. Here we are forced to rely on our understanding of Greek history and modern details of track and field to complete the mosaic. Only when the fragments are pieced together do we achieve a comprehensive picture.

Additional archaeological and artistic evidence is slow in coming. My interest in the literary evidence was piqued when a database, *Thesaurus Linguae Graecae*, became available on CD-ROM. Now known as TLG Digital Library, the project converted all surviving Greek literature, even the shortest of extant fragments, from the period of Homer in the 8th century B.C. through the 6th century A.D., into a readable format. The database has 80 million words. The very first word I typed in was pentathlon (πένταθλον) and I got 142 hits, a third of them from Pausanias. Here was a summary of evidence, although taken alone it was a bit sterile. Over the years, and while publishing various works about the modern decathlon and all-around events, I collected more than 200 books and journal articles on ancient Greek sport. They make up, for the most part, my bibliography.

Keeping in mind that the ancient pentathlon, like its modern counterparts, must be considered a discrete sport and not a collection of sub-events, I plowed through the evidence. I have tried to examine all of the evidence, ancient and modern. At least 80 modern scholars have weighed in on the pentathlon or the

The Greeks not only invented a combined events contest to determine their most versatile athlete, they also developed innovations like the *haltere* (held by the Greek jumper) to improve performances. This red figured pelkie, dating to 480–470 B.C., is found in the Louvre, Paris (Erich Lessing/Art Resource, New York).

sub-events and I concluded early on that many of the disagreements stemmed from a lack of understanding of either the history or presentation of combined events or of kinesiology, or both. Many outstanding scholars with classical training, most of whom were track and field literate, had little or no experience with combined events. Their scholarly claims, normally useful and even astute, occasionally raised the hackles of modern coaches. One needed a healthy skepticism of earlier conclusions.

The earliest modern sources I found were an 1827 University of Berlin doctoral dissertation (in Latin) by G.F. Philipp and a surprisingly modern book in German by Eduard Pinder (1867). Sources used were both ancient and modern. Since the early 19th century numerous (last count, 82) scholars have weighed in on pentathlon related issues. Much of what is published today amounts to reinterpretations with no new information. I have found that the most persuasive conclusions come not only from the overlapping fields of archaeology, literature and language but the realistic fields of history, kinesiology and management. All were used, for example, in the examination of the Greek jump (a running jump with a short approach).

The opening chapter reviews the nature of combined events and concludes that the pentathlon, for the Greeks, represented an opportunity for excellence through temperance. Four credible influences have been cited for the origin of the pentathlon: religious, military, gymnastic and philosophical. Each explains a piece of the event. I conclude that the event was likely not premeditated with lots of weighty thought. It likely evolved out of a way of life. The event was widely copied and, even though the Greeks eschewed standardization of weight and distance, the sub-events, their order and the overall conduct were standard and never controversial.

Two longstanding questions are investigated: the order of events (Chapter 2) and how the winner was determined (Chapter 3). With the help of the Rhodes inscription, kinetic logic and evidence from modern combined events procedures, one may conclude that the order of discus, jump, javelin, sprint and wrestling is the most logical and its standardization became a coordinating mechanism for the Greek world of festivals. The question of determining the winner was never an issue for the Greeks. Begun in an oral, mostly illiterate society with little understanding of numbers (8th century B.C.), the pentathlon procedure had to be simple and easily comprehended by athletes and spectators alike. H.A. Harris was almost correct in his answer to this question (Harris' explanation was first detailed in his 1966 Indiana University Press book, *Greek Athletes and Athletics*). That is, the ancient pentathlon was actually a triathlon (three unique events) with two tie-breakers. Victories were paramount to the Greeks and the first contestant with a majority of sub-event wins was declared the overall winner. Harris was mistaken only in the use of a *repêchage* tie-breaker event.

Chapters 4–8 examine the techniques and administration of the five sub-events in the order they were contested. There is sufficient evidence to conclude that athletes were allowed five attempts in the field events. Three attempts is a modern custom invented by the 19th century Scots. And these efforts were marked but—and here the evidence is overwhelming—not measured. Techniques are discussed. The Greeks used a running long jump. The ultimate use of the *haltere* seems to turn as much on balance as it does distance. References to 55 and 52 foot jumps are treated as literature only.

The biomechanical throwing errors of earlier scholars are revealed. It is obvious to me that the discus was a standing throw with lots of torque and the javelin used a rather short approach. The size of the sprint field could only have accommodated two or three runners and probability tells us that the need for a fourth (sprint) or fifth (wrestling) event was high and increased with the number of contestants.

The history of the ancient pentathlon during the Archaic, Classical, Hellenistic and Imperial periods (Chapter 9) attests that ancient athletes had all of the notoriety and temptation of their modern counterparts. Indeed, one might say it sounds like the modern sports page or website. As the Greeks bumped up against other groups they left a cultural imprint. Notably the ancient pentathlon was exported and practiced by the Phoenicians.

Part Four presents a "record" of the event. Chapter 10, using extant data, might be called the "official ancient pentathlon record book." Chapters 11 and 12 provide a list of all known pentathlon statues of antiquity and the surviving victory odes by Pindar and Bacchylides.

I draw on earlier works, most notably David C. Young, in determining the value of pentathlon prizes (Chapter 13). Since the value of a monetary prize is what it can be exchanged for, the estimates of ancient prizes are thorny but feasible. Young sets a high bar for all succeeding scholars.

Part Five constitutes an attempt to connect the ancient pentathlon with the modern world of sport. My study on the development of modern combined events demonstrates (Chapter 14) that the link between the ancient pentathlon and its modern counterpart, the decathlon, is a good deal less solid than most observers and writers have assumed. The 1906 Intercalated Olympic Games of Athens demonstrated the scoring/place problems wrapped up in preserving an ancient format in a modern world of measurement. Yet the ancient pentathlon (Chapter 15) has gone a long way in how we define all-around excellence.

Appreciative of earlier scholarly contributions, the author welcomes those with differing viewpoints which test of the assertions and conclusions here. Facts are most consequential within some context. The framework used here, the procedures and techniques of combined events, has provided meaningful answers to "ancient" questions.

PART ONE : THE PENTATHLON

1. The Nature and Origin of the Event

Mythology tells us that the pentathlon was invented by Jason, the leader of an excursion to retrieve the Golden Fleece. The voyage of the Argonauts was set in the heroic age, a generation before the Trojan War. An account written in the 2nd century A.D. by Philostratus states that before the time of the Argonauts, the discus, jumping and javelin were independent and unrelated events. Prizes were awarded for each of these contests.

At the time of the Argos journey, Telamon was the best man in the discus, Lynkeus in the javelin, and the two sons of Boreas, Zetes and Kalaïs, at running and jumping. Peleus was second in all these, but could beat everyone at wrestling. When Jason wanted to award the prizes, therefore, he combined the five events out of a desire to honor his friend Peleus, to whom he gave the victory; in this way he created the pentathlon.[1]

Virtually all modern texts on the ancient games begin with this tale, and today the civic fathers of the northeast Aegean island of Lemnos claim this to be the birthplace of the pentathlon in their promotional and travel literature.[2] Yet this appealing story clarifies nothing about the event's origin.[3] For that we must first examine, through the eyes of the Greeks, the nature of the pentathlon event. It should reveal more than a myth about Argonauts.

Character of the Pentathlon

Some Greeks recognized that there was a type of talented athlete who was not quite as good as specialists but who could excel in a variety of events. These became known as pentathletes, athletes who displayed skills in as many as five events. Eighth century B.C. organizers at Olympia had seen a combined event as a decisive test for an all-around athlete and the event was held in high regard. But it would be misleading to say that this belief was universal among

Greeks. For example Plato, failing to see that the pentathlete himself was also a specialist, concluded that the pentathlon was the opportunity for only the second-rate performer.

The pentathlon was a staple of the ancient Olympic Games program as well as that of other Crown Games and Panhellenic athletic festivals for over 1200 years. It consisted of five events contested in two stages, and wins in three events were necessary for overall victory. The first three events (today we would call them "field" as opposed to "track" events) were only ever part of the pentathlon: the discus, the jump and the spear throw. These three made up the "first triad." If a single athlete won all three events the pentathlon winner was decided. If an athlete did not win the first three events, additional events were added—a sprint and ultimately a wrestling match—to help determine the winner. The latter two events were also discrete contests at Greek festivals.

Despite their versatility, pentathletes were often not as respected as combat athletes, runners, or charioteers. There is some surviving evidence about the size of the prizes at Panhellenic festivals. It gives us an idea of the relative importance and popularity of the pentathlon, even though at Olympia, the reward for all athletes was the symbolic olive wreath.

Compared to winners in running, combat or equestrian events at money games, pentathletes seem to have earned a bit less.[4] For example, in the boys' events of the Panathenaic Games of the 4th century B.C., the pentathlon winner received 30 large jars (*amphoras*) of olive oil, the same as the wrestling winner. The pankration winner received 40 and the highest prize, 50, went to the winner of the sprint (*stade*).[5] In one set of figures, from a local games in Asia Minor in the 2nd century A.D., the pentathlon winner received, by far, the lowest monetary sum.[6] Other evidence spread throughout antiquity does not place the pentathlon winner at the top of the prize list.

Why, then, would the ancient pentathlete choose (and train) to become the best all around rather than the best at a particular event?[7] Why, in other words, would one choose versatility over specialty? The answer emanates from Greek philosophy. For example, Socrates strongly condemned excesses in physical development. A clear note of practical moderation pervades the ethics of Aristotle, whose doctrine defines virtue as the mean between two extremes. "Every virtue lies between two vices, which are the excesses and defect of appetite respectively."[8] For Aristotle this concept applied to all facets of life, including athletics. Aristotle was critical of the athlete's overemphasis (including the extent of his training and the individual's physical enhancement) on a single athletic event. The 4th century philosopher tells us that "he who excels in everything is fit for the pentathlon."

At times the pentathlete was held in high regard, not only by philosophers but by poets and artists as well. Aristotle said that "pentathletes are the most beautiful" and sculptors frequently relied on pentathletes as prototypes because of their well-balanced muscularity. Some of the most celebrated statues of antiquity, depicting athletes with discuses or javelins, are actually statues of pentathletes. The statues that are usually attributed to Naukydes and the *Doryphoros* by Polykleitos (with javelin) were constructed to display the pentathlete's proportions.[9] The most famous (and most copied) statue of antiquity is Myron's *Discobolos* created in the 5th century B.C.[10] Myron, from Eleutherae, a small town north of Athens, was the first Greek sculptor to succeed in giving life and motion to his figures. *Discobolos* is a figure of a pentathlete whose proportions are both harmonious and realistic. By capturing the balanced physical development of the pentathlete artists became public relations agents for the event. It is one of the reasons why the pentathlon survived throughout antiquity.

Temperance, that is moderation of every facet, was promoted as a way of Greek living. The priests of Apollo at Delphi encouraged Greeks to be temperate, to avoid unreasonable extremes, and this notion even applied to the overdevelopment of athletes. The pentathlete strove most to achieve a middle course between different types of athletes.

Our initial mythical description (written by Philostratus 900 years after the invention of the event) is apocryphal and of no help in explaining neither why the pentathlon was created nor why it survived and flourished. It's just a good story but nothing more and does not answer the questions on the order of events, the selection of a victor, or why there were five events. The pentathlon story begins with religion.

Origin of the Pentathlon

Four plausible influences have been given for the introduction of the pentathlon: religious, military, gymnastic and philosophical. Each rationalization likely contains a fraction of the truth.

The first explanation of its origin, like the ancient Olympic Games themselves, has its roots in religion. The festival at Olympia, the site and the contests were all sacred to the Greeks. "They (the contests) were a religious act in honor of a deity. Those who took part did so in order to serve the god and the prizes which they won came from the god."[11] When placed on the winner's head at Olympia, a wreath, woven from the branch of a sacred olive tree, symbolized and conveyed life-giving properties.

The southern peninsula of Greece, the Peloponnesus, is named for Pelops, a mythical king and patron tied to fertility and agriculture. Pelops, the grandson of Zeus, won his wife, Hippodamia, by winning a chariot race. Annual religious and fertility rituals at Olympia were held in his honor at Olympia, a grove

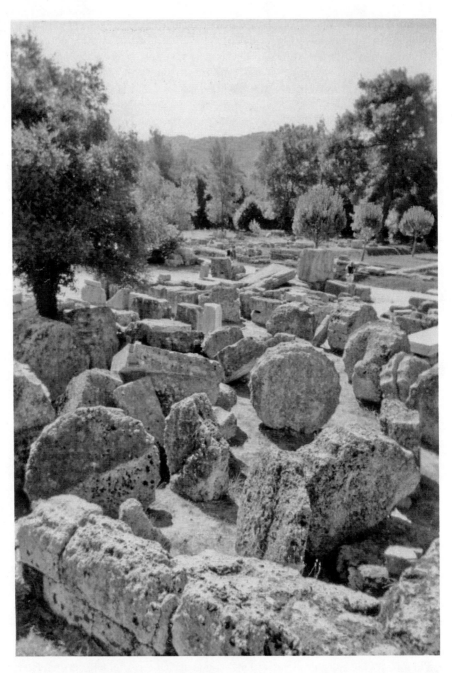

Blocks of grooved columns from the Doric colonnade are all that is left in a field of ruins at one of the Seven Wonders of the Ancient World, the Temple of Zeus (Don and Sharon Boyer).

approximately 35 miles from Elis, a major town in Peloponnesus. We have some fleeting references to these annual festivals, which date to the very late 2nd millennium B.C., yet it is improbable that they were immediately accompanied by sporting events.[12]

Sporting events were also well known and documented by the 8th century B.C. In Homer's *Iliad* and *Odyssey*, wrestling, foot racing, leaping, discus throwing and spear throwing all occur in funeral games and other challenge contests.[13] Athletic contests conducted in conjunction with funerals were common in Greek society. The fact that they all show up as contests in Olympia in the 8th century B.C. is to be expected. That they became part of a combined events contest should not surprise us. Some scholars have concluded that the light athletic contests (running, jumping, throwing) were seen by the Greeks to be representative of a renewal of life, that is, an attempt to convince the god to return from the dead. It was a fertility rite, in this case a praying for the return of spring after winter.

It may be that the Olympic Games, in honor of Zeus, replaced earlier funeral games dedicated to the old fertility god Pelops. That is not important here. The usual starting date of the games at Olympia is 776 B.C., because this is the date for which a winner has been recorded. It has been reasonably assumed, however, that such games were held at Olympia and elsewhere well before that date.[14] As the sacred games at Olympia progressed, additional events, representative of life and agriculture renewal, were added. During the 8th century B.C., many of these early events at Olympia may still have been dedicated to the hero Pelops.

The second and third explanations are interrelated. The 7th century B.C. witnessed both military innovations (a reliance on the heavily armed but mobile soldier) and changes in urban civic life of Greece. It became the duty of each young man, in his preparation for citizenship, to be physically ready to defend his city state. Much of the military preparation for young men who had turned 18 (*ephobos*) took place in the *gymnasion*, "the nude place," literally the place of nude exercises. This training, called *ephebic*, included but was not limited to physical and military exercises.

Every city-state provided a gymnasion and an accompanying *palaistra,* "the wrestling place." Larger cities had several. For our purposes this is of consequence since some writers tie the origin of the pentathlon with military preparation. Wolfgang Decker asserts that "one can hardly err in assuming that a former military necessity—the surefooted legs of an attacking hoplite— was here turned into a sport as, indeed, was the case for the entire ancient pentathlon, whose other disciplines—-the discus, the javelin, running and wrestling—originated in the need to prove the citizen-soldier's many sided preparedness."[15] A less weighty but related military argument suggests that the pentathlon was an outgrowth of all of the events practiced in the gymnasium.

By the 3rd century B.C. there had already been 400 Olympic pentathlon winners. After the 3rd century B.C. this is what the athletes would have seen at Olympia. A reconstruction of the ancient Olympic sanctuary shows the Temple of Zeus in the center, Treasuries in upper right and entrance to stadium (not shown; would have been in the upper right) and Palaestra extreme left (DeA Picture Library/Art Resource, New York).

The resulting and convenient combination (the pentathlon) represented most of what was practiced there. Since the Greeks had not yet discovered high jumping, pole vaulting, hammer throwing or hurdling, the five events of the pentathlon represented nearly the complete range of athletic exercises. For some scholars this seems to be an adequate explanation of the origin of the pentathlon, that is, the pentathlon roughly coincides with the birth of the gymnasium and palaistra, both of which served as a bridge to public competitions. In an almost Veblen-like ideal, the leisure class, in the para-military atmosphere of the gymnasium, re-enacted the civilization of the archaic warriors.[16]

The pentathlon was representative and an outgrowth of the Greek way of life. It had been integrated into the Olympic program early. The initial games had but a single event, a race of approximately 200 meters, called a *stade*. A double stade (*diaulos*) was added in 724 B.C. and a distance race (*dolichos*) in 720 B.C. At the 18th Olympiad (708 B.C.) Elean organizers added additional contests from the old fertility-funeral inventory (discus, javelin, jump, and wrestling), but, in an innovative moment combined them so that they constituted a balanced and proportionate exercise.[17] All of the individual events appear in Homer, so they were not new.[18] But combining the five events into a single contest was. The discus, jump, javelin, stade and wrestling were now elements of a new event, the pentathlon, which fulfilled the Greeks' desire to avoid the excesses of a single event. By doing so the Greeks promoted balance and proportion. The pentathlon was an avoidance of the disproportionate. It was a simple notion and it worked.

Each of the above explanations, in itself, is too simple. Taken together they may tell us a good deal of the story of the pentathlon's origin. Yet social scientists and sporting historians would have a different take on the event's formation. It is doubtful that there was an official committee (à la the International Olympic Committee today) which debated its inclusion in the Olympic program.[19] Social and political scientists as well as economists would view the origin of the pentathlon as analogous to what they refer to as "spontaneous order," that is, a creation without anyone thinking very hard about it. Greek organizers hit upon a good thing and efforts to uncover a profound motivation for the pentathlon are likely to be unproductive.

Other explanations by scholars about the combination of pentathlon events are unconvincing. For example, there is absolutely no evidence that the three field events (discus, jump, and javelin) were grouped together because field events were unpopular to the Greeks. The conjecture that Greek behavior toward field events mirrored that of the 20th century British sports fan is pure bunkum.[20] We find the answer to the origin of the pentathlon in religion, philosophy and expediency, not in the whims of modern-day track and field spectators. It may have been that the Greeks offered a combination of discus, jump and javelin as an event because, individually, they did not enjoy the status of running, the only pre-pentathlon events. Collectively they enjoyed an elevated status. Make no mistake; the unique pentathlon events were not unpopular. Surviving literature and art confirm this.

In fact the inclusion of a pentathlon into the Olympic program represents an effort by the Eleans to move their festival beyond a simple religious picnic with a few foot races toward something more universally Greek, more Olympic. The Eleans accomplished this in an unconventional way: by collecting the most popular forms of gymnasium exercise of the day and linking them. So they were combined. The pentathlon then became the event *most Greek* since it represented the ideal of balance and moderation.

Legend has it that the pentathlon made its appearance in the late 8th century B.C. It may have been a bit later, that is, in the mid–7th century B.C. At the same time, military innovations, the widespread use of the Greek gymnasium, and formality in athletic contests occurred within the Greek world. It is unlikely that the origin of the pentathlon was merely coincidental to these other developments. We will never know who ultimately made the "pentathlon" decision. It may not have been a smooth process, deliberately "thought out" or "planned." More likely it simply flowed from the Greek way of thinking while officials ironed out the details. Greek mythology offers numerous examples of combined tasks. The pentathlon was a contest that fit the Greek mindset and its invention should not surprise us. We would be more surprised if the Greeks had not conceived a combined-event contest.

Combined Events in Greek Myth

The warrior-athlete was a common Greek mythological figure. For example, Homer's *Iliad* frequently describes two of the Greeks' mightiest heroes, Ajax, son of Telamon, and Achilles, son of Peleus, in athletic terms. The former was always characterized for his extraordinary size and strength, having wounded the Trojan Hector twice by hurling boulders. He became a cult hero, and a sporting festival at his home in Salamis was conducted in his honor for centuries. Achilles was continuously described by Homer as the fleetest of the Achaeans.

Even more compelling, some of the greatest of the Greek warrior-athletes were painted with a multi-event history. The 12 Labors of Herakles (Latin, Hercules), while not specifically athletic, required the skills of a modern day decathlete: strength, speed, spring and smarts. His mythological connection to the ancient Olympic Games (some considered him the founder) continually cast him in a sporting light.

Herakles[21] was an early member of the Argonaut crew, and its leader, Jason, is said to have created the pentathlon for his friend Peleus, father of Achilles. Jason reportedly pooled the five events of the pentathlon to orchestrate a victory for Peleus.

Perhaps the most sporting active of the legendary "warrior-athletes" was Odysseus. Broad of shoulder and speedy, Odysseus took part or witnessed the pentathlon's five events either at the funeral games for Patroclus (*Iliad*), or at the recreational games of Phaecia (*Odyssey*). All of the pentathlon's events were, it seems, known to Homer, whose writing (likely mid–8th century B.C.) predates their inclusion into the pentathlon's recipe. But Odysseus could be considered a sort of patron saint of combined event athletes. He is the earliest known mythological figure with a background in all five events. A lighthearted description of the athletic career of Odysseus, as if prepared by a modern day track statistician, is provided in Appendix E.

There is even a modern day combined events connection to Odysseus. James Joyce, the author of the novel *Ulysses* (1922), was the son of an early and prominent multi-event athlete, John Stanislaus Joyce (1849–1931). As a young man John S. Joyce won numerous track and field medals at the Annual Sports at University College, Cork, in 1869 and 1870.[22] At the time in Ireland combined event athletes were know as all-round men or general athletes.

Standardization

Even though we are uncertain of the origins, we do know that the ancient pentathlon was widely copied and standardized. Additional Crown Games began in the early 6th century B.C. and adopted much of the Olympic program, including the pentathlon. Gradually more and more civic festival games were held, many of them annually. They served as preparations for the major games. Many offered valuable prizes to the winners. By the second century A.D. we find as many as 500 different athletic festivals celebrated in the vast Mediterranean–Black Sea region, and virtually all of them conducted a pentathlon.

The pentathlon's homogeny made it easy to understand and export to the rest of the Greek world. The order of events and the process of determining a winner were, in a sense, a coordinating mechanism which allowed all festivals to attract pentathletes from far-away settlements. The athletes themselves would have found it easier to prepare knowing that all festivals were on the same page. We have absolutely no ancient references as to controversies as to how the event was conducted. It must have been straightforward and simple, so uncomplicated, in fact, that the Greeks found it unnecessary to write down the rules. They were simply understood.

There is a modern analogy. It has been a century since the decathlon has been in place, yet its events, their order and winning procedure have never changed.[23] Only the scoring tables have been altered occasionally.[24] Modern scoring tables have been altered because of technical improvements in some events. But the decathlon of all Olympic champions—from Jim Thorpe in 1912 to Bruce Jenner in 1976 and for Ashton Eaton in 2012—was always the same, the same events, the same order and the same process to determine the winner.

Part of the explanation for the ancient pentathlon's standardization is that, for the millennium of ancient athletics, there were precious few technical advancements. The 7th century switch from stone to bronze disci and minor alterations to the weight and shape of *haltere* (jumping weights) could be considered technical. Yet neither resulted in a change in the pentathlon's program or procedure. Yes, there may have been minor variations from festival to festival, in, for example, the length or start of the *stadion* race, the weight of the *disci* or the length of the long jump pit. But these were inconsequential and did not alter the basic format of the event. The pentathlon did not change and the Greeks, in fact, felt that its structure and conduct were satisfactory.

Some Related Issues

Three additional issues surround the origin of the pentathlon: what came before it, that it was novel, and why the Greeks selected five events to determine their all-around champion.

First, it should be noted that the pentathlon pre-dated virtually all other Olympic events. Since it was preceded only by foot races, its inclusion in the Olympic program may be an indication of the importance of moderation and balance in Greek culture. The pentathlon was added to the Olympic program before boxing, chariot and horse racing, and the pankration, all of which came in for heavy criticism about their extremes during antiquity. Over the years the pentathlon may have been surpassed in popularity by other sports, but its early inclusion is significant.

Second, the pentathlon was one of only two sports the Greeks can claim to have invented or institutionalized. The pankration, a no-holds-barred combination of boxing and wrestling, was the other. All other ancient Olympic events originated from natural movements or preparation for warfare. Anthropologists may argue whether combining ideas was in the Greek nature. And we may quibble about whether the Greeks invented the discus throw, but the point is made.

Finally, why did the Greeks choose five events, and not say, four, or six or some other figure? The number five had no mythical meaning in Greek life.[25] The Greeks were simply a practicable and efficient lot and five events were enough to prove the point.[26] As a matter of fact, winning three (a triad) was satisfactory to the Greeks in a day when there were a limited number of events.[27] One would have thought that the Greeks would have invented a decathlon, knowing how taken they were with the number 10. Pythagorians, for example, felt that "the number 10 is thought to be perfect and to comprise the whole nature of numbers."[28] Yet by the late 8th century B.C. (even before Pythagoras) there were not even ten track and field events. Five was a convenient and suitable number.

Pentathlon Evidence

Ancient pentathlon evidence is archaeological, artistic and literary. Some excavated items have inscriptions, most frequently written in stone, which offer a glimpse of how the pentathlon was conducted. Many of the engravings have not survived in full, forcing scholars to speculate what is missing and its meaning.

Artwork, either in the form of statues or paintings on vases (*amphorae*), helps us in the analysis of how the pentathlon events were performed. Victor statues and amphorae date to the middle of the 6th century B.C. Sculptors had a high regard for pentathletes and the amphorae, on occasion open to different interpretations, have been immensely helpful.

As to the surviving written word, victory odes, especially those of Pindar and Baccylides, have been most useful. The lone ancient treatise on athletics, by Philostratus and written in the 2nd century A.D., is unreliable. A far more trustworthy document is the traveler's guidebook of Pausanias; much of what we know of the ancient pentathletes was provided by his eyewitness (2nd century A.D.) reports of statue inscriptions in the sacred *Altis* at Olympia.

None of the catalogues of Olympic victors—initially provided by Hippias in the 5th century B.C., updated by Aristotle a century later and reworked in A.D. 217 by Sextus Julius Africanus—have survived. Church historian Eusebius copied much of Africanus's work, and that still exists. We find from these lists that early pentathlon winners, like those of other events, were local to Olympia, coming from Elis, Sparta, Messene or other cities in the surrounding region. As the games became more important winners came from all corners of the Greek world. For example, there were at least five pentathlon victors at Olympia in the mid–5th century B.C. who hailed from the Italian island of Sicily.

The ancient pentathlon lived for at least 1200 years, and probably longer. For that period of time one could hope for more data from any genre. But, overall, the evidence is meager and we are forced to rely on our understanding of Greek history and the modern details of track and field to complete the mosaic we call pentathlon.

2. Orchestrating the Pentathlon

From the time of Homer (8th century B.C.) to the time of Roman conquest (146 B.C.), Greece went through a continual political and cultural revolution. Few things in Greek life went unchanged. Yet the ancient pentathlon was a constant. It had emerged from prehistoric shadows and pre-dated the flowering of intellectual and artistic Greek culture. It was universally accepted as the test for the versatile athlete and lasted well over a millennium. William Blake Tyrrell has summarized it best: "Like other rituals, Greek athletics resisted change, with continuity reinforced by the period games and their imitators."[1] And so, too, it must have been with the organization of the pentathlon, which was quickly institutionalized, and by the time it was copied by the crown and other games in the early 6th century B.C., it was set in stone. It may have seen minor scheduling adjustments from time to time, but it remained essentially the same format from its beginning until ancient athletics disappeared in the early days of the 6th century C.E.

Scheduling

Conventional wisdom reveals that the pentathlon was initially offered at the 19th Olympiad, 708 B.C. Whatever the accuracy of this date historians accept that the pentathlon was the first non-running event of the ancient Olympic Games. Archaic officials, much like their modern counterparts, must have always been concerned about where the pentathlon fit within the remainder of the program. It is reasonable to expect that over the span of a millennium the schedule would be modified on occasion as other sports were added, dropped, or became more or less popular. It now appears, given the recent research by Hugh M. Lee, that pentathlon scheduling at Olympia went through three stages.[2]

For the ancient organizers, where to insert the pentathlon within the festival schedule of events was paramount. Because of Pausanias we know a good deal about scheduling at Olympia. In the first phase (708–472 B.C.) the Olympic festival lasted only a few days with most events held within a short period of time. But at the 77th Olympiad (472 B.C.) the schedule was so packed and the pentathlon ran so long that the subsequent pankrationists had to compete into the night. The blame was put on the length of the equestrian events and the pentathlon. Thereafter (phase two of the five day festival) the equestrian events and pentathlon were given a separate day, the second, so as not to be an impediment to the remainder of the program.

To modern track meet organizers, this should sound all too familiar.[3] It is well known that combined events—decathlon, heptathlon, pentathlon—require many officials, involve most of the facilities and consume a good deal of time. And so it was in ancient times. The ancient pentathlon did not have the 30 minute rest rule required for modern combined events but proceeded continuously from one event to the next.[4] The *Hellanodikai* had to keep the event moving. Yet the very nature of the pentathlon required extra time as these jocks-of-all-trades moved from event to event. The pentathlete would *strigil* himself, re-oil, and limber up frequently between events. Even the best organized meeting could drag. Large fields created a scheduling problem since all field event athletes were allowed five attempts in each of the first three events. The time constraints, then, are yet another reason why, we will see later, the throws and jumps were neither measured nor recorded.

The Olympic schedule remained at five days until Roman times, when the festival was stretched to six days. By 256 B.C. there were six different horse and chariot races and the imperial desire to focus on these equestrian events forced festival organizers to place equestrian and pentathlon events on separate days. Lee argues convincingly that the final change in the schedule came "in the time of the first Caesars" whose partiality to equestrian events was well known and whose patronage and prestige was crucial for the ancient games.[5]

The following table summarizes its major scheduling changes at Olympia.

Pentathlon Scheduling Phases

Phase One:	pentathlon, equestrian and combat sports on same day	(708–472 B.C.)
Phase Two:	pentathlon and equestrian events on same day	(472–1st century B.C.)
Phase Three:	pentathlon on separate day	(1st century B.C. to 4th century C.E.)

Order of Events

Unlike modern scholars, the ancients did not agonize over the order of events, which was traditional and did not change. Yet few issues have attracted as much academic attention as this one. Since the mid–19th century, writers have debated the ancient pentathlon's order of events without consensus.

Probability theory tells us that, within a five event contest, there could be a maximum of a 120 possible orders or five factorial (5!).[6] But since there is overwhelming evidence that wrestling was the final pentathlon event, the number of possible orders before wrestling can be reduced to 24 or four factorial (4!). One can find 9 of these 24 possibilities in the modern literature. More than five dozen modern scholars, researchers and writers have weighed in on this issue and two notable scholars even claim that, as long as wrestling was last, the order did not matter.[7] Two additional scholars maintain that the order of the first three events did not matter, so long as running was 4th and wrestling 5th.[8] In due time we will see that the Greeks rationally selected the sequence of events. Appendix A summarizes the claims of a sampling of modern scholars, and their diversity of opinions on the pentathlon sequence is vast.

I have used two avenues to settle the sequence issue. The first relies on ancient sources, and the second on the lessons of modern combined events and kinesiology.

Event Order Using Ancient Sources

Archaic sources imply a customary order but offer no consensus. As modern scholars go, Gene Waddell offers the best summary of the ancient evidence.[9] But I reach a very different conclusion than does he. The table below lists the most important ancient references to this issue.

The earliest of the ancient evidence comes from an ode by Simonides in the late 6th century B.C. But his sequence is influenced more by metrics and can be discounted.

Artemidoros (ca. 140 A.D.) uses the pentathlon as a way to interpret dreams. His order is summarized in the table below. Yet one must question, 20 centuries later, whether a dream interpretation, using superstition, symbolism and imagination, offers proof of the order of events. Victory odes from the 5th century B.C. imply relationships between pairs of events. For example, Pindar's "Ode for Sogenes of Aegina" at the boys' pentathlon at Nemea implies that the javelin preceded wrestling, while Eustathius offers a Pindaric interpretation 17 centuries after the poet's career. The table below summarizes some selected ancient sources.

Summary of Selected Ancient Sources for Pentathlon Order
[in chronological order]

Name	Date	Events				
Simonides	(ca. 500 B.C.)	run	jump	discus	javelin	wrestling
Pentathlon Victory Odes						
Pindar (7th Nemean ca. 460 B.C.)					javelin	wrestling
Baccylides (at Nemea ca. 450 B.C.)*		[discus	javelin]			wrestling
Xenophon	(4th century B.C.)				[run]	wrestling
Rhodes inscription	(1st century B.C.)	discus	jump	javelin	run	wrestling
Artemidoros	(ca. A.D. 140)	run	discus	jump	javelin	wrestling
Pausanias	(2nd century A.D.)		[run	jump]		wrestling
Philostratos	(3rd century A.D.)	run	jump	javelin	discus	wrestling
Pindar via Eustathius	(12th century A.D.)	jump	discus	javelin	run	wrestling

The order presented here is the order in which the events are mentioned in epigrams, odes or inscriptions. Brackets [ ] are used for the order when all events are not mentioned.

*It is likely that Baccylides lists the three events that Automedes won in Nemea.

The best evidence on the pentathlon's order is supplied by a fragmentary inscription from the island of Rhodes dating to the first century B.C. It appears to be a sort of rule book offering instruction on how the pentathlon was to be conducted. Enough of the inscription survives to allow us to draw conclusions on the sequence of pentathlon events. Taken with what else we know about how the Greeks conducted events, the ancient sequence issue is no longer in question.

The first translation of the Rhodes inscription appeared in 1956 in *Rivista de Filologia* and is reproduced here from Stephen G. Miller and Donald G. Kyle.[10] The sections enclosed in brackets have been lost.

1. [-----------------] they are to be in charge of [-----------------]
2. [- in] turn until each five times [has thrown the *diskos*----]
3. [first] shall jump the one who threw the *diskos* farthest [--]
4. [---------] they have ? the *skamma* nor the [-----------------]
5. [------------] of the surface of the stadium [-------------------]
6. Let it be two feet. Similarly [-----------------------------------]
7. Of the *kanon* and the [---]
8. ? and the one at the *te[rma*-------------------------------------]
9. Of those who are [---]
10. Of the wrestler [---]

Key words have been italicized. Rules about the discus (*diskos*) appear first. The *skamma*, the landing pit for the jump, is mentioned next and some scholars suggest that this refers to the preparation of the pit on the stadium surface and softening it by digging the pit two feet deep. The *kanon* (a measuring rod) is next mentioned. Many standard modern works provide a glossary of Greek terms, but some do not include a reference to the kanon, knowing that the Greeks did not measure their competitive throws.[11] But the kanon was useful for the javelin event, not to measure the throw per se, but to measure the approach, the run-up. This is so standard a part of the javelin competition that anyone who has ever participated in, coached, officiated or just seen a modern javelin competition knows that today the javelins themselves are the measuring rods (the modern kanon). Today, without the immediate availability of a measuring tape, athletes, placing the javelin end over end, use the javelin itself to "get their steps." So to for the Greeks, the javelins themselves could be used as the kanon. The Greek word for the competitive, lightweight spear is *akon* (or *akontion*).

It is clear then, from the Rhodes inscription, that the three unique events to the pentathlon—discus, jump and javelin—were conducted first. We know that winning the first three events could produce the overall champion, so it is reasonable that these three should come first.

The next event reference in the Rhodes inscription is the *terma,* literally a "border," and usually translated as a finish line or starting line. This must refer to the fourth event, the pentathlon sprint race, or *stade,* and is verified by a passage from Xenophon: "They had already finished the horse races and the run in the pentathlon. The competitors who had advanced to the wrestling were no longer in the stadium but were wrestling between the stadium and the altar."[12]

And the final Rhodian reference explicitly refers to wrestling. We have our sequence from an ancient source: discus, jump, javelin, run, wrestling. This order was standardized.

Kinesiology and Modern Combined Events

Yet we need not have deferred to ancient literary or inscription evidence to answer the sequential uncertainty. We could have reached the same solution by applying the principle of alternating events and stamina, principles so accepted in athletics, no matter what era, that it is reasonable to assume that the ancients applied it to their pentathlon as well.

Ludwig Drees provides the best understanding of the alternate principle. "The order of events (of the ancient pentathlon) had been well thought out, for the first four tested the athletes' arms and legs in alternating sequence, while the last tested the whole body."[13] In 1956 George Highmore described this well, claiming, "It is extremely improbable that the Greeks consciously designed the (pentathlon) competition; more probably by their native intuition, they accepted progressively the principle of weight and counterweight."[14] He rightly maintained that the two throws were (using the terms provided by Philostratus) "heavy" events and the jump and run were "light" events and the Greeks would have configured them in a balanced way.

Kinesiology tells us that if the same muscles or muscle sets are used over and over again, that is, used uninterrupted, performances suffer. It is the reason why one would not conduct all the throws in a combined events contest consecutively. Tired muscles, asked to perform the same or similar skills, result in substandard performances. One can ask any combined-events athlete, coach, weightlifter, body builder or personal trainer. Tired or overused muscles test none of the desired skills of strength, speed, spring nor agility. Tired muscles test nothing. This is the reason why the tests, exercises, or events are separated by classification and why the stamina test is placed last. This only works, incidentally, if the number of events is greater that then number of classifications.

Today individual track and field events are customarily referred to as runs, jumps or throws.[15] It is here that modern combined events offer us a lesson. The sequence of events in the decathlon, pentathlon and women's heptathlon never offer the same "type" (muscle or skill requirement) back-to-back. The history of modern combined events can be enlightening. Without much of the historical detail it can be concluded that the first "modern" formal and institutionalized combined-event was the American amateur all-around, begun in 1884. After a few years the 10 events and their order became standard. The all-around event was held on one day and there was a deliberate attempt never to have similar events back to back.[16] So the order became:

(sprint) (shot) (high jump) (walk) (hammer) (vault) (hurdles) (weight) (long jump) (mile)
Race   throw   jump   race   throw   jump   race   throw   jump   race.
(4 races, 3 leaping events, 3 throwing events).

Another way of saying the same thing was that the all-around never tested the similar skills consecutively. This was quite deliberate by early organizers,[17] and when the all-around morphed into the decathlon in the early days of the 20th century, the same philosophy prevailed. For example, the modern decathlon order of events is:

	(100m	*long jump*	*shot put*	*high jump*	*400m)*
1st day:	run	jump	throw	jump	run
	(110mH	*discus*	*pole vault*	*javelin*	*1500m)*
2nd day:	run	throw	jump	throw	run

In the ancient pentathlon this principle would look like this:

(discus)	*(jump)*	*(javelin)*	*(run)*	*(wrestling)*
arms	legs	arms	legs	both arms and legs

Appendix B summarizes the sequence of events in modern combined events. Once can see that in every case runs, jumps and throws are separated and never required to be contested back-to-back. And the endurance test is placed last. These are the rock solid principles of combined events.

Modern scholars spend most of the time using the classification of events spelled out by Philostratus in the 3rd century A.D. But his classification as

A view of athletes' entrance to the stadium at Olympia from the west. As the athletes approached the tunnel on the stadium's northwest corner, they were reminded to play fair by Zanes, statues of Zeus paid for by fines levied against those who had cheated (Don and Sharon Boyer).

either "heavy" or "light" offers no clue in understanding the sequence of events and has more to do with the athlete's muscle mass than anything else. Philostratus classifies all running events, the jump and the javelin as "light," while boxing, wrestling, the pankration and the discus are "heavy" events. The pentathlon was a combination of both light and heavy.[18] This is a bit simplistic and helps little in discovering the pentathlon sequence.

In summary, most reasonable scholars now conclude that running (the stade) was indeed the fourth event and the pentathlon began with the trio of contests that were unique to it, namely the discus, jump and javelin. With this assumption our order-of-event possibilities is reduced to six, or three factorial (3!). If we also apply the alternating principle the sequence possibilities are reduced to just two. We also know that the javelin was conducted relatively late in the program, so it is not hard to deduce the definitive sequence. This was so well understood by the Greeks that there was never any discussion.

I maintain that the order of the pentathlon followed similar thinking. The order of the ancient pentathlon, given was inevitable:

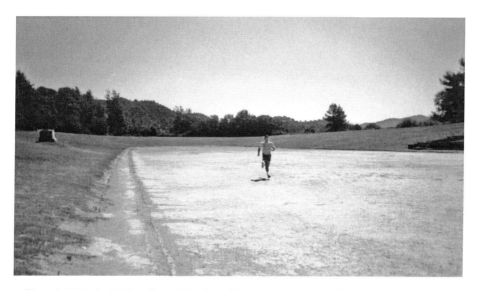

There is little doubt that the origin of combined events occurred here at Olympia, on this flat, open surface. Today the curious, Olympic aficionados, historians and athletes, like this lonely runner, visit the site (Don and Sharon Boyer).

- that a triad winner would discontinue competition;
- wrestling was always last since it was the stamina event;
- the run was next to last;
- the javelin was relatively late in the program;
- the three events unique to the pentathlon would be conducted first;
- and the alternating principle applies;

And it exactly corresponds to the Rhodes inscription:

- discus
- long jump
- javelin
- sprint
- wrestling

One must also be remembered that, as athletics developed in ancient Greece and as athletes were able to travel from festival to festival, having a standard event became a coordinating mechanism. That is, the pentathlon brought the best athletes together and they all knew what to expect.

Number of Competitors

Determining the number of pentathlon contestants, given the scanty evidence at Olympia and elsewhere, is complex. We know that Akmatidas of

Sparta, for whatever reason, faced no rivals at Olympia (ca. 500 B.C.) and won the pentathlon in a walkover.[19] But this appears unusual.

What we can conclude is that, given travel constraints and the evidence about preparation requirements at Olympia, the number of entrants was likely to have been smaller than those of local games. One writer maintains that the usual size of the Olympic pentathlon field was twenty.[20] This conjecture is way too high. Nigel Crowther conjectures that the average size pentathlon field at an Olympic festival was somewhere between 5 and 10, and this estimate is much more reasonable.

There is much evidence that there were larger fields at local festivals. One reference of 87 pentathletes at the Sebasta Festival in Naples in the 3rd century A.D. is probably a mistake and is more likely a reference to a footrace.[21] After all, there are limitations to the size of a combined event field. Imagine the Sebasta situation where, given what we know about the number of attempts in the field events, over 1,300 attempts had to be conducted, marked and officiated even if they were not measured. Given the modern standard (used in most track and field competition guides) of allowing one minute per attempt, this would mean that the first three events alone, assuming single facilities and no rest between events, would have taken over 21 hours. The 87 athletes at Sebasta must have referred to a footrace, not the pentathlon.

The biggest modern championship decathlon field ever accommodated was at the 1984 U.S. Olympic Trials where 53 athletes met the qualifying standards. Thirty minutes' rest was required between events and, over two days, more than 1,200 efforts were timed, measured and recorded. In spite of dual pits and circles at the Los Angeles Coliseum, half the field had to be shuffled off to a local university track to complete the event. Incidentally, the 1984 problem resulted from a soft entry standard.

The Olympic *hellanodikai*, by requiring a month's preparation prior to the games under their watchful eye, were, de facto, imposing an entry standard on the field. There are upper limits to combined event fields. Crowther's guestimate of 5 to 10 athletes at Olympia is certainly in the ballpark. My own would have been a few less, perhaps 4 to 8, remembering that a field of at least three makes the sequence of events necessary.

3. How the Winner Was Determined

Determining the winner of the ancient pentathlon has only been an issue for modern scholars. Donald Kyle reminds us that the question of how the ancient pentathlon winner was determined has lasted longer than the modern Olympic Games themselves.[1] For the Greeks it was never a problem. We have no evidence that selecting a winner was ever controversial. The Greeks must have had a system that was straightforward and uncomplicated, the victor being clear and obvious to the spectators. Remember, the pentathlon was created in the late 8th century B.C., even before the Greek language was established and before the Greeks had a formal numbering system.[2]

In fact, the ancient pentathlon was a triathlon with tie-breakers. It was designed to test the skills of three events (*diskos, halma, akon*) which were only offered as part of the pentathlon. The tie-breakers, running (*stade*) and wrestling (*pale*), events in their own right, were added when necessary to determine an overall winner.

Over the years there have been a myriad of solutions to the victor question. Scholars have proposed a system of absolute wins, relative wins, systematic or chronological eliminations, *repêchages*, semi-finals, randomly selected pools, and even an old all-around points-for-place system. And still the issue of how the winner was determined, debated now for over 140 years, has no consensus. The table at the end of this chapter, although not exhaustive, lists 30 different theories by 24 modern writers and scholars (some of them changed their minds) as to how the pentathlon winner was established. From this list I'll focus on half a dozen of the major influences on what I call "pentathlon determination scholarship." Many were attracted to the problem because our thinking is influenced by the relative fairness of modern sport. Our belief has been that the Greeks, too, had to be fair and tidy in their own staging of athletics. Today we are obsessed with "getting it right," or what Kyle calls a "modern rulebook fetish."[3] Today automatic timing devices split hairs at the

finish line, instant replays allow decisions to be reviewed, sophisticated measuring devices measure jumps and throws, and scoring systems are computer-
ized.

The Greeks had no such technical devices to help determine a winner and
played at a more basic level. Ancient Greek sport does not fulfill many of the
characteristics of modern sport, as identified by Allen Guttmann.[4] The Greek
guidelines used for determining the pentathlon winner had to be simple and
uncomplicated. Yet from the mid–19th century to the turn of the 21st, eclectic
theories on this question abounded: they ranged from conducting the pentathlon
in tournament fashion (think tennis) to using a points system to always requiring a field of 24 athletes because there were 24 letters in the Greek alphabet.

In 1994 Victor Matthews provided the correct interpretation to a Plutarch
reference, written in the 2nd century C.E. Plutarch, a Greek historian and essay-
ist who was born near Delphi, used a pentathlon metaphor to explain how he
determined that *alpha* was a superior (winning) letter. Alpha "1) is superior to
most letters in being a vowel, 2) among the vowels it has two quantities, 3)
of those with two quantities it is superior by always coming first (in diph-
thongs). Thus [Matthews explains] the 'competitors' in the alphabet are suc-
cessively reduced from 24 to the seven vowels (as by the first triad), then the
three with two quantities (as by the footrace), and finally to alpha alone (as
by the wrestling)."[5] Matthews is quite correct is concluding that Plutarch would
not have made the effort to compare a prominent letter and a pentathlon winner
if there was no analogy to be drawn. And Plutarch points us in the right direction in solving the problem.

A Myriad of Theories

Yet there have been any number of victory determination theories from
modern day scholars. Emblematic of the peculiar and outlandish proposals
was a 1903 idea from E. Norman Gardiner (1864–1930), the dean of his pro-
fession (classical sports history at Cambridge University), who argued that,
in case there was no triad winner, second and third places were counted and
used in the determination of the overall winner.

Gardiner proposed that all entrants compete in each event, that wrestling
was the final event and that the order of the initial four was inconsequential.
From a management and organizational standpoint Gardiner's system can be
dismissed on three grounds. First, it would have taken forever to conduct. The
wrestling alone would have seemed endless. For example, in a field of eight
athletes, three rounds or a total of seven bouts would have been necessary to
determine the event winner. These bouts could not have been conducted simultaneously since there were few judges (at Olympia before 496 B.C., only one

If an athlete won the first three events: discus, jump and javelin, he was said to have won the triad, and the pentathlon was settled then and there since he had already won a majority of the events. Adapted from Panathenaic amphora, 520–510 B.C., in British Museum (*Greek Athletic Sports and Festivals*, 1910).

for the pentathlon). Second, Gardiner supposes that it would be possible for five different athletes to each have a victory apiece so that, to decide on an overall winner, 2nd and 3rd place event finishes would have been used, although he does not explain how. This would have been very unlike the Greeks, who were interested only in winners, and implies that places must have been kept. How, for example, does one decide who was 3rd in wrestling? And this suggests that for the three field events (discus, long jump, and javelin) measurements were taken or at the very least implies that 2nd and 3rd places would be known. The amount of record-keeping to fulfill his thesis would have been considerable.

Third, from the viewpoint of the spectators, Gardiner's system would have been overly confusing. We can, perhaps, excuse Gardiner, for in his world of British athletics the history of combined events was a blank page. To use his own words, "Unfortunately, in too many cases the writers have set about to improvise a system of athletics out of their inner consciousness with no practical experience to guide them."[6] Gardiner's admonition should have applied to himself. His background in athletics was minimal and his knowledge of combined events was imaginary. It is fair to say that Gardiner never witnessed a pentathlon, decathlon or all-around in his lifetime because the British athletic establishment simply ignored the genre. Britain's experience with combined events was nonexistent during Gardiner's lifetime, the second half of the 19th and first half of the 20th century. Britain was one of the last participants to offer a national decathlon meeting and first did so in July 1928, two years before Gardiner's death.[7] When the modern Olympic Games were held in London in 1908 (within the prime of Gardiner's scholarly productivity), no combined event appeared on the program. In fact, the 1908 London Olympics are the last modern games not to have included combined events. Further, the combined event record in Britain is so void that the last documented combined athletic event contest held in Britain prior to 1928 would have been in 1868, the final year of the Much Wenlock Games pentathlon. Gardiner would have been four years old.

The literature on combined events in Britain (newspaper, books, and meet results) is also a blank page from the advent of modern track and field (for argumentative purposes, say, 1860) to 1936: no British literature exists on the subject. As far as combined events were concerned, the UK had virtually no interest. For example, in the modern Olympic Games, from 1906 to 1936 (of which there were 150 decathlon entrants worldwide from every continent), the British entered exactly no one in Olympic decathlon or pentathlon events.[8] Not a single entrant. Because the British lacked interest and experience with combined events, we probably should not hold Gardiner, who has been labeled a "second class scholar" for other reasons,[9] accountable for his gaffes. He lived virtually his entire life without the background of combined events. Unfortunately, for our purposes, he was the best known of classical scholars in the first half of the 20th century and his influence on the thinking about the ancient pentathlon, often right, often wrong, was enormous.

In 1925 Gardiner teamed with Lauri Pihkala of Finland to promote an indefensible scheme of "comparative victories" to determine the pentathlon winner. Outright victories were unnecessary, they maintained, and only comparative ones helped determine who would advance to wrestling. Their format was so complex that it can be rejected outright for spectatorship reasons. Unfortunately Gardiner had the embarrassing misfortune of claiming that Pihkala's system had "a very practical application to the pentathlon of the modern Olympic Games," since his statement came a year after the International Olympic Committee dropped the pentathlon from the modern program.[10] He clearly was not paying attention. The theories of Gardiner and Pihkala held sway for the first half of the 20th century when other major figures (Bean, Ebert, Harris, Sweet and Kyle) entered the argument. Each had a significant following.

George E. Bean proposed five different victory schemes, each more and more intricate, since they included second place finishers. Four of them are listed in the table below.[11] My tongue in cheek favorite is his "Third Theory" in which athletes could choose the distance of the run and in which the winners of a 200m (*stade*) and a 400m (*diaulos*) met in a wrestling final. Joachim Ebert performed the first comprehensive look at the ancient pentathlon in a manuscript which found its way out of East Germany in 1963. His rather naïve conclusion that an athlete was eliminated after showing that he was deficient three times (relative, not absolute victories) would have required intensive record keeping and would have provided, for the athletes and spectators, a complicated finish.[12] Yet his stature as a scholar, like that of Gardiner, claimed converts.

In 1966, H.A. Harris offered the most reasonable scheme to date. A fine classical scholar with little athletic background,[13] he made certain simplifying assumptions and came closest to the actual system. He correctly concluded that Greeks were only concerned with first places, and wins were necessary for the overall victory. As soon as that occurred the pentathlon concluded. He correctly assumed that the sprint and wrestling were the 4th and 5th events.

Harris ran into trouble in only one situation, that is, when three competitors remained after four events, with A claiming 2 event victories and B and C one apiece. He hypothesized that B and C would engage in a semi-final wrestling match, and the winner, now with two wins, would meet A in the wrestling final. This notion can be rejected on practical grounds and it is here that he drew much criticism. Waldo Sweet, a leading scholar from the University of Michigan, correctly pointed out that Harris's system would draw "heavy" (to use the ancient term of Philostratus) athletes to the event who could reasonably expect to win the discus, the semi-final wrestling bout and the wrestling final, virtually pre-determining the winner.

This situation, to Sweet, seemed unfair and he claimed that the Greeks would have thought so as well. And he is right. The Greeks may not have had the same concept of fairness as moderns, but they would not have stacked the pentathlon with heavy events.[14] I offer as evidence the fact that there are no known double winners at Olympia in the pentathlon and wrestling. Ancient pentathlon winners have also won the *stade* (ca. 200m), the *diaulos* (ca. 400m) and the *hoplitodromos* (race in armor). But there are no recorded double winners in pentathlon and wrestling. The pentathlon did not attract wrestlers who could take advantage of the Harris system. It just did not happen. The fact that many pentathlon winners were also outstanding runners helps us reject Harris's contention and allows us to confirm a later theory.

The Harris position, less common today, continues to appear. In 1991 Lee came to the defense of Harris' wrestling *repêchage* scheme, by arguing (rather unconvincingly) from the standpoint of spectators, that another wrestling match had much to offer.[15]

Sweet offered his own theory allowing all competitors to compete in the

If the pentathlon had not been settled after three events, all athletes with at least one individual event victory proceeded to the stade, a sprint the length of the stadium. Thus, there could be no more than three pentathlon sprinters. From a Panathenaic amphora (Metropolitan Museum of Art, New York, 1914).

run, for, according to Sweet, the order of the first four events was inconsequential. First, this is highly improbable. With large pentathlon fields this would have involved sections of the sprint or one large race entertaining the entire field. In the former case this would have involved heats and as many as three total races would have had to be contested to ascertain a *stade* winner. This is not only confusing, it is irrational and there is no evidence that the pentathlon race was run in heats.

Or, all competitors would have to be placed in one section and the difficulty of judging at the finish line with, say, a dozen athletes, is daunting and the Greeks would have not been able to handle it. Sweet did not give the management aspect of the pentathlon much thought. But there is more. If, after three events there is a triple winner (one athlete who won all three initial events), the final two events are cancelled. But without a definite order it would have been possible, using Sweet's scheme, not to conduct one of the three core events (discus, jump or javelin). This would defeat the very purpose of the pentathlon outlined in our introduction.

It gets even more complicated with Sweet. If there was a different winner in each event after four, or if one athlete had won two and two had captured one event apiece, under Sweet's system, all athletes with one victory would be matched by lot and compete again in an event that he had not won earlier, also determined by lot. This would resolve who would advance to the wrestling final. Understand? This procedure would have been difficult for spectators to follow and for the judges (*hellandakai*) to administer. De facto, there could be two different discus competitions (the initial one and a *repêchage*), or two jump competitions, or two javelin events, and so on. Needless to say, Sweet's system, which offers no new (or even old) supporting evidence, has been the most confusing and unreasonable one to date. Kyle laments this because of Sweet's stature: "By his scholarship and his years of teaching ancient sport at the University of Michigan, Sweet has done much to legitimize and promote the study of ancient sport. However, his interpretation of scoring the pentathlon may mislead future readers, given Sweet's authority and the probability that his will be *the* sourcebook for generations, generations growing up with even more complex and modern systems of sport."[16]

A Final Solution

So where does that leave us? How was the ancient pentathlon victor determined? The Harris system covers most of the possible scenarios and is likely correct with one exception. It is here that Kyle injected himself into the debate.[17] He offers a convincing solution when, after four events one athlete (A) has two event victories and two others (B, C) have one apiece. Harris had proposed that B and C compete in a semi-final wrestling bout, something dismissed on fairness grounds. It is obvious that A has won the run and Kyle suggests that the semi-final match be a race, another *stade*, between B and C, on spectatorship and management grounds. It would have been understandable to spectators, easy to manage, and would not have exhausted one of the competitors before the wrestling final.

It is important to recall two elements of this debate. First, as I will argue in Chapter 7, this final scenario would be infrequent; the probability analysis suggests that the number of times officials would have to resort to a second race would have been relatively small and unworthy of the amount of attention it has attracted in the journals.

Second, a convention of modern combined events is to place the stamina contest last. For if it is not, the athletes will not be able to perform the speed, skill and strength events with any proficiency. The ancients tested stamina (one may use endurance, fortitude, energy, staying power, grit) with a five fall wrestling match. Today combined event stamina is tested with a distance race and one would not think of holding a distance race before other events. It hurts me just to imagine this. It is not a coincidence that every modern combined event ends with a stamina event—*every one*, from the 1860s Wenlock pentathlon of William Penny Brookes (an 880 yard hurdle race), to the All-Around (mile), to the modern decathlon and pentathlon (1500 meters), to women's combined events (800 meters) to the modern pentathlon (cross country race). The laws of both bio-mechanics and kinetics applied to the ancients as well. Performances suffer where one is tired and so the semi-final wrestling match of Harris would have been debilitating if one had to then wrestle again.[18] The Greeks would have understood this. Harris did not. The advantage of Kyle's method is its simplicity for all concerned.

So, the ancient pentathlon winner needed three individual event wins. He was the overall pentathlon victor if:

1. He won the first three events (discus, jump, javelin)
2. He won two of the first three events, then won the sprint
3. He won one of the first three events, then won the sprint and wrestling
4. There were 3 athletes (A, B, C) with a victory apiece after 3 events. If A won the sprint, giving him 2 wins, B and C would then compete in a *repêchage* sprint, with the winner meeting A in the wrestling final.

That's it.

What to Do About a Tie?

Kyle leaves the door open for local modifications or variations over time, yet I would downplay their significance. But the rare issue of a tie should be mentioned. The victory method used dictates whether or not a tie in combined event was possible. In modern times decathletes compete against a scoring table which uses enough digits that ties are a rarity. When tables were introduced in 1912 they included points and fractions of points with decimals of up to four places. It would be a virtual impossibility to have two athletes with identical scores, say of 7567.3875 points. The decimals were dropped after 1935 and there has only been one significant decathlon meeting, the 1964 US Olympic Trials, in which the top two athletes finished with identical scores.[19] The IAAF uses a three-tier tie-breaking system for duplicate scores. Using the tie-breakers, in nearly 100 years of the modern decathlon, there has never been a tie. The National Collegiate Athletic Association (NCAA), up until 2013 incidentally, did not break ties.

For the ancients a tie resulted in a "sacred victory," that is, the victory was dedicated to the festival god(s). We have record of this happening at Olympia, but not for the pentathlon event. A pentathlon tie was technically possible for two reasons. First, injuries could occur, preventing any single athlete from achieving three event wins. A "sacred victory" would then be declared. Second, it is possible that bad weather could prevent a finish or the event could simply run out of time and daylight. Weather and time constraints accompany combined events no matter what the era. For the ancients pentathlon ties were technically possible, but unlikely.

4. The Discus

(Discos / δίσκος)

Myron's *Discobolus* (the discus thrower), the most famous athletic statue of antiquity, was a representation of the ideal male form. The bronze original (470 B.C.) has been lost but thousands, perhaps hundreds of thousands, of replicas from Roman times dot modernity.[1] At Olympia the discus was not contested as an individual event. Rather it was always a sub-event of the pentathlon and now there is little doubt that it was the first pentathlon event contested.

Discus throwing was popular and often required in gymnasium training for young men. Every Greek youth was familiar with the event and we should give no weight to the conjecture that discus throwing was illogical since the implement was neither a weapon nor round for use in ball games.[2] The event was so popular in the Greek world that Cicero, commenting in the 1st century B.C. about the Greek gymnasium, claimed that athletes preferred the discus to the lectures of philosophers.[3]

The Discus

About twenty discs survive from antiquity. Eight have been found at Olympia. The ancient discus was initially shaped of stone but by the 6th century B.C. bronze discs were normal. Marble and lead discs have been unearthed but they are larger and likely to have been votive (ceremonial). Ancient metal discs were initially created by smelting molten ore and pouring it into a circular mold, perhaps hollowed out of sand. They often had a flat top. And, whether flat or elliptical, they were sanded for a better grip.

The ancient discs, although similar in shape, varied greatly in size, ranging from 6½ inches to 13½ inches in diameter, and in weight from 3 to 15 pounds. Each festival used its own equipment and the implement was not standardized. And boys (and possibly young men) threw smaller discs. We should not be confused by all of the variation. Indeed, if, a millennium from now, someone had unearthed disci from the 21st century, they would range from approximately 7 to 8½ inches in diameter and 2.2 to 4.4 pounds. Today, considering gender and age, there are five (and this excludes veterans' track and field equipment) official size disci in use.

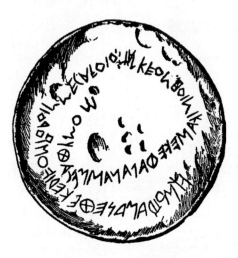

This drawing depicts a competition discus (2 inches thick, 1.245 kg/2.74pounds, 16½ inches in diameter) found at Cephallenia from 6th century B.C., which was also used as a votive offering. It states, "Exoidas dedicated me to the twin sons of Great Zeus, the bronze discus wherewith he conquered the high-souled Kephallenians." So we are sure Exoidas won the discus, but uncertain if he won the pentathlon. British Museum, 1910 (*Greek Athletic Sports and Festivals*, 1910).

Some scholars have noted the similarity of weight between the modern disci for men (ca. 4½ pounds) with that of the ancients.[4] Yet this does not seem to square with the nearly two dozen amphora depictions of the ancient discus thrower we have in today's museums.[5] Here the discus is always portrayed as significantly larger than its modern counterpart, at times reaching halfway up the forearm. Two explanations take care of this anomaly. First, the ancient implements, although nearly the same weight, were flatter, more planed. This made them harder to grasp. Second, modern discus throwers are significantly larger, in height, weight and mass, than the ancients. It is not unreasonable to say that ancient Greek pentathletes were at least ca. 20 percent smaller in both weight and mass than modern discus throwers. This would make the discus appear about 20 percent larger on illustrations.

The Event

Pausanius tells us that three *discoi* at Olympia were hung in bags and kept in the Treasury building of the Sikyonians for use in the pentathlon.[6] The discus, the initial pentathlon event, would begin at the conclusion of the hippic (equestrian) events around noon of the second day of the festival. Spectators would move from the hippodrome, located just south of the stadium, and stand or sit on the grassy stadium embankments while a herald introduced the pentathletes.

At Olympia the pentathletes would line up within the tunnel at the northwest corner of the stadium. There was not a little bit of Atlantic City in the procession.[7] A herald would announce each athlete who would parade, unclothed, toward the eastern end of the stadium while the *Hellendoakai* called for the disci from the Sikyonia Treasury. Similar to modern major meetings, the athletes did not provide their own implements. The athletes threw from the *balbis* (starting line used for the sprint).

Many early scholars have mistakenly claimed that the throwing area was a heaped up mound of earth large enough for a single athlete. This erroneous notion was so ingrained in late 19th and early 20th century scholarship that, when the modern games were returned to Athens in 1896 (and again at the Athens Intercalated Games in 1906), an elevated and sloping (toward the landing area) platform was used. J. Kenneth Doherty tells us that this was soon deemed impractical and discontinued, but not before (for a few years) it was an official modern Olympic event.[8]

It would be another 70 years before the literary mistake was caught. David C. Young tells us that is was simply a transliterated mistake by Philostratos, a 3rd century A.D. observer who used the term *diakechôstai* (a heaped up area) for *diakechôristai* (a marked off area) while describing the ancient throwing area.[9] Early Hellenistic scholars and Greek officials at the early Olympic Games thus re-created a discus throw from an elevated platform, an event which had never occurred in antiquity but which did not deter Americans Robert Garrett (1896) and Martin Sheridan (1906) from becoming Olympic champions.

The throwing area was a small, rectangular spot fronted by the *balbis* which served as the forward foul line. It was marked on both sides and open at the back. There was no V-shaped landing sector like today. The acceptable landing area was width of the stadium and this varied from venue to venue. At Olympia the stadium was approximately 90 feet wide. Athletes were given five throws which were marked by a small peg (*sema, semion*), but not measured.[10]

Greek Measurement Was Ordinal, Not Cardinal

It is a modern misconception that the ancient Greeks measured their efforts. Measurement of athletic effort would have applied only to the core pentathlon events, the discus, jump and javelin. Some writers have criticized the Greeks as careless measurers.[11] Nothing could be further from the truth. The Greeks marked their jumps and throws. A visual inspection of the *sema* farthest from the throwing area or take off area was all that was necessary to determine who had won, and knowing the winner was all that was necessary. A few vase paintings show rods (*kanons*) and some modern scholars have

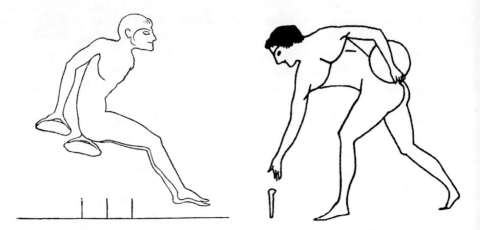

The jump effort was marked by a semeion or peg. There was no need to measure the effort and in the first image the athlete is about to surpass the leading mark, which may be his own or belong to another. From a 6th century B.C. amphora in British Museum (drawing from 1904 *Journal of Hellenic Studies*). The discus attempt was also marked by a semeion but also not measured. This youth is either placing or pulling up a mark. From a kyslix, about 525 B.C., in Würzburg Museum (drawing from 1907 *Journal of Hellenic Studies*).

assumed that they were used for measurement. The rods displayed appear to be 4 or 6 feet long. It would take dozens of rods (or the same rod turned over dozens of times) to measure one discus effort and scores of rods to measure a good javelin throw. This would have been time consuming and unnecessary. E.K. Brothwick, although he initially assumed throws were measured, unwittingly stumbled upon the truth when describing the ancient Gymnasium of Bromius. He concludes that "there seems to be no literary evidence for how throws were measured."[12] Indeed, they were not.

In 1948 Professor Paul Tasch complained, in a scientific paper about Greek measurement, that there were very few reported measurements in any field by the 4th century B.C. He wondered aloud why there were no athletic measurements and noted that the first recorded attempt to apply direct measurement of physical laws to biological phenomena did not come until the 3rd century B.C. Tasch's field was physics and he should not be criticized for being unfamiliar with athletics.[13]

Ernest W. Adams, in a seminal paper, "On the Nature and Purpose of Measurement," succinctly reminded us that the users of measurement must question what can legitimately be done with measurements and what meaningful can be said about them.[14] The non-standardization of linear measurement is but one part of the explanation why the Greeks did not measure field events. For instance, a foot at Olympia was not the same as a foot at Delphi. We will see more of this when we examine the Greek long jump. The lack of pentathlon standardization extended to the length of the sprint and the size and weight of both the discus and jumping weights.

Non-comparable measurements would have been hollow. For example, a twenty foot jump at Olympia and a similar mark at Delphi would have been significantly different marks. No sport goes to the lengths track and field does to compare measured physical efforts. *Track and Field News*, for example, has concocted an elaborate system to make sprint times comparable by adjusting them for wind measurements and altitude. Some studies have even gone so far as to take into consideration air temperature, humidity, hardness of the track and even the time of day.[15] For the Greeks and the pentathlon events, the only important "measure" was ordinal, not cardinal. The only important number was "first," as in "first place."

The Field

The discus efforts were accompanied by music from the *auletes*, a flute player. There is more than sufficient evidence from vase paintings that music was used throughout the triad of the pentathlon.[16] In reality the *aulos* was an oboe, a reed with holes pierced along its length enabling the musician to change the pitch of the note by stopping one or more holes with his fingers. None of the ancient music survives. Terrell tells us that a good *auletes* player was always in demand, and Pausanias says that one Pythokritos played for the pentathlon at six Olympic Games.[17]

If Nigel Crowther is correct about the size of the pentathlon fields at Olympia (5–10 athletes),[18] this would result in 25 to 50 throws, and without measurement, would take no more than 30 to 60 minutes, often less. The time taken in administering the discus is in the measuring of the attempts.

Throwing Technique

It is uncertain which ancient pentathlon event, the jump or the discus, is the most misunderstood. For my part, I believe it was (is) the latter. For the better part of the 20th century the conventional wisdom of how the ancient discus throw was performed, as explained in a comprehensive article by Gardiner in 1907, was incorrect.[19] Using the 5th century B.C. sculpture *Discobolus* by Myron as a starting point, Gardiner explained in detail (and incorrectly) that the thrower took one advancing step with his left foot and tossed discus in a forward direction, that is, to the right. This description of the discus throw was the standard explanation for many years. And it was never challenged. But, in fact, it was completely erroneous. In actuality the throw went in the

opposite direction, requiring a counterclockwise unwinding of the torso to create torque and a pivot over the left foot. In Myron the thrower is initially facing
the landing area. In modern terms, Gardiner's explanation was wide of the
mark and his discus would have landed in the back of the cage.[20]

Imagine, for several generations modern observers could not figure out
in which direction the throw went. The fact that the error was not caught until
recently only validates that coaches and scholars are discrete groups. Any
coach or athlete who had read his description of the Myron *Discobolus* would
have guffawed.

There was no monopoly on the misunderstanding of how the ancient discus was thrown. Two additional samples of confused scholars, one early and
the other more recent, will suffice. The first, by H.A. Harris in 1972,[21] is a daz-
zling array of biomechanical errors. He contended that in the ancient discus
throw: (a) there were two moments of rest within the throw; (b) that there was

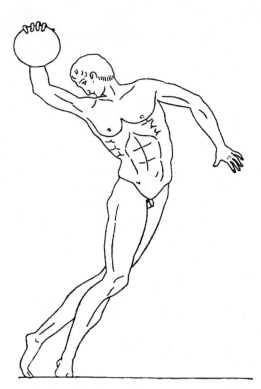

a rotary movement of the legs
much like that of the modern
thrower in the circle, (c) the
forefinger imparted a spin on the
implement upon release; (d) the
throw was a horizontal one; and
(e) the athletes' aim is at the
greatest possible speed of body
revolution. Unfortunately he was
wrong on all counts. Yet for
years, this too was an unfortu-
nate and misleading description
of the ancient throw.

To compound his mistakes,
he offers a suggestion that the
discus should be bowled, as in
cricket, with the throwing arm
bent back immediately before
release. Track coaches and athletes would find this recommen-
dation outrageous, since given
what we know about discus
release (straight arm, long pull,

The pentathlon's first event was the discus throw. Athletes threw for distance, similar
to today, and each contestant was allowed five attempts. Today we would call the effort
a "stand." Here the thrower has completed his backward swing and will step forward
with his left leg before throwing. From a Panathenaic amphora, 450 B.C., in Naples
National Archaeological Museum (1907 drawing, *Journal of Hellenic Studies*).

and grip on top of the discus); it would require a broken arm. The description was outlandish but at the time passed for good and sufficient truth. One thing is for certain: the author himself could claim a world record for the number of kinetic errors in a single paragraph.[22]

An equally embarrassing technique description was provided in a set of sequence drawings in 1999.[23] With the exception of improper position of the head, left hand, right (holding) hand, feet, body posture and angle of release, there is little to nitpick about these illustrations. And the claim that today the discus is thrown with 2½ turns in the circle confirms unfamiliarity with the modern event.

Some modern experts claim that it is difficult to describe the ancient throw since there is not enough literary or artistic evidence. Yet today there are some adequate descriptions of the ancient throwing technique. The best can be found in Tyrrell's 2003 description for a right handed thrower[24]:

> The thrower began, as does *Statius Phkegyas*, by rubbing his hand and the discus with sand. He assumed a position facing the *balbis* and the stadium beyond it in which the discus had to land for the throw to be valid. His arms were extended before him with the discus in his right hand. The left steadied it and kept it snug against the right. His left leg was forward of the right, which bore his weight, counterbalancing the discus. With the discus in his right hand, he swung his arms up and down before him ... he wound the discus by turning his torso to the right. His throwing hand rotated so that the discus was held from above by his fingers over the rim and by the motion of his arm. He shifted his weight onto the toes of his right foot. At the same time the left foot pivoted toward the right. Both feet remained in nearly constant contact with the ground [some would question this]. He continued the wind until his arm and the discus were fully outstretched behind his back. As he moved his arm, he bent his torso further to the right and at the waist and his knees toward the ground. His head turned backward with his body allowing him to see his ribs. In the stance immobilized by Myron's *Discobolus*, he was now coiled for the delivery phase.
>
> In delivery, the discus was unwound by being pulled around in a wide arc and accelerated by the rotation of the body and right arm. The wider the arc the more force generated ... the left arm guided the thrower through the arc as he turned clockwise to face the stadium [this is a major flaw]. He shifted his weight forward and pivoted on his left foot. He cast his right side into the throw as he projected the discus upward. The discus rolled off his fingers ... his was a flowing, seamless movement.

Few will quibble with this description. Today's coaches may question the foot placement. And Tyrrell obviously has no concept of the late left arm, the creation of torque (it does not happen automatically) and, what is commonly called "the block." But it is the best example in today's literature and essentially an accurate portrayal of what happened.

There are three things to remember in the ancient discus technique. First, it was a standing throw, what is currently and simply called a "stand." Today world class throwers can toss over 200 feet from a stand. For many a combined event athlete, 150 foot stands are ordinary. Given a similar size implement and a thousand years of experience with the event, my guess is that some good Greek throwers achieved comparable distances.

The discus competition, like the jump and javelin, was accompanied by music; a flute player (*auletes*) is on right. The middle athlete is affixing the *ankyle* to the javelin (*Journal of Hellenic Studies*, 1907).

Second, in ancient times, because of the implement (shape and weight) and less centrifugal force exerted (because it was a stand) the angle of release was necessarily greater. The ancient discus was essentially "scooped." Finally, given the parameters already described, there could have been little variation in technique. There was no step or full turn, no reverse, so time-honored was the style. With an emphasis on restricted yet elegant and graceful movement, the full potential of distances would have been limited, muted. On the practical side, shorter, controlled throws were easy to administer. The Greeks did not build a cage at the throwing area.

Given available literary and artistic evidence and an understanding of biomechanics, it should not have been difficult to describe the ancient throw. Yet we have even more evidence of how the Greeks performed the event. Recently a film of Martin Sheridan (the 1906 Modern Olympic Games winner of the Greek style discus) has been discovered. At the end of his versatile and successful career (approximately 1910) Sheridan demonstrates, on perfectly preserved film, the techniques for numerous track and field events, including the Greek style discus. The 1906 Olympic contest in Athens used a raised platform and there is no guarantee of accuracy, but after viewing the film one can readily conclude that Sheridan's technique must be very close to the ancient style. It is the closest we have to a demonstration of the ancient Greek discus style. We will deal with Sheridan later.

It is unknown how the order of throwing was determined (likely by lot) and whether athletes alternated throws or took them all at the same time. We can be certain that the athlete did not mark his own throws. One of the judges would do that and, since the pegs (*sema*) would be placed on the stadium floor it would have been obvious who led the competition. Marks near or beyond the *sema* would have been obvious and appreciated by the spectators. When everyone had taken his allowed throws, the furthest mark determined the winner and the pentathletes moved to the *skamma*, the jumping area.

5. The Jump

Halma / ἅλμα

There is more written and less understood about the ancient pentathlon jump than any other sub-event. Tyrrell reminds us that an academic fascination with a reported extraordinary leap "has preempted serious discussion of the jump itself."[1]

There has been much discussion about the type of jump (*halma*, literally a leap or bound) used by the Greeks. In modern times there have been at least nine different types of formal jumping events.[2] The Greek jump itself was a running long jump, although it was never referred to by the Greeks as "broad" or "long." It should be remembered that each of the pentathlon events were likely preparations for warfare, and crossing Aegean terrain necessitated leaps over gullies, rifts or water. Today it seems irrefutable that the ancient jump was anything but a running one. We know this because of the innumerable references to a take-off board (*bater*) and an earthen landing pit (*skamma*), neither of which would have been necessary for a standing jump. Yet contemporary writers have differed greatly, and the following table offers a sampling of views.[3]

A Sampling of Ancient Jump Opinions

Running jump	standing jump	triple jump	series of standing jumps
Terrell (2004)	Gardner (1880)	Hyde (1938)	Harris (1972)
Kyle (2007)	Schöbel (1965)	Harris (1964)	Valavanis (2004)
	Swaddling (1980)		
	Sim (2000)		
	Perrotte (2004)		

The athletes landed in an area of softened earth, skamma, literally "that spot which has been dug." We will, for convenience, use the misleading term "pit" for the skamma. There is no agreement among scholars as to the placement of the skamma, who did the digging, its length, the placement of the toe-board and the length of the approach. In other words no other sub-event requires more biomechanical understanding and needs additional academic investigation than the jump.

Conduct of the Jump

Most likely the skamma was prepared in the day(s) before the pentathlon began. There has been little discussion about the location of the pit. Harris makes the strange mistake of placing the pit, both at Olympia and Delphi, in the middle of the running area of the stadium, nearer the curved end, forgetting that the same area may have also been used for the wrestling matches—pentathlon and open—later in the day and, ultimately, the pentathlon *stade* and all of the running events.[4]

At Olympia the position of the pit is unknown and literary and archaeological evidence is of little help. It was most likely prepared somewhere near the middle of the stadium (to accommodate more spectators), but to one side or the other (to stay away from the running area). A safe and suitable landing area was necessary. A surviving inscription from the stadium at Rhodes orders the *skamma* be dug to a depth of two feet.[5] Picks for digging are frequently depicted in pentathlon scenes in vase paintings.

The winner of the discus was the first jumper. The order of the remaining

The jump was conducted for distance with the use of hand weights, called haltere. Here a youth practices under the watchful eye of a trainer-coach, on right. This scene is taken from a vase dating to about 500 B.C., Boston Museum (*Greek Athletic and Sport Festivals*, 1910).

jumpers may have been chosen by lot. Each athlete was allowed five jumps. The tradition of allowing three attempts for field events was developed in the 19th century by the Highland Scots and somehow erroneously found its way into modern Classical scholarship. There is no evidence that attempts were restricted to three but there is literary evidence for five attempts.[6]

The jumpers' effort was marked by a peg (*semeion*), but not measured. Some scholars maintain that the *balbis,* the marble starting-turning point for the running events, served as the takeoff mark, the toe-board so to speak, for the jump. If this was the case at Olympia then the takeoff was configured from west to east at the east or open end of the stadium. The west balbis could not have been used since there was insufficient space for either an approach or pit. A 1971 reenactment of the ancient pentathlon at Delphi insisted on using the balbis at the closed end of the stadium with a congested run-up utilizing a 90 degree turn. Miller reveals a more practical explanation. A *bater*, literally "that which is trod upon," was used and functioned like a modern toe-board. It may have been a "simple board embedded in the surface of the stadium track for the *halma* and then removed."[7] It could be placed anywhere.

There are innumerable modern scholarly references to "sand" in the Greek pit,[8] but there appears to be no reference to it in any literary sources. The skamma was simply dug up soil. The use of sand in a jumping pit is a late 19th century invention.

Likely an official stood at the skamma, and both marked the jump with a *sema* and smoothed the ground for the next jumper. Some scholars have suggested the unlikely case that the athletes marked their own jumps.[9] When a peg or sema was not used, as the Scholiast to Pindar tells us, "that after every leap a fork was drawn across to marks its length so that he who leaps beyond all marks distances his rivals."[10]

There is plenty of artistic evidence that the sema were used and these simple marking pegs provide a powerful argument against "measuring" the jumps. If the jumps were measured there would be little need for the sema. One ancient representation of a jump shows three sema and this has confused scholars.[11] One scholar mistakenly maintains that this must have meant that second and third places were kept.[12] The three pegs may have simply determined the throwing order of the next event, the javelin. But all of this is guesswork.

One has to start with the presupposition that the Greeks were only interested in winning. In a society is which only first place mattered the placement of the marks told everyone (pentathletes, officials and spectators alike) all they needed to know, who was winning or who had won.[13] Determining leaders or winners of the jump could also have been accomplished by a less accurate procedure of drawing a line in the dirt and having officials watch closely.

One scholar maintains that each effort was measured by rod called a *kanon.*[14] This is doubtful. This does not mean that they could not do it, but there would be little reason for measurement if winning the event was the only goal. More likely the kanon served another purpose, that of smoothing the landing area after each jump. Given what we know of modern jump competitions the only piece of equipment missing in the artistic evidence is a rake, and the kanon may have served that purpose.

The Greek jump was uncomplicated. The sema simply did its job. Those who maintain that the Greeks were sophisticated about measurement should be reminded that the ancient pentathlon pre-dated the Greek numbering system as well as all of the Greek advances in mathematics. By then the pentathlon had been established and was well entrenched.

Technique

The distinguishing feature between the ancient and modern jump is that athletes in the former hand-carried jumping weights (*halteres*). Often shaped like dumbbells or a telephone receiver, the function of the halters may have been to lengthen the leap, but modern experimentation has netted inconclusive results. Philostratus tells us "The *halteres* are an invention of the pentathletes and were invented for jumping (*halma*) from which they take their name. Considering the jump to be one of the more difficult events in competition, the rules permit encouragement of the jumper by means of a flute and also assist him even more with the *halteres*. For the guidance of the hands is unfailing and brings the feet to the ground without wavering and in good form. The rules show how important this is for they refuse to have the jump measured [counted] if the mark is not correct" (Philostratus, *On Athletics* 55).[15]

The *halter* (singular) was made of stone, lead or metal and often was designed to fit the hand.[16] The *halteres* were not standardized even within the pair. Rather they were personal equipment usually weighing between 3½ and 5½ pounds each. Many have survived, often with inscriptions indicating that they were frequently used as a votive offering after victory. The *halteres* dedicated by Olympic pentathlon winner Akmatidas of Sparta (ca. 550 B.C.) now displayed in the Olympia Archaeological Museum were fashioned of stone and weighed over 10 pounds. The inscription reads, "Akmatidas of Lakedaimonia, having won the 5 without dust dedicated ...."[17] It is unlikely he used these in the competition.

The technique of the *halma* can be recreated using the four stages of the leap, many of which are portrayed in vase paintings. The approach was short by definition because the pentathlete carried weights. Likely the run-up amounted to no more than six to ten strides, about 50 feet. The run-up would have been vigorous, stylized and rhythmic. Because of the weights there could not have been the vigorous pumping of the arms as done by modern jumpers. A shortened penultimate step would have been as important in ancient times as it is today.

Law of Motion

Newton's 3rd Law of Motion states, "To every action there is always an equal and opposite reaction: or the forces of two bodies on each other are always equal and are directed in opposite directions." Whether the Greeks discovered an application of Newton's third law of motion (ca. 1666) by using haltere is problematic. Two issues are paramount, the weight of the haltere and the force with which they are thrust backward immediately before landing. Ancient Greek long jumpers would have had to make several compromises about the weight, which we know was somewhere in the neighborhood of 2 to 3 pounds each. Heavier weights would allow more force in the final motion, but also act as a deterrent to the athlete's speed of approach. In the running long jump the athlete essentially transfers horizontal speed into lift at the point of takeoff (in athletic terms, the take-off board). One hears often of "running off the board."

Speed is an essential element. Ancient jumpers carrying heavy haltere could only lumber toward the take-off and any force imparted by thrusting the implements backward would have been lost earlier by the slow approach. Very light jumping weights might have little impact of the speed of approach but also would have little impact using the effect of Newton's 3rd law. So the weight of the haltere was always a compromised decision, and it is no coincidence that the weight of the extant ancient haltere varied by athlete.

The second issue, the force of the backward thrust of the haltere, is also a compromise. Vigorous backward pulls could be unbalancing. Tepid thrusts would not help. This part of the long jump technique had to be practiced and it is no wonder that the Greeks believed that the jump was the hardest event to master. The consequence of this Goldilocks technique (not too heavy—not too light—not too strong—not too weak) would have been virtually negligible (perhaps a small positive distance) on the outcome. Nothing more.

The second function of the haltere was likely much more important ... that of aiding in a balanced landing since distinctive footprints had to be left in the dirt in order for the jump to count.

The Jump

In spite of numerous scholars claiming that the running starting line, the balbis, was used as the jump take-off point, this opinion is unreliable.[18] In all

The haltere were difficult to master. At the beginning of the leap the weights had to be thrust upward, which is presumably what the trainer-coach on right is teaching. From vase, Boston Museum, circa 480 B.C. (*Greek Athletic and Sport Festivals*, 1910).

of track and field there is no single moment of kinetic stress on muscles and joints as when a jumper slams his foot upon the toe-board. It is a crushing movement and the thought of using a marble slab as a toe-board for barefooted jumps makes the author wince. The Greeks were smarter than this.

The leap in the air was timed so as to coordinate body posture, the hands holding the halteres and the feet. The athlete bound into the air swinging the halteres forward to add momentum. On the descent the athlete keeps the halteres in front of him with his feet stretched out, then swings the halteres behind him and drops them immediately before landing.

The landing placed a premium on balance. The athlete had to tip forward, and in a modern gymnastics sense the jumper had to "stick" the landing, meaning that the footprints in the skamma had to be distinctive for the jump to count. A tumbling forward could not be avoided but the footprints were crucial. Philostratus tells us that the jump had to be made in good form and officials refused to have the jump count if the feet placement was incorrect.[19] Artwork (sculptures and vase paintings displayed at the New York Museum of Art as early as 1925) strongly suggest that the jumper landed on his feet.[20]

This is a significant difference between the ancient and modern jumps. Today the long jump is measured from the mark closest to the toe-board, however made. Today balance on landing is unimportant and many combined-event athletes considerably extend their feet upon landing so that the last mark made in the pit is by the buttocks, back or shoulder.[21] Modern measurements would be noticeably shorter in length if ancient landing procedures were in force.

The best single sequence reconstruction of the ancient halma from vase paintings is provided by Stephen Miller.[22] Some modern scholars have reasoned that the halma must have been a triple jump or a series of standing leaps. Neither is correct. Carrying weights or controlling the second or third steps from a soft surface would have precluded a triple jump. A triple jump would have been unworkable.

And a standing jump would have made it impossible for the known and required arm and hand movements while hauling the halteres. Despite the claims of some scholars, the Greeks could not defy the laws of physics. For example, the typical standing jumper would have no more than five to seven tenths of a second to execute all that is known about the movement of the, legs, the arms and the halteres; thrust forward, tuck, thrust backward to drop, then move the arms ahead of body for the landing. No athlete, however gifted, would have had time to accomplish all of that in a fraction of a second. And so a standing jump would have been equally unworkable.

It is also often contended by modern writers that the addition of music to the ancient jump distinguished it from its modern counterpart.[23] Nothing could be further from the truth. The Greek pentathletes indeed relied upon an auletes, a flute player, to provide music and rhythm during the attempt. The Olympic pentathlon flute player was usually the winner of the *aulos* (flute) competition at the Pythian Games, where music competitions were common. A Pythrokritos of Sikyon won the aulos competition at Delphi six times and thus played at the Olympic pentathlon on six occasions, likely a record.[24]

The tempo of the flute music was designed to aid the jumper in establishing cadence and to coordinate the actions of his hands holding the halteres. But the use of music in aiding a jump is not unique to the Greeks. Today, at every major combined-events international, athletes supply their own music on compact disks which are played during the long jump, high jump and pole vault attempts.[25] At major meets where music is not played (for example: Olympic Games, world and national championships), the event cadence for athletes is provided by rhythmic clapping, offering the same aid as the aulos did for the ancient jumpers. Standing at the end of the long jump runway, athletes will begin the clapping themselves, in effect asking the spectators for rhythmic acclamation to begin. The noise gets louder as the athlete approaches the toe-board. At major meetings the stadium literally rocks. This practice is long-standing, universal and unmistakable. It is the modern aulos and modern scholars seem to have overlooked it.

Greek Jump Haltere, Over the Years

Using artistic and archaeological evidence, six examples of *haltere* used in the Greek jump are displayed here, in the chronological order in which they were used in ancient festivals.

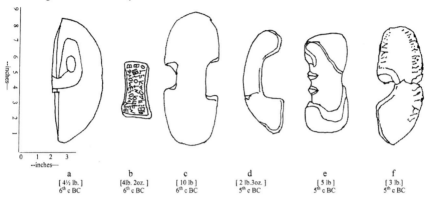

a	b	c	d	e	f
[4½ lb.]	[4lb. 2oz.]	[10 lb]	[2 lb.3oz.]	[5 lb]	[3 lb.]
6th c BC	6th c BC	6th c BC	5th c BC	5th c BC	5th c BC

(a) Stone halter. One pair found at Corinth. National Museum, Athens. Commonly shown on 6th century B.C. vases. (b) Halter of lead. Found at Eleusis. National Museum, Athens. 6th century. Inscription says, "Epainetos by means of this won the jump." (c) Stone halter, found at Olympia. Olympic Museum. Unlikely used for competition. (d) Halter of lead. British Museum, London. Type usually depicted on 5th century B.C. vases. (e) Stone halter, found at Rhodes. British Museum, London. (f) Marble halter found at Sparta. 5th century B.C. (drawings by author).

Phaÿllos and 55 Feet

Phaÿllos was a well known 5th century B.C. athlete who never won at Olympia but did win a pair of pentathlons and one *stade* at the Pythian Games.[26] In the first century C.E. an anonymous ditty appeared in a book of Greek poetry: "Phaÿllos jumped five feet more than 50 feet and threw the discus five feet less than 100 feet."

Much of the confusion about the ancient jump can be traced to this epigram. Phaÿllos was from Kroton, a Greek city on the instep of the Italian boot. Fascination by modern scholars with a fifty-five foot leap has forestalled critical dialogue about the jump itself. Classical scholars, willing to believe that someone jumped fifty-five feet, have gerrymandered their research to make the epigram stand up, perhaps as a triple jump or a series of standing jumps.[27] Internal logic and lack of evidence preclude these explanations. What we are left with are two possible explanations for the purported length of Phaÿllos' leap.

First, the point of the epigram has eluded scholars unfamiliar with characterizations of combined-event athletes. Today, if one were asked to describe a decathlete, something like "good thrower, weak runner," or "great jumper, can't hurdle" comes tumbling out. Cheeky characterizations of decathletes (and presumably pentathletes of antiquity) offer both the good and the bad. A portrayal of the 2008 Olympic decathlon champion Bryan Clay, for example, might go "great thrower, no endurance."[28]

And they are not modern. Ask any coach to describe his multi-event athlete and these coincident compliments and come downs are normal. In baseball we all know the meaning of "good field, no hit."

I am reminded of how Jim Phelan, a famous collegiate basketball coach, described more than one collegiate protégé: "looks like Tarzan, plays like Jane."[29] So it was with Phelan, so it must have been with Phaÿllos, who inspired a simultaneous compliment-slap epigram. Modern scholars have simply missed the point about this flippant and arithmetical statement. It was never about "55 feet," an extreme hyperbole. In the 3rd century C.E, Pausanias, via a Phaÿllos' statue at Delphi, knew of his athletic and his military reputation. He omits mentioning the jump either because he did not know of the story or did and dismissed it summarily.[30] So should we.

A second explanation which seems to have gained favor with some scholars is that the numbers were simply copied incorrectly. The numbers 2 and 5 in Greek are very similar are easily confused: $2 = κ$, $5 = υ$. The same point could have been made with Phaÿllos leaping 25 feet instead of 55 feet.

There are more angles to Phaÿllos story than a billiards tournament. First, the initial reference to a 55 foot jump does not occur until 600 years after the alleged fact. One would think that a fabulous feat would have been reported a bit sooner.[31] Second, we should be careful about the meaning of a "foot" in Ancient Greece. Some naïve modern writers have assumed that a foot was a foot and converted Phaÿllos' distance to the modern 16.76 meters.[32] Even if the jump was legitimate, the conversion to modern "feet" would not be.

Units of measurement were not standardized and differed in Greece from city to city. The length of the ancient foot varied considerably from place to place.[33] We know from the length of the stadium in Delphi that a Pythian foot was .2965 meters, but at Olympia a foot amounted to .3205 meters.[34] In other words, the presumed leap of Phaÿllos amounts to a modern jump of 16.30 meters or 53 feet, 53/4 inches using an imperial conversion. Yet it is not the longest reported leap of antiquity. That distinction belongs to a 52 foot jump at Olympia by Chionis of Sparta allegedly made in the mid–7th century B.C. Using the "Olympic foot" of .3205 meters, this distance converts to a modern 16.66 meters or 54 feet, 8 inches.

Ancient Leaps of Faith

date	athlete	festival	site	ancient feet	local conversion meters/foot	meters	modern feet
5th century b.c.	Phaÿllos of Kroton	Pythian G	Delphi	55'	.2965m	16.30m	53'–5¾"
7th century b.c.	Chionis of Sparta	Olympic G	Olympia	52'	.3205m	16.66m	54'–8"

The first modern writer to note that it was Chionis, not Phaÿllos, who owned the longest purported ancient leap was Heinz Schöbel (1965).[35] Unfortunately he miscalculates the Pythian-Delphic measure, creating an error that has been replicated by subsequent writers.[36] Interestingly, the leap by Chionis, who was a three time Olympic stade champion, must have occurred in the Olympic pentathlon, which he did not win. And, since it is virtually certain that he won the pentathlon stade this means we can hypothesize that he lost the pentathlon 3–2. It is peculiar that we might have the score of the meet and the name of the loser but not that of the winner.

Next, it is curious that the reported leaps by Phaÿllos and Chionis are rounded off to even feet, 55 and 52 in this case. Perhaps it is simply modern skepticism of any mark reported in even feet. But I think not. One must wonder what the chances were that two longest jumps were reported in even feet. It seems unlikely that the Greeks would just round off a jump to the nearest foot. The concept of unit fraction was well known to the Greeks (although the only number they used in the numerator was 1). The "foot" was not the smallest measurement available to the Greeks. In the modern history of track and field no single long jump record (starting in 1829) has ever been recorded imperially without fractions of a foot.

The reason is that the Greeks did not measure their jumps—there was no need.

6. Javelin

Akōn or Akontion / ἄκων or ἀκόντιον

The spear or javelin throw was the pentathlon's strongest link to military preparation. Indeed, in antiquity the javelin was an offensive weapon. Unlike wooden military javelins normally made of cornel, the implement for competitions was made from the branch of an elder tree. Its length was roughly equivalent to the height of a man, and its diameter about three quarters of an inch.[1] The javelin event was the least controversial of the pentathlon's three subevents.

As the third pentathlon event the javelin competition took place in the stadium and, like the discus, used the *balbis* as the foul line. It is likely that the winners of the earlier events threw first. There is some evidence that the javelin thrower's movements, much like the jump, were accompanied by the *aulos*. A legal throw had to land on the stadium floor. The pentathletes were allowed, as in the discus, 5 throws.[2]

Light and aerodynamic, the ancient javelin flew! Lucian describes the ancient javelin as "carried by the wind."[3] There is still a debate about whether the pentathlon javelin was pointed or blunt. For ancient competitions it is likely that the tip was blunt.[4] Although Pindar describes the athletic javelin as "bronze tipped," this is not confirmed by any of the many vase paintings which depict, in gymnasium and competition settings, blunted and tapered spears at the forward end. The number of paintings is so numerous that this could not have been an oversight. No metallic tips.

Modern metallic javelins are pointed and this aids in the marking, but a pointed landing is never guaranteed and, like many modern throws, there may be considerable skid or bounce after initial contact with the landing area. Presumably throws were marked where the javelin initially came in contact with the ground.

The throw was marked, like the discus, with a *sema*, a peg. The placement of the pegs may answer a concern scholars have had about what determined a winning throw, distance or accuracy. Virtually all modern scholars come down on the side of distance, yet there has always been lingering doubt since some literary sources suggest the opposite.[5] In fact, both were needed.

The fair landing area in antiquity was the entire stadium floor. At Olympia this was about 32 meters in width, at Delphi 25½ meters in width. An angle of 26 degrees determines the modern legal landing sector. In antiquity it was critical to keep the throws within the allowable landing area and as close to the middle of the infield as possible. A Pindaric Ode confirms,

> And I.......
> .....do hope
> Not to cast wide of the course
> The bronze cheeked javelin I whirl in my hand, but to throw it far
> And beat out my rivals [Pindar, "*Pythian Ode*," 1.42–45].[4]

An analogy can be drawn from the world of golf which simultaneously puts a premium on distance and accuracy.

A pentathlete preparing to throw a javelin. Because of the lightness of the implement and the use of the ankyle, the Greek throwers achieved outstanding distances. The landing area was the stadium floor itself. This red figured cup, which dates from approximately 470 B.C., resides in the Louvre, Paris (Erich Lessing/Art Resource, New York).

At ancient Greek festivals it was important that the javelin throw be long, but also, so to speak, down the middle. Judges would eyeball the position of the sema for length. Throws to the left or right of center might have been technically longer (in our modern view), but viewing the landing area diagonally (from one side of the *stadion* to the other) a shorter throw, that is, the way they are measured today, closer to the center of the landing area appears longer. Accuracy counted to a degree since throws down the middle appeared longer than wayward tosses far to one side or the other.[7] Moderns, who are much more technical and consistent, would be aghast at the manner in which the Greeks determined the javelin winner. But the Greeks kept it simple. Since there were no measurements, judges looked for the throw that was farthest down the landing area from the middle of the stadion floor. A simple diagram should suffice.

Outline of an Ancient Stadium
[Conduct of the Javelin]

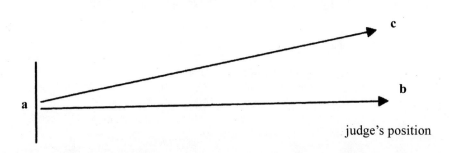

a–c is technically longer than a–b, but a–b would be judged the winning effort since it appears longer, since there were no measurements. For example, if a–b were 50 meters (164 feet), and the stadium width was 32 meters (about 105 feet) then a–c (depending upon the angle abc) could be as long as 52 meters (170 feet, 7 inches), yet judged as the lesser of the two throws.

Since the entire surface of the stadion was the landing area, this had to be the case. Bear in mind that the pentathlon-javelin contest was viewed and judged in a straightforward manner. It predates the science of geometry; something moderns take for granted and for which modern track and field has accounted for with measurements and sector lines.[8] The Greeks used neither. As in golf, distance is crucial but it pays to be accurate. Neither an inaccurate long driver nor an accurate short one wins many golf tournaments. Both were important.

Even though accuracy was important and practiced, wayward tosses and injuries may occasionally have occurred. So it paid to "groove" the toss to the center of the landing area. To aid in this accuracy and to enhance the distance of the effort, the Greeks used a leather strap or thong (*ankyle* in Greek, *amentum* in Latin). From 12 to 18 inches long, the strap was meticulously wrapped around the mid-point of the lightweight wood, near its center of gravity. Any number of ancient *amphorae* illustrate the pentathlete wrapping the strap with care and skill, since it played an important role in the success of the throw.[9] Keeping it taut the athlete placed one or two fingers (usually the index and/or middle fingers) of his throwing hand through a loop at the free end of the thong. As soon as the implement was released, the "wrapping came undone at lightning speed, which resulted in a twisting motion of the javelin. By quickly

The javelin was the 3rd pentathlon event. Like the discus, each athlete was allowed five throws. Much like modern throwing, the athlete glances back at his grip. Stemless cup, around 420 B.C. The pillar on the right is likely a leftover turning post at the balbis, which was used as the foul line. Berlin (*Greek Athletic Sports and Festivals*, 1910).

turning around on its own axis, the javelin's flight was stabilized and lasted longer, which resulted in greater distances."[10]

The best description of the ancient throwing technique is provided by Tyrrell, whose explanation occasionally references depictions on red-figure amphorae.

The thrower approaches the *balbis*, the same start/finish line used as a foul line in the discus, at a quick, short run. He aims at transferring the energy of the run smoothly through the rotating body into his arm and the throw. He keeps the javelin at the level with his ear ... the transition begins for a right-handed thrower on the fall of his left foot at a point near the *balbis* but not near enough to induce a foul after release. His shoulders and head turn to the right, and his right arm is extended, drawing the javelin back behind him. He stretches his left arm forward to maintain balance ... he rotates his arm so that the javelin rests in the palm of his hand, and the fingers hold onto the strap. Landing on his left leg, he rotates his right hip in the direction of the throw ... the arm pulls the javelin from behind and whips it at full extension toward a point down the stadium. He releases the javelin at an angle of about 35 degrees from level for maximum distance.[11]

Tyrrell's description is decidedly modern and there is little to quibble about.[12] He does not mention the length of the approach other than to describe it as "quick and short." Today's javelin throwers can afford a much longer approach, often as much as 25–30 meters, since they have less to worry about in the carry. Ancient throwers had to keep the *ankyle* taut until immediately before release and push the javelin back with the left hand. A long approach would have caused problems here.

Tyrrell mentions that the ancient pentathlete kept the javelin level with his ear, something that can be found in all modern technique manuals but which is also depicted on extant amphorae. Tyrrell does not spend much time on the use of the left (non-carrying) arm, claiming only that it is stretched forward for balance. In fact, this is an oversight, since the left arm is crucial in the beginning of the block, when during hip rotation, it is brought close to the body and pulled violently back, creating torque.[13] He claims that the optimum angle of release is 35 degrees, but this is a decidedly modern estimate.[14]

At Olympia the javelin could be thrown in either direction; east to west or west to east, but the former is more likely for the latter stadiums since it afforded a longer approach. It is incorrect to believe that the javelin was a standing event and athletes stood on an elevated balbis.[15]

Modern javelin throwers do not use the ankyle. For the Greeks, who experimented and practiced the javelin toss for well over 1000 years, the strap served a dual purpose. First, it allowed a longer pull on the throw, much like the discus, by increasing the radius of the throwing arm by the length of the strap. The longer pull produced more power at the point of release. Second, as it unwrapped in the early moments of the throw, it generated a spin to the javelin, much like bullets rifling from a gun barrel. The rotation kept the javelin from wobbling in flight and thus improved its distance. Philostratus (in *Gymnasticus* 31) tells us that the longer the fingers, the greater the results. The spin did not, however, guarantee that the spear would land on its point.[16] A bit too much is made of this aspect by modern writers.

The leather strap was twisted around the shaft but was otherwise not attached to it. There are no depictions from antiquity of un-gripped, free javelins with straps attached. When the javelin was unleashed the strap simply fell off. A fixed strap would flop around in flight, hindering both the accuracy of the effort and its distance. Modern seat-of-the-pants experiments on javelin distance using straps have been inadequate and resulted in questionable conclusions.[17] But, in and out of warfare and for 1000 years, the Greeks used the ankyle so there must have been something to it. We have no ancient standards of performance. Greek javelin achievement is speculative. Only a roundabout reference to javelin distance comes to us in the description of the length of a chariot race course: "In length it was three times a bow (arrow) shot, and four times a javelin throw."[18]

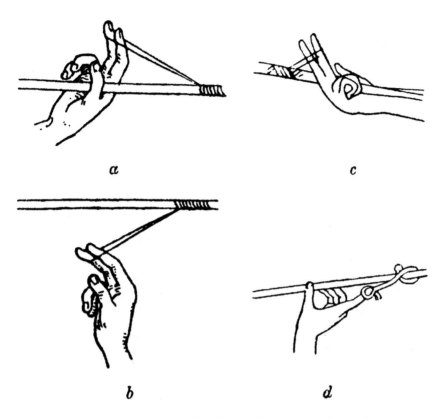

a

c

b

d

The ancient javelin throw was aided by a leather strap, the ankyle, which was wound around the center of gravity of the implement and helped in both accuracy and distance. All modern experiments confirm that the strap facilitated the javelin throw. These four early illustrations were prepared by German scholar Julius Jüthner (Julius Jüthner, *Antike Turngeräthe*, Vienna, 1896).

Given that ancient hippodromes (Circus Maximus of Rome, Olympia and others) were as long as 600 yards and shorter courses 400 yards, this would seem to imply that the ancient throwers, using lighter implement with a strap, were capable of throws 100 to 150 yards (91–136 meters or 300–450 feet) covering the largest part of the ancient stadium, but there is no conclusive evidence of such distances. Yet, overlooked by all modern writers is the evidence provided by the modern Finns. In a land where the javelin has been adopted as the national event, Finns experimented with the ankyle and many of throws over 80 meters were recorded.[19]

The smaller the stadium, the more danger the javelin throw presented to spectators. Wayward throws outside the track made accidents inevitable. Ulrich Sinn claims that this may have happened on occasion.[20] Yet we have not a single reference to a stadium javelin accident. This may be because the javelin, although tapered, did not need to be pointed, nor did it have a metallic tip.[21] There is no reference that the implement had to stick.

The javelin contest concluded the pentathlon core of three related "gymnastic" events. A victory in the javelin would have ended the pentathlon if a single athlete had also won the discus and jump as well. If not, then all athletes with at least one event victory would have headed to the east end (at Olympia) starting sills for a test of speed, a race the length of the stadion.

7. The Sprint

Stade / στάδιου

    The running event of the pentathlon was the *stade*, a sprint the length of the stadium. As an individual event it was the oldest of the "recorded" Olympic contests, and legend tells us that Corebeous, a Spartan cook, won the 600 foot race in 776 B.C. This simple race arose as a supplement to a religious-cultic gathering and may, in fact, be much older. For the next 13 festivals, as legend has it, the stade was the only event at Olympia. Then, in the 14th Olympiad, presumably 724 B.C., the *diaulos* (a double stade race—down and back) was added to the program. At the next games a *dolichos* (a distance race of 24 stades) was added. Finally, in 520 B.C., a race in armor, *hoplitodromos* (wearing helmet, shin guards and carrying shield, otherwise nude), was introduced, completing the program of footraces at Olympia. The sprint event was so important that the entire four year cycle was named for its winner. The 26 mile marathon is a modern creation and was never an event in antiquity.

    Since the sprint was already a stand-alone event, its inclusion into the pentathlon served as a sort of tie-breaker in case no single athlete had won the first three events. Its function was to help determine the overall winner (in the case that it became the 3rd victory for an athlete, or to whittle down the field). So there is little doubt that the pentathlon running event was the fourth event and not much controversy that it was a stade, a sprint one length of the *stadion*. Of major scholars, only Joachim Ebert maintained that the pentathlon race was longer than a stade.[1] He claims that it was five times the length of the stade, in keeping with the use of "penta" (five). Using a 1000 meter race before a wrestling match belies any appreciation of kinesiology.

    With the exception of the issue of starting devices and sills, most modern scholars have directed little attention to the preparation and conduct of the stade, taking for granted that a footrace is a footrace.[2] The length of the stade was 600 feet, but since the "foot" differed from festival to festival, the actual distance of the stade varied. But not much. Its closest modern counterpart

Frenetic sprinters in a stade (about 192 yards) race at Panathenaic Games. The artist has taken liberties with sprinting technique by illustrating the impracticable arm-leg sequence. This could not have represented the pentathlon stade since there would be no more than three runners. From a Panathenaic amphora, about 525 B.C., now in Metropolitan Museum of Art, New York (*Greek Athletic Sports and Festivals*, 1910).

would be the 200 meter dash. At Olympia the stade was 192.28 meters, at Delphi the distance was 177.5 meters. In all cases the distance is reasonably close to the modern 200 meter race distance.

The original running event at Olympia was part of a religious rite in which runners took their places 600 feet away from a priest, torch in hand, who stood next to a sacred altar. The contestants would race to the priest and the first arrival earned the right to light the sacred fire. At Olympia a flat running area was east of the sacred altar so the runners ran (Greely-like, "run west young man") east to west toward the altar. Even though, over the ages, five different stadiums were built, renovated or modernized in the same general vicinity at Olympia, the tradition of running east to west continued throughout antiquity. This was not necessarily the case in other ancient stadiums.

Lucian tells us that the sprinters trained by running in sand, a sort of modern day resistance training. Interestingly, in the late 1960s, Dave Thoreson, a Santa Barbara school teacher and national class decathlete, created an entire decathlon on sand. His conception was decidedly Greek in nature ... train the muscles by resistance. And, for the record, the ancient pentathlete did not run, jump and throw on sand, but the simple loose dirt of the stadium floor.

A number of ancient pentathlon champions were also outstanding sprinters. Four time Olympic pentathlon winner Gorgos of Elis (dates uncertain, some say 3rd century B.C.) also won the double stade (about 400m) and the race in armor at Olympia, a significant feat. At the 239th Olympiad (137 of C.E) the very busy Aelius Granianus of Sikyon (near Corinth) won all three of these events at the same games. Xenophon of Corinth (464 B.C.) and Demetrios of Salamis (233 C.E) both won the stade after winning the pentathlon at Olympia. A pair of ancients won several pentathlons at the Pythian Games and important sprint races: Phaÿllos of Croton (early 5th century B.C.), who is renowned now for his fictitious 55 foot long jump and Pythian stade victory, and Eupolemos of Elis who, in 396 B.C., captured the Olympic sprint. As today, the premium of combined events was on speed.

Size of the Field

The beginning of the pentathlon stade race was announced by a herald. The pentathlon sprint field would have a minimum of two or a maximum of three runners. Only those athletes who had won one or two of the previous three events would have been allowed to advance to the running event.[3] After the first three events there were only three possible scores (number of victories): 3–0, 2–1, or 1–1–1. Pentathletes without an event win at this point would have been dropped from the competition. Allowing anyone without an individual event win to advance to the stade would have been pointless, for, at this stage, they would have no chance for the overall win. Their presence would be needlessly complicating.

So the pentathlon stade field was small and, unlike the open races which would be contested two days later, was easy to administer. The remaining two or three pentathletes who had a chance for overall victory would limber up with calisthenics, run in place and prepare with brief sprints.

The Start

The initial start and finish lines at Olympia were likely lines drawn in the dirt. Later, as the stadiums were built and rebuilt, the lines were replaced by stone sills. Since all races at Olympia ended at the west end (in the direction of the *altis*, the sacred altar) there was a need for the sills at both ends of the stadium. The sills were oblong, made of limestone (in other stadiums marble was used) and contained shallow parallel furrows or grooves. Within the grooves, set between four and seven inches apart, the runners would place and grip their toes for a faster and balanced start. They were the ancient version of starting blocks. Numerous ancient sculptors portray stationary athletes at the start of a race with arms extended and one foot in front of the other.

Above: Renowned track and field coach Don Boyer, Middletown, Maryland, accurately demonstrates the sprint starting position at the balbis in Delphi stadium, site of the Phythian Games. The clothing and running shoes are not authentic, but the posture and hand position are precise (Don and Sharon Boyer). *Left:* The starting line for the sprint at Olympia, the balbis. Runners fit their toes into the stone sills and awaited the starting command (Borromeo/Art Resource, New York).

Frequent archeological excavations have located the starting sills. Some of them include post holes drilled into the ancient stone. These holes were used to construct starting gates, called a *hysplex*, or used as receptacles for turning posts for longer races. The numbers of gates varied from stadium to stadium. For instance, there were 21 of these starting gates at Olympia and 16 at Isthmia. Wooden barriers, resembling tollbooths, attached to strings were controlled by a judge standing in a pit behind the starting sills. He kept the string taut until a signal was given; he released the strings allowing the wooden obstruction to drop and the athletes were free to race. The scene was similar to the starting gates of a modern horserace. Statius tells us, "As soon as the bar fell, and left the threshold level, they nimbly dashed away and the naked forms gleamed upon the plain."[4]

At times the term "lists" has been used as a synonym for the starting gates. These starting gates may have been discontinued by the 5th century B.C. as awkward and simply too burdensome. Herodotus offers a hint as to their abandonment in a conversation between Adeimantes, an admiral from Corinth and Themistocles, the celebrated Athenian leader of the Greeks before the Battle of Salamis. In a tactical meeting and warning against engaging the invading Persians too soon, the Corinthian says, "At the games,[5] Themistocles, those who start too early (false start) are whipped."[6] It would seem that by this time (480 B.C.) the starting gates had been abandoned since a false start could not have happened with them. We are unsure what replaced the hysplex, perhaps just verbal commands.

The two or three pentathlon runners took their position on the stone sills. Presumably they would use the center starting positions and run side by side. Their toes were placed in the starting grooves, one foot in front of the other. We are told that runners at Corinth placed their toes into individual toe grooves instead of an unbroken groove running the length of the sill. They took a wide stance since the toe grooves were two to three feet apart. Then they leaned slightly forward awaiting the starting command.[7] There seems to be some disagreement on the starting position of Greek sprinters. Carl Diem has described the start: "By pressing his feet against the concave surfaces and the rear of the groove and gripping the front rims with his toes, while at the same time slightly extending and raising his arms he was able to attain the maximum angle of inclination. And so the runner stood poised for the start like a coiled spring."[8] On the other hand, a description by Gardiner has the runner lean so far forward that his upper body is virtually horizontal with the ground with one arm extended in front and the other backward. The former description, by Diem, matches a number of sculptures. The latter, by Gardiner, would be very hard to hold, and, with a slow starting judge, would result in some very tired toes and a plethora of false starts.[9]

False starts, themselves, were a problem for ancient sprinters, but especially pentathletes since the overall victory could hinge on getting away promptly. Legend tells us that Themistocles answered the earlier mentioned warning about false starters being flogged by claiming, "Yes, but he who is left at the start will win no prize."

False starts in the shorter running events are a way of life in modern combined events where one false start per athlete is allowed without punishment. As late as the 1940s it took 4 false starts to disqualify an athlete in the decathlon.[10] Today a second false start brings disqualification. Punishments were much more common in ancient Greece. Those who false started were flogged by the *alytes*, a guard. For the ancients, there were no limits on the number of false starts, just the humiliation of continual public flogging. Athletic contests provided one of the very few occasions in which a free Greek male could be publicly whipped.

In 1971 a pair of modern Olympic decathlon champions, Rafer Johnson (Olympic winner in Rome, 1960) and Bill Toomey (Olympic winner in Mexico City, 1968) re-created the ancient pentathlon at Delphi for the camera.[11] At the time both were still outstanding athletes in their mid–30s. Yale Classics professor Erich Segal both wrote and narrated the film titled *The Ancient Games*. In the stade Toomey false started. Segal, in an effort to be historically accurate, insisted that the ancient penalty be imposed, that is, a whipping. Johnson chuckled but Toomey winced when Segal produced a whip, and then reluctantly went along with the penalty.

A judge, attached to the *hellanodikai*, wincing a bit himself, cracked the whip on Toomey's bare back raising several welts on Bill's skin. Unfortunately there was a technical problem with the take and the director, Lou Volpicelli, sheepishly informed Bill that he had to be re-lashed. This time, trying to be too careful, the judge wrapped the whip around Bill's face. Toomey was not amused. On this take the picture was fine but the sound was bad.

Segal and Volpicelli were for whipping Toomey a third time but Bill had had enough and refused. A young Greek boy had been hired as a gopher for a few drachmas per day and someone suggested that they whip him instead, but the production crew decided to stick with what they had.[12]

The Race

Scholars are uncertain, without the hysplex, whether a verbal command or trumpet blast set off the runners. Ludwig Drees maintains that a trumpeter gave the starting signal for foot races at Olympia because it also held a contest for trumpeters.[13] The stade starting procedure must have varied from time to time and place to place.

What is virtually certain is that the pentathlon race was one length of the stadium, a stade, and not another distance. One scholar maintains that the pentathlon race was a distance race (*dolichis*) and this conclusion is to be ignored on practical grounds.[14] Running a distance race before a wrestling match would make the ancient pentathlon much more like the modern triathlon or double decathlon where endurance and survival were the main criteria and purpose. Today the Iron Man Triathlon combines a 2.4 mile swim with a 112 mile bike ride and a 26.2 mile marathon. It would seem that the primary goal of this "combined event" was to simply be alive at the finish. The double decathlon, now a contest in many nations with an annual world championship, requires the athlete to compete in 20 track and field events over two days and ends with a 10,000 meter (6.2 mile) run.[15] The Greeks were much more practical. Their pentathlon race was one length of the stadium (600 local feet). It was easy to administer, lasted less than half a minute, and conclusively decided who was fastest.

The ancient Olympia pentathletes started at the eastern stone sills and dashed west toward the *Altis*. Since the race would have been conducted in the late afternoon, after the field events were completed, the sprinters would have run directly into the Aegean sun. And, since the prevailing winds off the Aegean Sea come from the west at Olympia, there would be no wind-aided races. And there would have been no requests from athletes or coaches to run the event with the wind.

The track surface would have been hard on the athletes' feet. Running, jumping and throwing barefoot was no easy feat. Some scholars have concluded that a thin layer of sand was spread over the stadium floor in preparation for the athletic events.[16] But, as Miller tells us, this interpretation is surely incorrect.[17] For example, at Olympia where the stadium surface encompassed more than 73,000 square feet, even a sprinkling one quarter inch thick would have required more than 76 tons of sand.[18] Remember that the surface of the ancient stadium was approximately 50 percent bigger than the surface of the modern track.[19]

The sprinters would have run in clearly marked lanes. There is enough anecdotal evidence for running lanes. Sweet reminds us of a quote by Eustathius, a 12th century A.D. scholar, "Just as with runners, so in the orchestra there are lines marked out so that the chorus will stand in a straight line."[20]

Few scholars have ever seriously addressed the issue of lanes, but their importance would have been as clear to the ancient athlete as to his modern counterpart. They reduce the possibility of fouls and assures that the runners do not "drift," guaranteeing that they run the shortest distance between the start and finish lines. Miller argues convincingly that a form of lime or whitewash (much of which has been found in the remnant excavations at Nemea, for example) was utilized. As of today there is no irrefutable proof, "but the evidence appears sufficiently strong to make the suggestion that ancient stadia were marked out by lime or gypsum into lanes primarily to guide the competitors."[21]

A few modern writers claim that the lanes in the ancient stadium must have been roped, a modern practice that began in late 19th century England.[22] This notion is unthinkable and should be disregarded.

So down the stadium track the remaining pentathletes pounded, barefoot, nude, and arms pumping. Fatigue would become a factor since the athletes would have been on their feet for several hours. One can be sure that they made vigorous use of their arms to build and maintain speed. Indeed, ancient vases depict Greek sprinters using high arm and knee action. It is no different today. One famous amphora depicting five Greek sprinters has confused observers and takes some getting used to. After one stares at it for awhile, the viewer realizes that the artist has reversed the arm-leg action and depicted the runners raising the left arm and left leg simultaneously. This is done for artistic purposes and no one should conclude that the ancient sprinters actually attempted to run without alternate arm-leg movement.

The Finish

With approximately sixty meters remaining the runners passed the *cathedra* or judges stand on the left.[23] As the athletes approached, the finish would have been clearly visible. The purple robed *hellanodikai*, or pentathlon judges, stood at the finish line, likely the starting sill at the western end of the Olympia stadium. In the early days of Olympia, before there was a formal stadium, and at less formal festivals, a line drawn in the dirt would have sufficed as a finish. There is no evidence of a finish string, nor any indication of what constituted the exact end of the race. Today the race technically ends when the lead runner's torso reaches the front end of the two inch (5 cm) finish line, drawn or painted on the track. Head, neck, arms and legs do not count. It is the torso, defined as the bottom of the neck to the waist, which has to reach the finish line first (technically today the runner does not even have to "cross" the line, just "reach" it, and this becomes important for runners who are falling at the finish). Fortunately we have cameras which aid in the judging.

The pentathlon judges had no such help and had to make decisions visually. It is unlikely that the Greeks were as formal about which body part crossed the line first and most races would have been easy to decide. Picking a winner in a close race of two is infinitely easier than selecting a winner in a close race of, say, six or eight. Yet some of the races could be exceedingly close and the final decision was made by the pentathlon hellanodikae. Before approximately 400 B.C. one judge would be stationed at the finish line and his decision on a close race would be final. It is unknown if he could declare a dead heat.[24] After

400 B.C. the number of officials was increased and there could be a difference of opinion between or among officials. Disagreement could lead to a re-run, but this would have been rare. There is no evidence that this ever occurred at Olympia, but in the 1000-plus years of ancient pentathlon competitions, it may have cropped up on exceptional occasions.

If there were two runners, A (with two previous victories) and B (with one previous victory) and A won the stade, the pentathlon was concluded since A now had the necessary three event victories (the triad). If, on the other hand, B was victorious, then each had a pair of wins and both athletes proceeded to the wrestling pit to settle matters.

The Need for a Race

How necessary was the pentathlon running event? Probability theory offers insight. Probabilities can be computed for various size fields if one assumes that the field was evenly matched, that is, each athlete had an equal chance to win each event. See the accompanying table. For example, if the initial pentathlon field was made up of three athletes, the probability that a stade would be needed would be nearly 90 percent.

That is:

$$1 - [(\tfrac{1}{3} \times \tfrac{1}{3} \times \tfrac{1}{3}) \times 3]$$
$$1 - 11.1\%$$
$$88.9\%$$

As the size of the field increases the necessity of the stade also increases. By the time the field is enlarged to 10 original pentathletes, the chances that a stade would be necessary to help determine a winner grows to 99 percent.

$$- [(\tfrac{1}{10} \times \tfrac{1}{10} \times \tfrac{1}{10}) \times 10]$$
$$- .1$$
$$99.0\%$$

Column 6 offers how frequently the pentathlon stade would be run for various size fields.

This could also be expressed as 1 minus the probability that the pentathlon was decided by having one athlete win each of the first three events (Col. 3). Again, and assuming an evenly matched field, the probability that one athlete would win the first three events decreases as the size of the starting field is enlarged.

Table 1. Probability Theory and the Ancient Pentathlon
After Three Events:

(1) initial size of field event*	(2) possible outcomes	(3) ← .... Probability .... → one athlete wins first 3 events	(4) that the score stands 2–1	(5) that the score is 1–1–1	(6) need for 4th event	(7) need for 5th
2	8	25.0%	75.0%	0.0%	75.0%	37.5%
3	27	11.1	66.6	22.2	88.9	55.5
4	64	6.25	56.25	37.5	93.75	65.6
5	125	4.0	48.0	48.0	96.0	72.0
8	512	1.56	32.82	65.62	98.44	82.0
10	1000	1.0	27.0	72.0	99.0	85.5

*-Col 7 = .5(Col 4) + Col 5.

There is a debate in the literature concerning the situation of having 3 different athletes with a victory apiece after the third event (javelin). The trio would advance to the stade which would result in one athlete with two victories and the remaining two still with one win each. Although this issue has been treated earlier, as a reminder, this is a bone of contention with many scholars. Virtually all modern scholars agree that three event wins were necessary for overall victory. But determining the procedure in the above situation has been a sticking point. Many maintain that the two loosing runners would then contest a semi-final wrestling match.[25]

This notion of a semi-final wrestling bout began with E. Norman Gardiner at the beginning of the 19th century. It has been picked up by numerous other writers and has enjoyed a century-long life. Yet it is an unfair notion for any number of reasons, not the least of which is that a heavy athlete could become the pentathlon champion by winning the discus, the *repêchage* wrestling and the final wrestling without demonstrating much versatility. Only strength would be necessary. There is no evidence that this occurred in antiquity.

More reasonable academics have concluded that a wrestling semi-final would not only be unjust, but also debilitating for the athletes and confusing for the spectators. Kyle argues persuasively that, instead, a second stade would have been staged.[26] The athletes would be allowed an appropriate time to recover, then re-race. It is a procedure that would be convenient, understandable, easy to administer and fair.

The winner of the second (call it a semi-final, repêchage, 2nd chance, whatever) race, who now also owned a pair of victories would advance to the final event, wrestling, while the slowest runner, since he has now lost two races, would be eliminated. A second race would not fatigue the athletes as a semi-final wrestling match would. This would not have been rare. In a field of five athletes of roughly equal ability, for example, it would have occurred

48 percent of the time (see Table 1). With larger fields the probability that this would occur would be even higher. Another procedure would be to advance the first two in the sprint since any re-race would only involve the 2nd and 3rd place finishers who had just demonstrated their speed.[27]

Table 2 below offers the probability of additional pentathlon events when 2 or 3 athletes remain after the discus, jump and javelin.

Table 2

# of remaining athletes (score after 3)	— 4th event	Probability of repêchage	— 5th event
2 (score: 2–1)	100%	0%	50%
3 (score: 1–1–1)	100	100	100

In actuality the chances of a repêchage stade would be far less. In our calculations we have assumed that all athletes were of equal ability. Although a simplifying assumption, it is in fact, naïve. If, for example, there are two very good athletes, the size of the effective field is essentially two and there would be never be a need for a second race. If there were, for example, three dominant athletes, the effective field size would be three and there would be a need for a second stade only about a fourth of the time. The history of combined events (both ancient and modern) tells us that fields rarely, if ever, contain athletes all of reasonably equal ability. Of course minimum standards, first imposed by the watchful eye of the *Hellanodikai*, and today by minimum qualifying scores, help winnow out the mediocre or unprepared. But even within qualifying groups for a combined event, it is once in a blue moon that everyone has an equal chance. And so the number of times officials would have to resort to a second race would have been relatively small and unworthy of the amount of attention it has attracted in the journals.

8. Wrestling

Pale / πάλη

Wrestling was added to the Olympic program in 708 B.C., both as an event in its own right, and, because its practice was widespread, as a way to decide the pentathlon winner. One concept agreed upon by all modern scholars is that wrestling was the final pentathlon event. Although wrestling skills allowed Herakles to complete one of his 12 labors (against Libyan giant Antaios[1]), the first detailed description of Greek wrestling appears in Homer's *Iliad* at the funeral games to honor Patroclos. Homer's description of the wrestling bout between Odysseus of Ithaca and the giant Aias (often Ajax) of Telamon captures the flavor of the sport: "And then their backs cracked as they locked with one another, hooking their heavy arms, and rivers of sweat poured down and welts in great numbers appeared on their ribs and shoulders, swollen red with blood."[2]

The combat sports of wrestling, boxing and the pankration were symbolic sports of the Greek athletic tradition, born from military training. The former was eventually practiced by every able bodied male citizen in the town *palaistra*, literally, the "wrestling place." Ludwig Drees notes that the first four pentathlon events were alternating tests of arms and legs.[3] For Greeks, if these contests did not produce an all-around winner, then a final battle, wrestling, utilizing both arms and legs, would.

Greek wrestling was not particularly vicious, yet it could be dangerous and painful, especially for athletes who had endured the previous four pentathlon events. Injuries were common, and fatalities in the open wrestling event were not unheard of, although there is no evidence that this occurred in the ultimate pentathlon event. Wrestlers, incidentally, were exempt from homicide charges.

The most famous wrestler of antiquity was the huge Milo of Croton who, among innumerable victories in a long career, won five times at Olympia (a record), seven times at the Pythian Games, nine times at Nemea and ten times

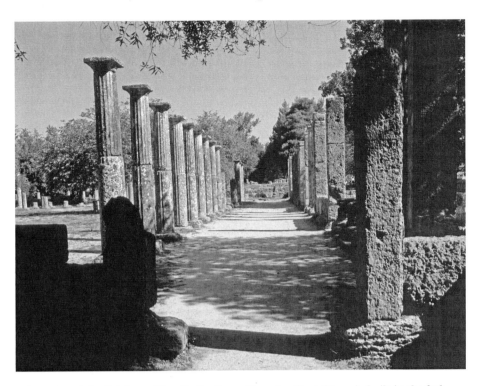

Remains of the Palaistra (literally the "wrestling place") at Olympia built in the 3rd century B.C. This was a practice-training venue located at the southwest corner of the ancient site. Wrestling pentathletes competed in the stadium proper (Scala/Art Resource, New York).

at the Isthmian Games. Counting an Olympic victory in boys' wrestling, Milo won a remarkable 32 *periodnes* wreaths. A modern analogy might be winning 32 world or Olympic titles or winning 32 of the major golf tournaments. His was a career unsurpassed in either ancient or modern times. An epigram was inscribed on the base of his statue at Olympia claiming him to be simply "the best amongst the best." I use Milo as a reference here because of his size. By ancient standards he was described as simply enormous. Milo, as the legend goes, once carried a 4-year-old heifer around the stadium, then slaughtered, roasted and ate the entire animal himself.[4]

Greek wrestlers, like Milo and others at Olympia, tended to be heavy since there were no weight classes and the heavier athletes held an advantage. So too in the pentathlon, the benefits could go to a heavier athlete who would have used his strength in the throws—discus and javelin. Yet it is rare in ancient texts to find an athlete winning both the pentathlon and the open wrestling contest. To the best of our knowledge it happened but once at Olympia, in the boys' pentathlon and boys' wrestling, when Eutelidas of Sparta won both in

628 B.C. The record is clear. Oversize wrestlers were not attracted to the pentathlon.

The Greeks were enthusiastic about wrestling and considered it an art. Pentathlon wrestling may have been more exciting to spectators since the athletes would have had to rely more on agility and the correct application of the holds than on brute strength. With the exception that the field had been reduced to two, the rules and conduct of the event would not have differed from the discrete wrestling event.

Preparation

The pentathlon wrestlers, like their open counterparts, prepared for their bout by scraping their body of all of the sweat and dust accumulated from the previous four events. Here a small curved scraping instrument called a *strigil* was used. Cleansed, they rubbed olive oil onto their torso and arms and then were "dusted" by one another, that is, they tossed dust onto their opponents to insure a solid grip during the bout. At the conclusion of the bout the strigil was again used to remove the caked sand, dirt, sweat and dust. On occasion pentathletes won the overall victory *akoniti*, "without dust," meaning that wrestling was unnecessary and that the pentathlon had been determined within the first 3 or 4 events. An inscription found on a *halter* at Olympia about 500 B.C. claimed that Akmatides of Sparta won the pentathlon akoniti.

The wrestlers moved into the *skamma*, a non-standardized pit which was dug up sandy soil.[5] Some scholars maintain that the wrestling pit (*skamma*, the same name as the jumping pit) at Olympia was not placed in the stadium but rather was located in the *Altis* or sacred grove of Zeus.[6] This is the result of a passage in Xenophon dating to the mid–4th century B.C.: "They had already finished the horse races and the run in the pentathlon. The competitors who had advanced to the wrestling were no longer in the stadium but were wrestling between the stadium and the altar."[7]

This was likely a temporary situation in 364 B.C., perhaps for some logistical or scheduling reason. To conclude that the wrestling event did not occur, as did all of the other combat events, in the stadium proper is illogical.[8] W.W. Hyde estimates that, in its heyday, there were nearly 500 monuments in the sacred grove surrounding the temple of Zeus.[9] In 364 B.C. the Altis would have been a bit less crowded but certainly did not provide much room for either the wrestlers or spectators.

Technique

The wrestlers dodged, feinted or often, with heads down, leaned into one another and locked arms as rams lock horns in battle. Homer likened the wrestlers to ceiling rafters, and their starting stance was called the *statasis.*[10] The wrestlers usually had their hair cut short or wore a skullcap tied under the chin to prevent opponents from grabbing hair. Greek wrestling was upright with holds above the waist. Tripping was allowed and the match ended when an opponent was thrown three times, whence the victor was referred to as *triakter.* A fall was declared when an opponent's back, shoulder, hip, torso or knee touched the ground. The winner had to remain standing or fall on top of his opponent. It was not necessary to pin an opponent's back to the ground. Kicking, punching, gouging and biting were not part of Greek wrestling. Holds on male organs were forbidden but strangling and breaking of fingers were not. The modern counterpart, Greco-Roman wrestling, is similar in that the athletes start in a standing position. But today tripping is banned.

Vase paintings, often depicting mythological heroes like Theseus (the legendary inventor of wrestling) and Herakles, illustrate many of the holds which were developed to place an opponent on the ground. The waist-lock, for example, involved seizing one's opponent about the waist, hoisting him up and tossing him to the ground. The "flying mare" was no different than today's version wherein a wrestler would grasp his opponent's arm and fling him over his shoulder, sending his victim crashing onto his back. Other classic holds focused on the neck, head, wrists, arms and body. Pentathletes, especially smaller ones, were probably adept at all of the throws and moves, since their agility had to overcome lack of size.

Various schools of wrestling developed over the centuries. Spartan, Thessalian and Sicilian methods were well known. Spartans tried to prevail by virtue of their strength alone. "The Sicilians were very crafty in their wrestling and did not have the reputation of being honorable athletes."[11]

Scoring

Probability theory from the previous chapter suggests that there was high likelihood that a wrestling bout would be necessary to determine the overall winner. Pentathletes were expected to be competent wrestlers. Nothing could be more discouraging than reaching the wrestling finals only to face a champion wrestler. It is akin to being tied in the modern decathlon after nine events only to face a champion distance runner in the 1500 meters.[12] Pentathlon wrestling lasted a maximum of 5 falls and there were but three possible scores, 3–0, 3–1 or 3–2. When the final fall was completed the pentathlon victor was declared the game's most versatile athlete. This position is consistent with both Herodotus and Pausanias, both of whom tell us, "Competing in the pentathlon he [Tisamenos] was within one wrestling match of winning the Olympic crown against Hieronymos of Andros."[13]

In Greek wrestling, contestants started in an upright position, then attempted to throw their opponent. Three clean throws meant victory in the overall pentathlon. There is no evidence that the bout ever continued on the ground. This drawing, featuring a bout between Herakles (left) and Antaios, is from a late 6th century B.C. amphora in the British Museum (*Greek Athletic Sports and Festivals*, 1910).

It seems that Tisamenos, via a prophecy that he would win five glorious crowns, entered the Olympic pentathlon. He won the jump and stade while Hieronymos won the discus and javelin. When Hieronymos won the 5th and final wrestling bout (making the final score 3–2 in his favor), Tisamenos, who later became a Greek military general, realized that the prophecy referred to five *military* victories, a prophecy that came to fruition.

It was that simple. Wrestling made the winner a "triple victor" and the pentathlon ended. At the crown games the champion would have a ribbon tied around his forehead signifying the victory, and he would receive his wreath on the festival's final day. Wrestling brought to a close a combined event competition, which had the "virtue of not being overly ingenious."[14]

PART THREE : A HISTORY OF THE EVENT

9. The Story of the Ancient Pentathlon

The story of the ancient pentathlon parallels that of the Olympic Games themselves, for the pentathlon was purportedly created at Olympia near the end of the 8th century B.C. I have divided my story of the pentathlon with a standard classification of Greek historical periods: early and late Archaic, Classical, Hellenistic, Greco-Roman and Imperial.[1] These divisions are used for convenience and signal changes (although certainly not abrupt) in Greek art, literature or politics. The scheme will help readers who are unfamiliar with Greek history.

The ancient pentathlon has a lengthy report card since it was a standard event for all or parts of 14 centuries. It outlived, for example, the history of both ancient Greece and ancient Rome.[2] This chapter will revolve around the ancient pentathletes themselves, and much of what we know about them comes from victory odes or from the descriptions of the bases of their statues which Pausanias, a Greek traveler and geographer, recorded in the 2nd century A.D. in his *Description of Greece*.[3]

The Early Archaic Age (776 to 600 B.C.)

The conventional dates for athletic events attached to the religious festival in honor of Zeus (776 B.C.) and the date of the initial pentathlon at Olympia (708 B.C.) are accepted here, although archaeological evidence confirms they are only approximate. After 17 festivals the Eleans, likely because the festival had grown in popularity and importance, expanded the program to include more than a few footraces. In 708 B.C. both the pentathlon and wrestling were added to the Olympic schedule. Modern scholars deduce that these dates may be a bit early, pushing back the actual beginnings by as much as a century.

The initial dates of 776 B.C. and 708 B.C. flow from the work of Hippias, a 4th to 5th century B.C. sophist, self-proclaimed expert and contemporary of Socrates. Hippias supplies us only with the name of Olympia's first pentathlon victor, a certain Lampis of Sparta. Unlike the origin of modern combined events, when coverage was prolific there was no ESPN or *USA Today* at ancient Olympia hanging around to interview the winner or report the results. In 1884, for example, the first amateur all-around was reported by 13 New York newspapers and magazines. And the initial Olympic pentathlon and decathlon in Stockholm in 1912 drew worldwide attention. But for Lampis we know virtually nothing. An unconfirmed modern source suggests that Lampis won the jumping event.[4]

The rationale for the pentathlon is covered in an early chapter. That many of the early Olympic winners (including the pentathlon) come from well known Spartan families have made some scholars suspicious that Hippias may have stretched his historical tale to ingratiate himself with his Spartan benefactors.[5] Regardless, lacking any additional evidence, we will use the standard 708 B.C. as the starting point and Lampis as our first champion. His victory came well before it was acceptable for winners to dedicate statues of themselves in the sacred Altis next to the stadium at Olympia. Pausanias saw an honorary statue of the son Lampis, one Timoptolis, dedicated by the inhabitants of island of Cephallenia, located in the Ionian Sea off the west coast of Greece.

We know of only three other pentathletes of the 7th century B.C., all Spartans. As a young man Philombrotos of Sparta was an athletic prodigy. At the 24th Games, 676 B.C., and a time in which Sparta was engaged in the 2nd Messenian War, he was accompanied to Olympia by his father and his coach, Kratistos. In 1974 a fanciful story appeared in a modern Olympic magazine telling us that Philombrotos arrived a month early because that was protocol (in 676 B.C. it was not!), that he won the jump, was second in the discus (taking only two throws), won the sprint by a wide margin, then lost the javelin to an Argive, who had also won the discus. Philombrotos then won the wrestling with an extensively depicted waist hold so that his final score was 3–2. There are absolutely no ancient references and the story was fabricated.[6] But we do know that he was a well known champion since Philombrotos repeated his pentathlon win in 672 B.C. and again in 668 B.C. A threepeat!

At the next three Olympic Games (664, 660 and 656 B.C.), one of Sparta's most remarkable athletes won each of three different running events: the stade (about 200 meters); the diaulos (about 400 meters) and the dolchis (a distance race of up to three miles). His triple-triple at Olympia came well before honorary statues were erected. Two hundred years later the Spartans hired the renowned Myron, sculptor of *Discobolous,* to create a statue of Chionis and dedicated it at Olympia with an additional plaque listing his accomplishments. They were still in the sacred Altis when Pausanias passed through around 150 A.D.

Although known primarily as a sprinter, Chionis is also reportedly the

A pentathlon scene from a Panathenaic amphora (about 525 B.C.) depicts, from the left, a discus thrower, javelin thrower, a jumper and a coach. The Panathenaic Festival nearly rivaled the Crown Games in importance to the Greeks. The amphora from which the drawing is taken is in Amsterdam Rikjsmuseum (*Greek Athletic Sports and Festivals*, 1910).

author of the longest jump in antiquity, 52 Olympian feet or 54 feet, 8 inches in modern day parlance. Most scholars now conclude that the report, which came several hundred years after the jump, was a mistaken translation from Armenian Latin, confusing "52" feet with "22" feet since the lettering of the two are remarkably similar. Regardless of the misunderstanding, there is also a modern internet reference, without any basis, claiming that Chionis, somewhere in the year 656 B.C., jumped 7.05m or 23 feet and 1¼ inches. Since the jump was only contested as part of the pentathlon, Chionis may have been a prominent pentathlete. Even though there is no evidence, it is tempting to conjecture that his sprinting and jumping skills must have won him those pentathlon events, in which case he would not have won the discus, javelin or wrestling and thus lost the Olympic pentathlon (the only pentathlon in those days) by a score of 3–2. Of course this is all speculation.

It was in the mid–7th century that Greeks from the mainland began to set up distant, new settlements, mostly a mirror image of those of the homeland with the same political structure, law and religious temples which provided an eventual basis for athletic festivals. The colonies tended to be established on the coast as trading centers. Within a century Greek colonies had been set from what is now the southern coast of France, to Sicily and southern Italy, Libya and the shores of the Black Sea.

Meanwhile the festival at Olympia grew in status and popularity. The 7th century's last known pentathlete was Eutelidas, also a Spartan. He won the first and last boys' (generally 18 and under) pentathlon as well as the boys' wrestling competition at Olympia in 628 B.C. We are uncertain why the boys' pentathlon was canceled after just one try but some speculate that the Eleans may have thought the pentathlon was too difficult for teenagers. Yet it was common for later festivals to include not only a boys' division (*paides*, usually under 17 or 18) but also a young men's pentathlon (*aigones*, literally beardless youths) in addition to the men's (*andres*) pentathlon. Eutelidas was one of the very few ancient pentathletes who were not primarily runners. The dedicated statue of Eutelidas was the oldest Pausanias saw at Olympia and he remarked how the inscription had faded with time.[7]

By approximately 600 B.C. the pentathlon began to adopt its final form. Progressively metallic (iron, lead and bronze) implements (*disci* and *haltere*) began to replace stone counterparts.[8] And the pentathletes shed their clothing. Paul Christensen tells us that "the relevant literary and artistic sources make it clear that the incorporation of athletic nudity into everyday life did not begin until the middle of the seventh century."[9] There is a whimsical tale that the first athlete to compete nude was a sprinter from Megara, Orsippos, who, 12 years before the pentathlon victory of Lampis, lost his shorts or loincloth during the race. Another tradition finds that Spartans introduced nudity at Olympia. More likely the advent of the gymnasium ("the nude place") and the expectation that Greek men remain fit for warfare made working out or competing a civic responsibility, and doing so with an absence of clothing became a symbol of social stratification.

Up until approximately 600 B.C. most of the participants of the games at Olympia lived locally. From 776 to 700 B.C. half (12 of 24) of the recorded victors came from just two towns in the Peloponnese, Sparta and Messene. In the next century athletes from Sparta, located just 188 km (about 112 miles) southwest of Olympia, won more wreaths at these games than all other cities combined. Civically responsible, nude and armed with metal implements, pentathletes marched into the tumultuous 6th century.

The Late Archaic Age (600 to 480 B.C.)

During the first half of the 6th century B.C. Greek athletics became big stuff. Before this time participation in athletics was limited to the upper or ruling class (*basileis*). When the middle class began to participate in the socio-political community, that participation included the expansion of opportunities at the local gymnasium. Christensen concludes that being an athlete was strong claim to social-political privilege and the civic nudity, which began at the last half of the 7th century and made itself evident to everyone in the community, raised the public's consciousness of athletics.[10]

The result was a sharp increase in the number of festivals that had a significant athletic component. The Pythian Games at Delphi (founded in 586 B.C.), the Isthmian Games in Corinth (founded in 580 B.C.) and the Nemean Games in Nemea (founded in 573 B.C.), along with the games at Olympia, became a circuit of major Panhellenic (and not just regional) festivals or *periodes*. The ancient circuit eerily resembles the modern circuit of championship track and field meets.

Note:

Ancient Circuit

Date and Year	Festival and site
July/Aug. 480 B.C.	Olympic Games—Olympia
Aug./Sept. 479	Nemean Games—Nemea
April/July 478	Isthmian Games—Corinth
August 478	Pythian Games—Delphi
Aug./Sept. 477	Nemean Games—Nemea
April/July 476	Isthmian Games—Corinth
July/Aug. 467	Olympic Games—Olympia

Modern Circuit

Date and Year	Championships
Aug. 2008	Olympic Games—Beijing
Aug. 2009	IAAF World Champs—Berlin
July 2010	European Champs—Barcelona
Aug. 2011	IAAF World Champs—Daegu, South Korea
Oct. 2011	Pan American Games—Guadalajara
Aug. 2012	Olympic Games—London

As well, numerous local athletic festivals popped up, including the Panathenaia in Athens. In many cases stadiums were built or renovated in the 6th century. By the end of the 6th century the pentathlon (as well as other athletic events) was part of an enhanced promotional, media and spectatorship effort. Athletes could dedicate a statute at Olympia, have a victory odes written about them by Simonides, Pindar or Baccylides and have a flute player (*auletes*) accompany their actions on the field. Between 548 and 532 B.C. a small man, Pythokritos of Sikyon, won the flute playing contest at Delphi, thereby earning the right to play the flute for the pentathlon events at Olympia. The musical skill of Pythokritos was so renowned that friends erected a statue of him at Olympia. He was the only pentathlon official of antiquity to be so honored.

It is here that we subjectively insert Ainetos of Amyklai, a pentathlon winner who is difficult to date. A stone stele or tablet which dates to 475 B.C. commemorates his Olympic pentathlon victory. Pausanias tells us that there also was a portrait statue of him in his hometown of Amyklai, a very old settlement about three miles from Sparta. The relief stele is written in the local

Northeast view of the stadium at Olympia where pentathlons were conducted for 1100 years. This view is much the way it looked in the 6th century B.C. The stadium was rebuilt on three occasions and, in its heyday, could accommodate crowds of 40,000 spectators who would sit or stand on the northern and southern embankments (Vanni/Art Resource, New York).

script of Amyklaion, chronicles his career victories and tells us that the over-joyed Ainetos died while the crown was being placed on his head.

The only recorded pentathlon victor at Olympia during the entire century was yet another Spartan. But halfway through the 6th century Spartans disappear from the victor lists and the dominant athletic power becomes Kroton, a Greek settlement on the boot of Italy. Akmatidas of Sparta won the pentathlon at Olympia in 500 B.C. and the surviving base of his statue says that he did so *akoniti*, "without dust." When an athlete sewed up the pentathlon without having to dust himself in preparation for the final wrestling match, he was said to have won *akoniti*. The final score then was either 3–0 or 3–1. Today the Olympia Archaeological Museum displays a stone *halter* that says, "Akmatidas of Lakedaimonia [the region in which Sparta is located], having won the five without dust dedicates this." The stone jumping weight weighs 4.629 kg (10.18 lbs) and is most likely a votive offering and not used in the actual competition. The inscription tells us that Akmatidas was no mere Olympic pentathlon victor, but one who achieved his victory in the most superior fashion. He was the earliest recorded akoniti winner in any event.

An Olympic winner could win akoniti if there were a small number of competitors, all of whom had withdrawn because they had "sized up" their opponents in the preparatory period and withdrew before the event began. Potential contestants could withdraw before the festival began without fines or loss of reputation. Once the festival began a withdrawee would be fined, a disgraceful result. An opponent's injury during the pentathlon could also result in an akoniti finish. Interestingly, Akmatidas is the last known Olympic pentathlon winner from Sparta.

In 492 B.C. we know that Hieronymos of Andros defeated his pentathlon opponent by winning the fifth and final fall in the wrestling match, winning 3–2 in wrestling and 3–2 in events. Yet this is one of those out of the ordinary occasions in which we know more about the loser than the winner. At a young age, Tisamenos of Elis had an oracle foretell that he should win five most famous contests. Concluding this referred to an athletic career, he trained for the pentathlon at Olympia. He won the jump but Hieronymos of Andros won the discus and javelin. When Tisamenos won the stade, both then oiled down, dusted up and headed for the wrestling skamma to settle matters. After each had registered two falls apiece, it appeared that Tisamenos' fate would be prophetic. But Hieronymos won the final fall, and thus the pentathlon,[11] and it was here that Tisamenos finally understood the oracle's meaning, that the gods would grant him five military victories. The Spartans, realizing this and wanting to jump on the bandwagon, persuaded Tisamenos (by offering Spartan citizenship) to migrate from Elis to Sparta and to be a state-diviner, a military leader. Thirteen years later Tisamenos won the first of five military battles which helped end the Persian wars and start the Peloponnesian War against Athens. His five victories included:

479 B.C.	at Plataia against the Persians
	at Tegea against Tegeans and Argives
	at Dipaia (an Arcadian town in Mainalia) against the Arcadians
464	at Ithome against the Helots
457	at Tangara, against the Argives and Athenians

At the next Olympiad (488 B.C.), Euthykles of Lokroi, a Greek settlement near the toe of the Italian boot, won the pentathlon. He later served as an ambassador and once, in his later years, returned home with mules and gifts from a foreign land. The Locrians, thinking them a bribe, mutilated his statue in the Lokroin agora and threw him into jail, where he died. An ensuing famine ended only when the townsfolk rededicated the statue and erected an altar for Euthykles' worship as a Hero, that is, a mortal who was treated as a god.

Theopompos of Heraia, an ancient settlement near Olympia, won the next two Olympic pentathlon wreaths (484 and 480 B.C.). Today the region has not been systematically excavated; nonetheless the settlement was known to be important in antiquity and the birthplace of great athletes such as Theopompos, who became the first known repeat winner at Olympia in 188 years. His universally known athletic family included his father, Damaratus, a two-time Olympic champion in the hoplite race (520 and 516 B.C.) and son, another Theopompos, who won the Olympic wrestling wreaths in 440 and 436. Nothing in modern Olympic history compares to the three generation accomplishments of the family from Heraia.

A final pentathlete should be recognized for his accomplishments at the end of the Archaic era. Phaÿllos of Kroton was a well known pentathlete and sprinter who never won at Olympia, but he did win the pentathlon twice and the stade once at Delphi, likely around 490 B.C. And, through no fault of his own, he became the victim of a crafty and ambiguous epigram, written 600 years after his death, suggesting that he once long jumped 55 feet. Much of the long jump tale was covered in Chapter 5.

But the 600-year-old report of a fictional jump was not the only fabrication about the life of Phaÿllos. We do know, from the historian Herodotus, that in the summer of 480 B.C., Phaÿllos outfitted his own ship and fought on the side of the victorious Greeks against the invading Persians in the Battle of Salamis, perhaps the most important naval conflict in ancient times. But English Classical scholar H.A. Harris embellished Phaÿllos' role and motives to such a degree that David Young says, "Harris' Phaÿllos is no ancient Greek at all, he is a 19th century Englishman and Harris creates an imaginary career as a moral lesson to modern man."[12] More specifically, Harris maintained that Phaÿllos consciously gave up his Olympic dreams (for all of his wreaths and fame he never did win at Olympia) and fought for his fatherland. Harris says Phaÿllos "had seen where his duty lay and had done it. His Olympic hopes were still in the future."[13] Young persuasively argues that Phaÿllos had retired by the time of the battle, and while this was all a fascinating story, it was a sham, outright historical fiction, a creation of Harris' own imagination. Young and others recognize the influence Harris has had on modern sport but rightly chastised him for lack of historical accuracy, writing to promote values of his time, and for sloppy scholarship. The moral is that, 25 centuries later, writers who report on the Phaÿllos or his long jump remain novelists.[14]

Classical Period (480–323 B.C.)

More cities added or expanded athletic festivals and the beginning of the 5th century B.C. For many of these festivals organizers simply paid money, for with few exceptions—Sparta being the most famous—Greece in the Classical age was now a monetized economy. The value of coinage was based principally on silver. Merchandise like tripods were out. Coins were in. The phenomena clearly, although not overnight, created a new class of athlete, the professional, the athletic specialist who made his living competing at local games for money and reputation at the Crown games.

The Crown Games, like those at Olympia, grew in popularity, and although the athletic program was virtually set by this time, facilities were updated and added to accommodate the ever increasing number of athletes. In the middle of the 5th century B.C. a significantly new stadium was built at Olympia with room for 43,000 spectators.[15] At Olympia a palaistra ("the wrestling place") was built near the end of the 3rd century and the gymnasion ("the nude place") came a few years later. Both we necessary to accommodate and prepare the athletes at Olympia. In fact the gymnasion at Olympia, which measured 220 meters, was even larger than the stadium.

By the early part of the 5th century B.C. the seemingly timeless Persian invasions of the Greece mainland ended. Theopompos of Heraia had won the pentathlon at the 75th games in 480 B.C., a few weeks before the Battle of Salamis in which Athenian statesman Themistocles and Spartan commander Eurybiades destroyed the overwhelming Persian naval force of Xerxes. A year later, 479 B.C., the Elean Tisamenos, the 492 Olympic pentathlon runner-up, led his Spartan forces to a decisive land battle victory at Plataea to finally end the Persian invasion ushering in Greece's Golden Age and one of the greatest of the ancient pentathletes, Nicolades of Corinth. He may have been the best athlete in Corinth history, but another pentathlon winner, Xenophon, was the more famous. We will deal with Xenophon momentarily.

We are not quite certain of the competitive career dates of Nicoladas but because the poet Simonides (who lived from 556 to 468 B.C.) tells us of his successes, we are able to date the victories within the 480–470 B.C. range. As a pentathlete Nicoladas came closest to achieving the periodonikēs, that is, a victory at all four competitive festivals of the original periodos (Olympia, Delphi, Corinth, Nemea). A modern corollary might be winning the four golf majors or achieving the Grand Slam in tennis. This circuit was later expanded in the Roman Imperial era. Although achieved in other events, the periodonikēs was never accomplished by a pentathlete.[16]

Simonides says Nicoladas won the Pythian Games pentathlon at Delphi and, on three occasions, won both the Nemean and Isthmian Games,[17] seven major festival wins, the most ever on the circuit! In the modern era, only decathlete Daley Thompson of Great Britain comes close, winning six majors (two Olympic, one World, two Commonwealth and one European title). Nicoladas never won at Olympia and, although we do not have the specific dates for his wins, we do know that it would have taken him a minimum of six years to accomplish this.

We also know that he won pentathlons frequently elsewhere. For example, he was a victor at the important Panathenaea pentathlon in Athens, where he won 60 amphoras of oil, worth a small fortune.[18] An epigram tells us that

Nicoladas also won four pentathlons at Pellene, two at Lykaion, and one each at Tegea, Aegina, Epidauras, Thebes, Pythious, and Megara. He swept the pentathlon at Phlious after three events and frequently ended pentathlons by winning the stade race, achieving victory akoniti. It appears that he had at least 21 career pentathlon wins, something infrequently achieved in the modern era.[19]

When the statesman and naval hero Themistocles appeared at the Olympic Games in 476 B.C. he was cheered to the heavens. The games at Olympia had grown in size and it was around this time (judged to be ca. 470) that the Eleans decided to add more Hellanodikai to officiate. Three judges from the Elean elite were named to supervise the pentathlon at each games. Uniquely garbed in purple robes during the games, these judges lived for ten months in the *Hellanodikaion*, the judges' residence in Elis, culled the entry field of the unprepared, oversaw the pre–30 day training and led the 37 mile procession to Olympia. The program at Olympia became more formal and was expanded to 5 days with the pentathlon always being contested on the afternoon of the second day, after the equestrian events.

As an indication of the growing reach of the festival at Olympia, its next three pentathlon winners came from afar, two from the Spartan colony in Taras, in Italy, and one from Miletos in Asia Minor. About this time another Greek from the Italian settlement of Corcyra won pentathlons, so Simonides tells us, at both the Pythian and Isthmian Games. Diophon was the grandson of Glaucus, governor of Camarina in Sicily and son of Philon. Both father (500 and 496 B.C.) and grandfather (520 B.C.) had been Olympic boxing victors.

This was also the era of the ode, the commissioned lyric poem praising the achievement of victors at crown games. They were sung frequently at other festivals and gatherings and became akin to pop tunes. Poets like Pindar, Simonides and his nephew Baccylides, were paid handsomely for them. Baccylides penned a glowing tribute to Automedes of Phlious who won the pentathlon at Nemea ca. 450 B.C. The ode was found in the late 19th century on an Egyptian papyrus. Although the entire poem can be found in Chapter 12, a partial rendition is presented below and implies that the contest was decided by the wrestling event, meaning the final score was 3–2. It suggests that Automedes won the discus throw, javelin and wrestling.

> To Automedes,
> Winner outshining
> all pentathlon men—
> Those stars blacked out
> By the bloom of a brimming moon.
> In the Greeks tightening ring
> His magnificent body gleamed
> When he skirred the discus;
> Stabbing the shoot

Of a black-leaf elm
Through the steep sky,
He whipped cries that peaked
On the flash of his grappler's falls.[20]

Pindar, the most famous lyric poet of antiquity, produced 45 odes for winners at the four crown games, two for pentathletes. One was for Sogenes of Aegina, the son of Thearion, who as a young boy entered the pentathlon for men at Nemea because at this time they had discontinued the boys' pentathlon. Surprisingly, he won and drew the praise of Pindar, who penned "the glorious limbs of youth" and referred to but two events, the javelin and wrestling.

Xenophon, a well known sprinter from a well-to-do family in Corinth, won both the stade and the pentathlon at Olympia in 464 B.C. and was the subject of Pindar's other ode to a pentathlete. Pindar was commissioned, likely by the family, to create an ode in Xenophon's honor. It is presented in its entirety in Chapter 12. The poem honors an athletic clan (his father Thessalos had won the Olympic stade 40 years earlier) by recalling many of its festival victories. Xenophon himself had also won crowns at Isthmia and at Nemea, but it is uncertain if they were for the sprint or the pentathlon. In addition to the ode, Xenophon is remembered from a song written by Pindar, in which Xenophon promised to dedicate (purchase from a slave market) between 25 and 100 prostitutes and set them up at the town shrine of Aphrodite if he was victorious at Olympia. Corinth, situated on a busy isthmus, was a town well known for its sailors and prostitutes. Guaranteeing him historical notoriety, Xenophon kept his promise.[21]

The next Olympic pentathlon victory Pythokles of Elis, 452 B.C., is not remembered so much for his deeds but for what he may have looked like. We know of him because Pausanias identified his victory statue at Olympia, erected well after his pentathlon triumph. The statue has been lost to the ages but its base has shown up in Rome. Some scholars speculate that the statue itself, because of the foot placements surviving on the base, may have been sculptured by Polykleitos, the great innovative sculptor from Sicyon, who two years after the victory of Pythokles, created *Doryphoros* (the spear bearer), the perfect sculpture of a javelin thrower. Pausanias confirms that the victory statute of Pythokles was indeed made by Polykleitos (active ca. 450 to 420 B.C.), and the base found in Rome portrayed a relaxed athlete standing on the ball of his right foot, in the style of Polykleitos. There is the natural speculation that the surviving copies of *Doryphoros* (the original bronze has been lost) may have looked like Pythokles, making it the only surviving likeness of an ancient pentathlete. Because of the many extant copies, when all is said and done, we know more about the statue than the athlete.[22]

Another famous sculptor and a contemporary of Polykleitos, Phidias, was finishing the great statue of Zeus at Olympia. Having gained attention as the supervisor of the Parthenon in Athens and as the designer of its sculptural decoration (now known as the Elgin Marbles and now found in the British Museum), Phidias sealed his artistic legacy with the construction of the enormous chryselephantine (gold and ivory) sculpture of Zeus at the god's temple at Olympia, now counted as one of the seven wonders of the ancient world.[23]

We know nothing of the 448 B.C. winner except his name. In 2003 a Greek film company produced a ninety minute DVD entitled *448 B.C. Olympiad* which showed Keton of Lokroi winning 4 of 5 pentathlon events.[24] Lokroi was a Greek town founded in 680 B.C. on the toe of the Italian boot on the Ionian Sea. Four years later another athlete from Magna Gracea, this time Taras, won the pentathlon wreath at Olympia. Ikkos of Taras later became the most famous coach of antiquity and wrote a treatise on basic biomechanics. Plato tells us that Ikkos had an extraordinary sex drive yet never touched a woman or boy when training. Ikkos urged, for major meets, especially for prestigious games like those of Olympia, that athletes engage in seclusion, fasting and sexual abstinence. Plato praised Ikkos, who "never had any connection with a woman or a youth during the whole time of his training" (Plato, Laws, 1968, p. 407; Laws 840A).[25]

We have no records of pentathlon winners during the Greeks' Peloponnesian wars which ended in 404 B.C. with Sparta the undisputed leader on the Greek mainland. Almost immediately the Spartans sought revenge on the Eleans by invading their territory. But unfavorable omens and an earthquake halted their invasion and Elis maintained their control over Olympia.

In 400 B.C. the versatile Antiochus of Lepreon, who had won pentathlon crowns twice at both Nemea and Corinth, won the pankration at Olympia, demonstrating a most unusual combination of skills. The Greeks are credited with inventing only two sports, the pentathlon and the pankration (a combination boxing and wrestling, no-holds-barred combat). We have no record that the same athlete won both at the same festival. Nonetheless, Antiochus, later a diplomat, was a highly unusual athlete.

Having survived an impending invasion from Sparta, the pentathletes from Elis made most of the noise in the early 4th century. After having won pentathlons at both Delphi and Nemea, Eupolemus of Elis entered and won the stade race at Olympia. Maybe. His race was a virtual dead heat with Leon of Ambracia. The three judges were from Elis and two of the three gave Eupolemus the nod. Feeling that he had been cheated, Leon appealed to the Olympic Council, who allowed Eupolemus to keep his victory but fined the judges for homering. Unfazed, the Eleans erected a statue of Eupolemus in the Altis which was later seen by Pausanias.

Hysmon of Elis had been a sickly boy, diagnosed with childhood rheumatism, when Kleogenes, his father, and Lykon, his tutor, recommended that the withered boy take up serious physical training. He had grown to be a powerful teenager when Lykon brought him to Nemea and entered him in the pentathlon. Hysmon won (probably 386 B.C.) and was soon training for the pentathlon at Olympia. Not only did he win there, but he did so akoniti, winning the discus, jump and run. The Elians erected a bronze statue of him in the Altis, and represented him holding jumping weights.[26] Another statue of an Elean pentathlete was dedicated to Stomios of Elis, who won at Olympia in 376 B.C. Stomios became a cavalry general who challenged an enemy counterpart to a duel and slew a Sicyonian general.[27] In 368 B.C., Damiscus of Elis won the boys' stade at Olympia at the age of 12, making him the youngest athletics winner of antiquity at Olympia. As an adult he trained for the pentathlon and won crowns at both the Isthmian and Nemean Games.

There is a well consumed modern myth that wars stopped during the ancient Olympic Games. The truth is more subtle. The Olympic Truce only guaranteed the safety of travelers to and from Olympia and that the site and sanctuary at Olympia would be free from invasion. Nothing more. Warfare among Greek city states was common during the games. After Elis, normally a neutral city, became embroiled in eternal Greek politics during and after the Peloponnesian Wars, it relinquished its impartial status among warring Greek cities. Elis and Sparta always seemed to find themselves on opposite sides and there had been situations in which the games at Olympia had to be conducted under armed guard. For example, in 420 B.C., the Eleans had banned the Spartans from competing at Olympia, and fearing that the Spartans would retaliate, used several thousand troops to protect the athletes and spectators. When the Spartans emerged victorious in the civil war after 402 B.C., they took their revenge on the Eleans, annexing their slaves, cattle and much of their territory.

In 365 B.C. Elis fought a disastrous war against a pair of city-states, Arcadia and Pisa. The latter captured Olympia and conducted the games of 364, games from which the Eleans themselves were banned. What happened next is right out of a Hollywood script. War broke out *at the Olympics.* Although we do not know who the final two pentathlon competitors were, we can state unequivocally that they were involved in the most extraordinary scene in Olympic history, ancient or modern. The historian Xenophon tells us: "They had already finished the horse races and the run in the pentathlon. The competitors who had advanced to the wrestling were no longer in the stadium but were wrestling between the stadium and the altar" (Xenophon, *History of Greece* 4.29).

The Eleans conducted a surprise attack late on the second day of the 364 B.C. Games while the pentathlon was in its final stages. Their troops stormed into the Altis, were met by the Pisan and Arcadian forces and the fighting was close range.

A hard to believe scene ensued with side-by-side battles: one pair of athletes struggling for a prize, while others struggled for their lives. Simultaneous hand-to-hand battles occurred in front of the spectators, one fabricated and others genuine. It's intriguing to imagine—for example, what did the herald-announcer say? For anyone making the case that athletics were a way to prepare for war, no one would have thought the real test would come so soon. Imagine: within a short period of time, two types of javelins filled the air. The light elderwood flew for distance. Then heavy metal ones sought human targets. The javelin had morphed from a distance to an accuracy event. Presumably the Hellanodikai stopped the wrestling bout and quickly declared a draw. The Arcadian troops forced back the advance and the Eleans withdrew from the Altis.

When Elis regained control of Olympia a year later they expunged the records of the winners, declaring the 364 B.C. games void. Elis had always been an athletic powerhouse at the Olympic Games, but after the fiasco of 364 B.C., strangely (or perhaps predictably) their only victories for the next 56 years were in boxing.[28] No screenwriter could create a panorama like this. As humorist Art Buchwald was fond of saying, "I couldn't make this stuff up." There is no modern analogy unless one counts the 1972 slaying of Israeli athletes inside the Munich Olympic village in 1972. But a real war in the arena?

During the 4th century B.C., Olympia was a haven from the political turmoil within Greece. In 399 B.C. Socrates had been forced to suicide. The Peloponnesian Wars had ended but there were military rumblings from Macedonia to the north. The Greeks had always regarded the Macedonians as dangerous barbarians, people who were not quite Greek or not "Greek enough." As early as the mid–5th century B.C. Greek athletes had protested, saying they would not compete with barbarians. Macedonians began to appear as winners at Olympia in the early 5th century. The race horse of King Philip II of Macedonia won at Olympia in 356 B.C., the same year that his son Alexander was born.

It has been suggested that this 6th century B.C. marble relief was the base of a statue of a pentathlete who had won three events (depicted from the left: start of stade, wrestling and the javelin throw). National Archaeological Museum, Athens, Greece (*Greek Athletic Sports and Festivals*, 1910).

Philip became an "Olympic champion" since the crown went to the owner, not the jockey nor the horse. Noted for his foot speed, his son Alexander was once asked if he considered competing at Olympia. "Only if my opponents were kings," he replied. By 346 B.C. the Macedonians had gained control of most of the Greek city states. But when Philip II was assassinated, Alexander (the Great) rode off in search worlds to conquer.

The Greek Classical Age neared its completion in 332 B.C. when Olympia faced a rare cheating scandal. And it involved a pentathlete, Kallippos of Athens, who had bribed his pentathlon competitors to throw the victory to him. The field must have been small or the bribe occurred late in the contest. It's unlikely that, say, a dozen athletes could keep a secret about anything, so the violators had to be few in number. But eventually the fraud became known and the infuriated Eleans levied a heavy penalty on the competitors and an especially heavy fine on Kallippos.

Heavy fines were not unknown at Olympia. In 480 B.C. Theagenes had been fined two talents (in 2009 purchasing power approximately $45,000)[29] and he simply had paid it. But here the Athenians considered Kallippos' fine excessive and sent Hyperides, their top orator and negotiator, to Elis to request that the fine be rescinded or reduced. The Eleans turned down the appeal and the Athenians not only refused to pay the fine but boycotted the games at Olympia. The Oracle a Delphi then declared that he would not entertain any Athenians unless they satisfied the Eleans. In a huff the Athenians paid the fine, which was used to erect six statues to Zeus (called *Zanes*, placed at the entrance to the stadium reminding competitors not to cheat) with inscriptions by no means flattering to the Athenians.

Six hundred years after the incident the Roman critic Cassius Longinus (*On the Sublime*), in an evaluation of Greek orators, found Hyperides formidable in most of the important traits of an orator, but the best in none, and ironically compared him to a pentathlete.[30]

Kallippos himself must have been well known and highly regarded locally for the city fathers to be willing to pay his fine. Likely he earned a local reputation at the celebrated Panathenaea festivals as well the annual and formal athletic games of Athens to honor the city's war dead. Inscriptions for the 1st and 2nd century B.C. indicate that participation in the funeral Athenian Games, which had begun in 479 B.C., were mandatory for *ephebes*, young men.[31]

The Hellenistic Age (323 to 146 B.C.) and the Greco-Roman Era (146–30 B.C.)

The death of Alexander ended the Greek Classical age. Alexander's considerable conquests had a noticeable impact on the spread of Greek culture.

He and his surviving generals founded dozens of cities in Asia and northern Africa (Egypt's Alexandria for example) and as far east as the Indus River (modern day India), all of whom began to offer periodic festivals which included the distinctive characteristics of Greek athletes—prizes, nudity, gymnastic and hippic events, and the pentathlon. By this time the pentathlon was contested on 3 different continents, all part of Alexander's world.

The first known Olympic pentathlon champion after Alexander's death is another Alex, Alexibios of Heraia, who won the pentathlon in 312 B.C. and whose victory statue at Olympia was fashioned by Akestor. In the 3rd century Gorgos of Messene, son of Eucletus, won at Olympia in 232 B.C. Privileged by birth, wealth and good looks, he won so many other crowns that contemporary historian Polybius (*The Histories*) called him "the most famous athlete of his time." Theron of Boiotia fashioned his Olympia victory statue. Mark Golden says that he was no less distinguished as a statesman in later life, not a boor like so many other athletes.[32]

It is here we insert the name of Gorgos of Elis, one of antiquity's greatest athletes. Not only did he win the pentathlon at Olympia four times, an extraordinary achievement spanning 13 years, but he also won Olympic wreaths in the *diaulos* (double *stade* of about 400 meters) and *hoplites* (race in armor).

We know that Pausanias saw at Olympia his portrait statue (bust), which stood next to a Spartan king, but Gorgos is so very difficult to date since we know so little else about him. He must come later than 520 B.C., for that is when the race in armor was introduced. And Hyde tells us that portrait statues were virtually unknown before the 4th century B.C., so he likely belongs to Hellenistic Age, but frankly, we are guessing.[33] He may fit here because three of the eight known pentathlon winners between 384 and 200 B.C. are also Eleans. At ancient Olympia, over a span of a dozen centuries, only four athletes won more wreaths than Gorgos!

By the time Roman emperor Hadrian minted this coin (with the head of Zeus) to celebrate the 228th Olympiad in 133 C.E., the pentathlon had been a standard in sporting festivals for more than 800 years. Muenzkabinett Staatliche Museen, Berlin (bpk, Berlin/Art Resource, New York).

Olympic book-end winners of the 3rd century B.C. are known.

Timachos of Mantinea was the first (296 B.C.) while Timon of Elis (200 B.C.) was the last. The latter won pentathlons everywhere in Greece but at Corinth since, in that time span the Eleans were not allowed to participate in the Isthmian Games. In the early 2nd century B.C. the Greek city states continued to battle the Macedonians and Timon commanded a garrison at Naupaktas, a town on the Corinthian gulf, against the northern barbarians. Hyde dates his Olympic win a bit later, perhaps 196 or 192 B.C.

Winners of other crown pentathlons of the era included Nicomachus of Messene who won back to back pentathlons at the Panathenaia (around 190 B.C.) and won once at Delphi in 194 B.C. A few years later, in 182 B.C., Acastidas of Thebes won at the Panathenaia. The final known winner at Olympia before the Christian era was Aristonymidas of Kos (72 B.C.).

Imperial Period, (30 B.C. to ca. 400 C.E.)

Roman rule was firmly established when Roman legions marched through Greece and destroyed Corinth in 146 B.C., completing the harass and subjugation process begun by Phillip II of Macedonia. The city's people were massacred or sold as slaves (a Corinthian peace) as the once proud city states and kingdoms became part of the Roman world. But Greek culture did not immediately pass into history. Instead, Roman consuls and emperors alternatively looted and bullied Olympia on one hand, and on the other elevated the festival to new heights.

In 86 B.C. consul Sulla looted the sacred Treasuries at Olympia and moved the games for one Olympiad to Rome six years later. The tomfoolery of the megalomaniac emperor Nero in 65 C.E. (the 211th Olympiad) was an embarrassment for all concerned. After his death his name was expunged from the official Olympic records. But other Roman leaders—notably Augustus, Agrippa and especially Hadrian—returned the festival at Olympia to its classical glory. The current stadium which archaeologists have uncovered and which tourists visit today was built under Hadrian between (ca. 137 B.C.). King Herod I of Judaea (73–4 B.C.) and Roman Emperor Domitian (emperor from 81 to 96 C.E.) underwrote a general rebuilding program at Olympia. In the 2nd century C.E. an Athenian aristocrat, Herodes Atticus, built an aqueduct bringing fresh water to the Olympic site.

Under the patronage of these Roman rulers, much of Greek culture, including athletic festivals, boomed and the pentathlon went along for the ride. Instead of fading into history, the Greek combined events creation lasted another 500 years.

We know the names of five Olympic pentathlon winners from the Roman era. For example, the most successful Olympic athlete from Sikyon had been a 4th century B.C. pankrationist named Sostrator (three pankration wreaths) known as "the fingerer" for bending his opponents' fingers back until they surrendered. But in the mid–2nd century of the Roman era a renowned runner named Aelius Granianus went Sostrator two fingers better. In 133 C.E. Aelius Granianus won the boys' stade at Olympia. In 137, taking advantage of the new, elevated stadium at Olympia built by the emperor Hadrian, Aelius Granianus won the diaulos (ca. 400 meters), the hoplite footrace, and the pentathlon; and in 141 he repeated as the pentathlon victor, making 5 Olympic wreaths. In 197 C.E. Aurelius Metrodoros of Kyzikos won the pentathlon wreath at Olympia, no doubt kept fit by using the lavish annual funeral games in his hometown. Kyzikos was both a peninsula and city in the northwest corner of present day Turkey. It was a Greek settlement, founded in the 8th century B.C. and, legend has it, was on the route of the Argonauts who supposedly created the pentathlon.

The speedy Demetrios of Salamis was the fastest man of the 3rd century and he would have gained athletic immortality had he only won the stade at Olympia three times. After all, his feat was only ever duplicated by ten others in ancient history. Yet he could also lay claim to having been the best athlete of his time, having also won a pair of Olympic pentathlon wreaths (229 and 233 C.E.). At one of the pentathlons at Olympia he defeated Opatus, 3–2, winning the wrestling bout, likely the sprint and one other event. He did not, as George Bean and Harris have interpreted an epigram, dead heat with Opatus four times, winning the event on the 5th rerun, a sequence more than just improbable.[34] Demetrios also won sprints at the Pythian and Isthmian Games and once defeated 86 rivals at the Sebastan Games in Naples. Two emperors appointed him *Xystarches* (person in charge of an athlete's guild) for life.[35] Another well known 3rd century pentathlete was Aurelius Polycrates of Cibyra in Lycia (a city in southern Asia Minor that had been annexed by Rome) who had won stadion races as a boy but earned most of his fame as a pentathlete who would sometimes sweep the first three events, winning 3–0, not only akoniti but without having to race. In later life he enjoyed citizenship of many communities and was *Xystarches* for life at the festival at Philadelphia (now Alasehir), a city in western Turkey.

We know of Publius Asklepiades of Corinth not only because he was only his city's second pentathlon winner at Olympia (Xenophon was the other and Nicoladas did not win at Olympia), but he was sort of the "Jim Thorpe" of his day. When in 1912 after his Stockholm Olympic victories in the decathlon and pentathlon, the American Indian was told by Sweden's King Gustav V that he (Thorpe) was the "world's greatest athlete," Thorpe is said to have replied, "Thanks King." The response had a historical precedent. Seventeen centuries earlier, at the 255th ancient games (241 C.E.), Publius Asklepiades had left a votive discus at Olympia Altis whose inscription read, "Thanks Zeus." Aside from his wonderful economy of words, he is also notable as nearly the last known pentathlon winner in antiquity. The ancient games continued at Olympia for at least 150 more years and pentathlons were likely conducted as late as the early 6th century A.D. in cities like Antioch, Syria. But our evidence (literary, artistic, archaeological, victor lists) dries up here and that makes him one of the last known Olympic pentathletes of antiquity. How ironic that the very next Olympic pentathlon winner and the first of the modern era would be Thorpe.

The last Olympic pentathlon champion we have a record of is [Pa]nkratios of Athens, who won in 365 C.E., nearly seven centuries after the first known pentathlon winner from Athens, the well-known rogue Kallippos.

The Chronological Reach of the Pentathlon in the Ancient World

By the beginning of the Christian era it may have seemed that Greek athletics festivals and events like the pentathlon were on their last legs. Yet three additional factors pushed the festivals and the pentathlon deep into the new millennium. First, athletic guilds, a sort of union organized and managed by athletes which had been created on a small scale in the late Hellenistic age, surged in Roman times. Their function was to oversee preparations for the games, maintain athletic facilities and look after the interests of the athletes. By the 1st century A.D., for example, Olympia had an athlete's guild clubhouse on site. The guilds lasted until the end of the athletic era. In 1994 a bronze plaque unearthed at Olympia contained the names of guild victors of athletics and combat sports at Olympia from 28 B.C. to 385 C.E. The guilds were, simultaneously, a result of and a promotional arm for ancient athletics.

Second, Romans appreciated (some may say "were enthralled by") Greek culture, including its art, literature, oratory and sport. And given intermittent special treatment from the Roman emperors and other benefactors, the number of festivals (which included the pentathlon) swelled in the 1st century C.E. Mid–20th century estimates put the number of annual or periodic Greek athletic festivals at approximately 300, a figure which now appears to be on the low side. H.W. Pleket tells us that "local games expanded in the post-classical period. Without exaggeration one might say that each polis housed within its walls a number of local prize games, organized in honor of local deities or local VIPs, living or dead."[36] Considering numismatic evidence, it now appears that at least 500 annual festivals were being conducted within the Roman Empire by the middle of the 2nd century A.D. Competitions were so numerous that local calendars were constructed to allow athletes to compete in neighboring cities.

Third, the assimilation of Greek culture into the wider Roman world brought not only a considerable expansion of Greek athletic festivals but a franchising of the Crown games. Cities adopting the Olympic program (*isolympic*), or the Pythian program (*isopythian*) or the Isthmian program (*isoisthmian*) gave local competitions additional prestige and brought the pentathlon event to new corners of the Roman world. Unlike the modern era where the term "Olympic" is religiously protected, the ancient managing Eleans franchised the right for other cities to call their games "Olympic" for the proper (and substantial) fee.[37] German scholar Onno van Nijf has reported more than thirty known Isolympic festivals in the Christian era. For example, during the reign of Hadrian (117–136 C.E.), the city of Antioch (Syria) paid handsomely to attach the term "Olympic" to their annual festival, one which lasted approximately a century after the site at Olympia, harassed by earthquakes and floods, was closed down by emperor decree (Theodosius I closed all pagan sites in 393 A.D., Theodosius II ordered all pagan temples destroyed in 426 C.E.).[38] But, the games at Antioch were still being held in the early years of the 6th century A.D. The pentathlon had outlived Olympia itself.

The Pentathlon in Other Ancient Cultures

Finally it is essential to note that the pentathlon event had an extensive reach. Where, when and for how long the event was conducted in the Greek, Roman and Byzantine world is mind-boggling. From the western Mediterranean to the Black Sea, from northern Africa to eastern Persia, pentathlons were conducted from the elite to novice levels. Appendix D contains my estimate for the number of crown, iso-crown, and local festivals which were conducted over a 1300 year period. Remembering that many of the festivals included pentathlons for various categories (boys, beardless youths and men) there may have been as many as half-a-million different pentathlon contests at nearly a quarter of a million festivals from the end of the 8th century B.C., when the event was presumably created, to the early days of the 6th century A.D., a century after Rome fell. If we assume conservatively that the average size pentathlon field was five and that the typical pentathlete of antiquity participated in an average of five career meetings (the modern average), then we find that there may have been as many as a half a million ancient pentathletes.[39] Spread out over 1300 years, the figure doesn't seem quite so large, but the figure dwarfs the number of decathletes of the modern era. Since the modern decathlon was first created and conducted a century ago there have been approximately 160,000 decathlon meets worldwide (22 Olympic Games, 60 other major championships, about 7500 national championships and about 150,000 other regional, local and age group meets). Consider: one half of a million ancient pentathletes!

The pentathlons' reach may not have been limited to just to geographical or chronological reflection. The event also crossed ethnic barriers. The Jewish faith was generally not athletically conscious and found nudity insufferable. The term "pentathlon" appears nowhere in either the Old or New Testament.[40] But some modern scholars discuss an Etruscan pentathlon. There is no pentathlon evidence for the people who preceded the Romans on the Italian peninsula (pre–Roman Republic, ca. 400–500 B.C.) except a painting with "pentathlete" competing or training.[41] The evidence is razor thin and most scholars agree that the Etruscans did not conduct pentathlons, although the Etruscans were once involved in an ancient naval battle with a Greek leader named Pentathlos.[42]

There is no doubt that the pentathlon was adopted by the Phoenicians, who spread it to their colonies and trading centers within the ancient world. The Phoenicians thrived before the Punic Wars (before 264 B.C.) but, by the fall of their major city, Carthage, the pentathlon was a fundamental part of Phoenician athletic festivals. We are told by Pindar that the games at Tyre, an eastern Mediterranean city in present day Lebanon, were well known in his day (5th century B.C.). Athletes from Phoenician cities would participate in the Tyre games which were held in honor of Baal or Melkart. These games were revised in Roman times and lasted at least through the 3rd century C.E. Labib Boutros argues unconvincingly that the Phoenicians had a major influence on the origin of the Olympic Games and Greek sport, but his evidence on the pentathlon, which relies on Greek inscriptions found at Tyre, is quite correct.[43] Incidentally, the order of the Phoenician pentathlon, says Boutros, is identical to that we have derived: discus, jump, javelin, sprint, wrestling.

As to the Celts who lived to the north of the Greco-Roman world for a more than a millennium, little is known of their sports and there appears to be no sporting influence in one direction or the other. The pre–Celtic tribes in present day Ireland conducted a concurrent ancient set of annual athletic games which began, if it is to be believed, in 1829 B.C. and which was continued by the Celts into the early Middle Ages. The Tailteaan Games contained their own set of running-jumping-throwing events, including ones in which the Greeks never dabbled (pole vault, hammer toss). But there seem to have been very little contact and no sporting cross-pollination. The Irish did undertake a modern renewal of the Tailteaan Games (for those of Celtic descent), and for a few years (1924–1932) revivals of the ancient Olympic and ancient Tailteaan Games existed side by side. No pentathlon, nor any combined event for that matter, was staged in the ancient Celtic culture, but it would be their descendants, the Scots, who would be instrumental bringing back and popularizing combined events in the 19th century. We will save that story for the final chapter.

A Warning About the Interpretation
of Ancient Pentathlon History

It has been suggested by some scholars that, because we know something of the demonstrated skills of some of the ancient pentathletes, we can deduce what events they may have won within a specific pentathlon. For example, Reinhold Merkelbach has made the observation that the first four events often saw double victories of two sorts (it is uncertain how he knows this since there is no record), i.e., the same athlete might win the jump and the run (like Tisamenos) or a single athlete the two throws (like Automedes and an athlete from Ephesos who was undefeated in discus and javelin). Victor Matthews says this "is because the two pair of events call upon related abilities, e.g., the sprinter-jumper combination is common, as with Jesse Owens and Carl Lewis."[44] The discus and javelin throws are not quite as closely related, the latter placing less of a premium on size and bulk. Matthews concludes that many pentathlon competitions must have been decided in the final wrestling between two double victors from the first four events.[45] That is, he suggests that the "type" of athlete can be used to explain the manner of victory. This is a common mistake made by those who do not understand the difference between "multiple-event" athlete and a "combined event" athlete.

Having organized, officiated, announced or witnessed more than 1,200 combined event competitions worldwide in the past half century, to me the following axioms have become all too apparent.

(a) The closer one approaches the top in combined events, the less the "types" classification applies. By definition combined event athletes aspire to become "all types," and the closer they get to the podium, by definition, the less relevant the types classification becomes. Elite combined event athletes are successful in rising above classifications.

(b) One must distinguish the strengths and weaknesses of athletes as either relative or absolute. One can be an absolutely terrific runner and lose the sprinting event to an even faster runner and, conversely, be a weak thrower and win the event because the competition is even weaker. Ancient pentathlon victories depended not only upon an individual athlete's ability but that of his opponents as well. Reaching conclusions of what events athlete A must have won on the basis of A's reputation (absolute strengths) can often be misleading and result in faulty conclusions. What is important are "relative" strengths, not the absolute ones. This has led Merkelbach and Matthews to deduce ancient event winners without knowledge of the competition. They do it on the basis of what is known about one athlete and not the field.

Some examples may help. By definition, the very best combined event athletes have skills that transcend "types." How would, for example, one explain Bryan Clay, the 2008 Olympic decathlon champion? Is he a sprinter-jumper type as Merkelbach and Matthews would suggest, since he is one of the fastest of the current crop of decathletes (having run 100m in 10.34 seconds and rarely losing a sprint race) and an 8.00m (26–3) long jumper? Or is he the "thrower" type because, despite his small stature, he is, among decathletes, the world's best discus thrower (holding world decathlon record of 55.87m/183–3) and almost the world's best javelin thrower at 72.00m (236–3)? In Merkelbach and Matthews' parlance would we classify him as a sprinter-jumper or a thrower? The answer is "both." The examples of top combined event athletes who transcend the "types" is legion. If we investigate the best absolute events of former Olympic decathlon champions we find too many athletes who do not fit the Merkelbach and Matthews categories:

1912 Olympic champion Jim Thorpe (runner-jumper–shot putter)
1960 Olympic champion Rafer Johnson (sprinter–discus thrower)
1976 Olympic champion Bruce Jenner (discus-vaulter)
2004 Olympic champion and former world record holder Roman Sebrle (long jumper–javelin),
and the list goes on.

Of course there are some examples that fit the Merkelbach-Matthews categories. But far too few to make this a truism. By definition, the best combined event athletes have skills that defy types. That is what makes them combined event champions. For the very best athletes the traditional "types" do not apply. So, too, it must have been for the ancient Greek winners. The moral: be very careful in applying this line of reasoning to history. In athletics it is a common mistake. Just ask Bryan Clay and Roman Sebrle.

10. The Creation of a Pentathlon Record Book and Register

Victor lists for ancient Greek athletic winners have been around for a long time. The initial list of Olympic winners (*Olympionikai*) is normally attributed to Elean sophist Hippias and dates to approximately 400 B.C. A large number of individuals, from Aristotle to Sextus Julius Africanus, updated victor lists from Olympia, and many of these lists circulated in antiquity. Unfortunately none have survived in their entirety and we have only fragments and references from other literary forms. The victor lists of Hippias were said to be complete for all events, including the pentathlon, from 708 B.C. until 400 B.C. (78 winners). Yet we have, from other sources, the names (or partial names) of only 17 pentathlon winners for the same time period. Ancient Olympic pentathlon winners offered here are taken from Luigi Moretti, *Olympionikai, I vincitori negli antichi Agoni Olimpici*, 1959. Although there seems to have been much interest in victor lists from Olympia, there appears to have been no corollary efforts for the other Crown Games, at Delphi, Corinth and Nemea.

Modern scholars, beginning with Isaac Newton in 1728, have expressed reservations about the reliability of the early names and dates of Hippias' lists.

With the exception of *stadion* winners, victor lists for individual events, a subset of overall victor lists, have rarely been constructed. Berlin scholar Eduard Pinder published the first (and as far as I have been able to discover the only) list of pentathlon victors. In 1867 he identified 25 Olympic winners and 27 additional pentathlon winners from other festivals. Additions to this list have come haltingly ever since. In 1994, for example, a bronze plate was excavated at Olympia and has been identified as including the names of ancient winners at Olympia who belonged to a common guild. The statistical genre's (victor lists) most recent and notable scholar, Paul Christensen of Dartmouth College, graciously translated the bronze plate which revealed a partial name and a full name of pentathlon winners at Olympia, the latter Pankratios of

Athens in A.D. 365, making him the last known pentathlon winner of antiquity. It goes without saying that, as additional inscriptions and evidence becomes available, these lists will be revised.

The surviving information allows interpretative possibilities and I have, for the present chapter, structured the data as would modern track and field statisticians.[1] For example, Section I, the list of the 40 ancient Olympic pentathlon winners at 48 different Olympiads, would be referred to as a list of performers/performances since the same names could appear more than once. And, although there are no scoring table totals nor individual event marks as with, for example, modern decathlon information, we can arrange the ancient data in meaningful ways.

The surviving evidence allows us to provide three types of lists: victors at specific festivals; victors by location; and a register of ancient athletes. Section I provides all known winners, listed chronologically, of the major Panhellenic Games (Olympic, Pythian, Isthmian and Nemean) and several other noteworthy festivals (Panathenaic, Asklepedia at Kos). In many cases we have dates (or approximate dates) of the victory, the name of the athlete's father and city, and, on rare occasions, the name of the runner-up or the final pentathlon score. We have approximately 15 percent of the names from a millennium of Olympic winners. The lists are useful in ascertaining the reach and popularity of the festival. For instance, ancient Olympic winners (in all events) came from as far west as Marseilles and from as far east as Babylon. Even a local festival like the Asklepedia in Kos (located in the southwest corner of Asia Minor) drew winners from Egypt, Athens and the Peloponnese.[2] We can also create meet records. For example, we can be fairly certain that Gorgos of Elis holds the Olympic record for most pentathlon wins, at four. Likewise, Nicolades of Corinth almost assuredly won the most major titles, at 8. And we can list those athletes who doubled with wins in the pentathlon and another event.

Section II provides a count of major festival pentathlon winners by city. This information is useful since it reflects the rise and fall of an athletic dynasty. There is a local bias in the data, however. Elis provided the most known Olympic winners, but this may be more a function of local record keeping than dominance. As well, we are unable to ascertain if the incidence of a city's winners is a result of interest or opportunity.[3] Nonetheless, we can learn much from such lists. Providing information about athletes by national affiliation and at sites and festivals is a practice provided annually by modern combined events statisticians.[4]

Section III is a register of known ancient pentathletes, winners and non-winners, at a variety of ancient festivals. It is more demonstrative than all-inclusive. Today all modern track and field annuals end with a similar register of athletes.[5] Given the durability and reach of the ancient pentathlon (see Appendix D, which suggests nearly a half of a million festivals that likely included the pentathlon) my register is woefully limited. It includes the names (or at time fragments of names) of 111 ancient pentathletes who won a total of 175 pentathlons (performers/performances) at ancient festivals. That works out to less than one-half of one-tenth of one percent of all winners. In many cases we have rather complete data: name, city, date, festival, name of father. There are even a few final scores available.[6] Unlike modern track and field lists, no individual event marks are provided because the Greeks did not measure field event marks and had no timing devices.[7]

These lists allow modern historians to create "records," insofar as athletic records are available from antiquity. Rudolph Knab recognized the usefulness of victor lists in creating records like the *periodoniken* (winners of a circuit of Crown Games) as early as 1934.[8] The question of Greek record keeping has been adequately addressed by Tod, Young, and Christensen.[9]

Major Sources for This Chapter

Biers, William R., and Daniel J. Geagan. "A New List of Victors in the Caesarea at Isthmia," *Hesperia* 39, 1970, pp. 79–90.

Christesen, Paul. *Olympic Victor Lists and Ancient Greek History,* Cambridge: Cambridge University Press, 2007.

Dunst, Gunter. "Die Siegerliste der Samischen Heraia," *Zeitschrift für Papyrologie und Epigraphik,* bd 1, 1967, pp. 225–39.

Klee, Theophil. *Zur Geschichte der Gymnischen Agone an Griechischen Festen,* Chicago: Ares: 1980 (originally published in Leipzig, 1918).

Matthews, Victor. "The Greek Pentathlon Again," *Zeitschrift für Papyrologie und Epigraphik,* Vol. 100, 1994, pp. 129–138.

Pinder, Eduard. *Funfkampf der Hellenen,* Berlin: Verlag von Wilhelm Hertz, 1867, pp. 117–135.

Tracy, Stephen V., and Christian Habicht. "New and Old Panathenaic Victor Lists," *Hesperia.* Vol. 60, No. 2, April-June 1991, pp. 187–236.

Yalouris, Nicolaos (ed.). *The Eternal Olympics: The Art and History of Sport,* New Rochelle, NY: Karatzas Brothers, 1979. Contains Olympic victor lists from Luigi Moretti, *Olympionikai, I vincitori negli antichi Agoni Olimpici,* Atti della Accademia nazionale dei Lincei, 8, 1959, pp. 289–296.

I: Pentathlon Winners of Antiquity at Major Festivals

Olympic Games (Olympia)

Lampis of Sparta	708 B.C.
Philombrotos of Sparta	676
Philombrotos of Sparta	672
Philombrotos of Sparta	668
Akmatidas of Sparta (*akoniti*)	500
Hieronymos of Andros° (3–2)	492
Euthykles of Lokroi°	488
Theopompos of Heraia°	484
Theopompos of Heraia°	480
(...) of Taras	476

(...)amos of Miletos	472
(...)tion of Taras	468
Xenophon of Corinth	464
(....)nomos of (....)	456
Pythokles of Elis	452
Keton of Lokroi	448
Ikkos of Taras	444
Hysmon of Elis°	384
Stomios of Elis°	376
Kallippos of Athens	332
Alexibios of Heraia°	312
Timachos of Mantineia	296
(...) of Elis°	252
Gorgos of Messene°	232
Timon of Elis°	200
(Klee says ca. 330 B.C. for Timon)	
Aristonymidas of Kos	72
(...)mios of (....)	21 A.D.
Aelius Granianus of Sikyon°	137
Aelius Granianus of Sikyon°	14
Aurelius Metrodorus of Kyzikos	197
Demetrios of Salamis°	229
Demetrios of Salamis°	233
Publius Asklepiades of Corinth	241
[Pa]nkratios of Athens	365

OLYMPIC VICTORS OF UNKNOWN DATE

Ainetos of Amyklai (Lakonia)
Aischinos of Elis (twice)
Anaxander pappos (between 576 and 416 B.C.)
Gorgos of Elis (four times)
Klearchos of Elis
Kleinomarchos of Elis
Menalkas of Elis
Theodoros of Elis
Lykos of Messene (uncertain)

BOYS' VICTOR

Eutelidas of Sparta	628 B.C.

Pythian Games (Delphi)

Phaÿllos of Kroton	ca. 500 B.C.
Phaÿllos of Kroton	ca. 500 B.C.
Nicolades of Corinth	5th c B.C.
Diophon of Corcyra	5th c B.C.
Eupolemos of Elis	398 B.C. ?
Eupolemos of Elis	394 B.C. ?
Timon of Elis	ca. 200 B.C.
(Klee says ca. 330 B.C. for Timon)	
Leon of Messene	194 B.C.

Isthmian Games (Corinth)[10]

Kratippos of (...)	6th c B.C.
Kratippos of (...)	6th c B.C.
Kratippos of (...)	6th c B.C.
Diophon of Corcyra	5th c B.C.
Nicolades of Corinth	5th c B.C.
Nicolades of Corinth	5th c B.C.
Nicolades of Corinth	5th c B.C.
Xenophon of Corinth	466 B.C.?
Xenophon of Corinth	464 B.C.?
Antiochus of Lepreon	400–380 B.C.
Antiochus of Lepreon	400–380 B.C.
Damiskos of Messene	368 B.C.—boys'

OTHER WINNERS WITH UNCERTAIN DATES

Aristolas of Rhodes	perhaps 1st c B.C.
(...)tos of Kos	1st c B.C. (2nd half)
Onasion of Argos	2nd c C.E.—youth
Poplios Ailios of Antiocheus	2nd c C.E.

Nemean Games (Nemea)

Eurybates of Argos	500–490 B.C.?
Nicolades of Corinth	5th c B.C.
Nicolades of Corinth	5th c B.C.
Nicolades of Corinth	5th c B.C.
Sogenes of Aegine	487 B.C.—boys'
Xenophon of Corinth	465 B.C.?
Automedes of Philius	460–440 B.C.?
Antiochus of Lepreon	400–380 B.C.?
Antiochus of Lepreon	400–380 B.C.?
Eupolemus of Elis	397 B.C.?
Stomius of Elis	380–370 B.C.?
Stomius of Elis	380–370 B.C.?
Stomius of Elis	380–370 B.C.?
Hysmon of Elis	365 B.C.?
Damiskos of Messene	365–360 B.C.?—boys'
Timon of Elis	ca. 200 B.C.
Aristolas of Rhodes	1st c B.C. (1st half)
(...) of Kos	1st c B.C. (2nd half)

Panatheaea Games (Athens)

Nicolades of Corinth	5th c B.C.
Nicomachos of Messene	186 B.C.
Nicomachos of Messene	182 B.C.?
Acastidas of Thebes	182 B.C.?
Noumenios of Athens	166 B.C.
Unknown Dates	
Demetrios of Boetia	
Timochles of Sikyon	

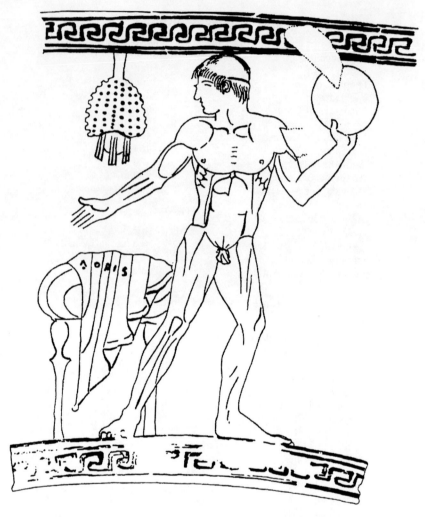

The ancient Greeks indeed kept records of their athletic accomplishments, for instance for most wins in a single event or most wins at a particular festival. Individual event records, for example, for this discus thrower, were not maintained. From a vase from Eretria, where the drawing first appeared in 1886 (*Journal of Hellenic Studies*, 1907).

(Some references maintain that Panathenaic victory lists survive for the following years: 202, 198, 182, 178, 170, 166, 162, 158, 150, 146 B.C.)

Alsekpedia of Kos

MEN

Thrasumedes of Rhodes	250	B.C.
Kallias of Kos	246	

MEN

Philonicos of Ptolemaieus of Barces	230
Timasianas of Rhodes	194
Nicomachos of Messene	190
Timasianas of Rhodes	182
Ermias of Halicarnasseus—2nd	182
Ant(...) of Assios	178
Nicarchos of Murinaios—2nd	
Artistomedes of Rhodes—2nd	

YOUNG MEN (BEARDLESS YOUTH)

Evanactidas of Rhodes	250 B.C.
Emprepon of Kos	246
Aristolas of Rhodes	230
(...) of Rhodes	214
(...) of Kos	198
(...) of Rhodes	194
(...)s of Achaios	190
Aristomedes of Rhodes	182
Menesstratos of Halicarnaseus	
Egeipp(os...) of Kudnou—2nd	
Armodius of Halicarnasseus—2nd	178

BOYS

Zopurion of Kos	250 B.C.
Nicostratos of Alexandria	230
Eracleitos of Kos	214
Aristodamos of unc	198
Timostratos of Kos	190
Andromenes of Kos	182
Apollodros of Kumas	178
Xenon(...) of Rhodes—2nd	
(10 wins for Rhodes, 7 for Kos)	

Heraclea Games at Chalcis

Moschion of Chalcis	2nd c B.C.
Phinlox of unc	2nd c B.C.

Records

Most major festival wins: 8
     Nicolades of Corinth   5th c B.C.
     (3 Isthmian, 1 Pythian, 3 Nemean,
     1 Panatheaen), (nb: none at Olympia)

The Olympic Doublers
Olympic pentathlon winners with victories in other events.

Olympiad	Name	Victory in Other Events
uncertain	Gorgos of Elis (4x)	diaulos
		race in armor

79–464 B.C.	Xenophon of Corinth	stadion
239–137 A.D.	Aelius Granianus of Sikyon	diaulos
		race in armor
252–229 A.D.	Demetrios of Salamis	stadion
253–233 A.D.	Demetrios of Samalis*	stadion

*won stadion 3rd time in A.D. 254–237

II: Major Festival Winners by Cities

Includes the 4 Panhellenic Games: Olympic (Oly), Pythian (Pyt), Isthmian (Ist), Nemean (Nem) plus the Panathenaic Festival at Athens (Pan).

Elis	24	[*Oly*- B.C.: 452, 384, 376, 252, 200, und-10×; *Pyt*: 398, 394, 200; *Nem*: 397, 380–70 (3×), 365, 200]
Corinth	13	[*Oly*- B.C.: 464; A.D. 241; *Pyt*: 5th c; *Ist*: 5th century (3×), 466, 464: *Nem*: 5th century (3×), 465; *Pan*: 5th century
Messene	8	[*Oly*-B.C.: 232, unc; *Pyt*: 194; *Ist*: 368; *Nem*: 4th c; *Pan*: 194, 186, 182]
Sparta	6	[*Oly*-B.C.: 708, 676, 672, 668, 628, 500]
Lepreon	4	[*Ist*-B.C.: 4th century (2×); *Nem*: 4th century (2×)]
Heraia	3	[*Oly*-B.C.: 484, 480, 312]
Taras	3	[*Oly*- B.C.: 476, 468, 444]
Athens	3	[*Oly*-B.C.: 332; A.D.: 365; *Pan*: und]
Sikyon	3	[*Oly*-A.D.: 137, 141; *Pan*: und]
Kos	3	[*Oly*-B.C.L. 72; *Ist*: und; *Nem*-B.C.: 1st c]

III: Alphabetical Register of Known Ancient Pentathletes

122 names or fragments of names from 19 different festivals. Greek name spellings provided by Classics Department, Dartmouth College, Hanover, New Hampshire.

Legend

und . . . . . . unknown date
unc . . . . . . unknown city
ufs . . . . . . unknown festival site
° . . . . approximate date
Men . . . . . andres (ανδρας)
Youth . . . . ageneioi (αγενίεους=beard-less youths)
Boys . . . . . paides (παιδας)
< . . . . after

All winners unless otherwise noted by (2nd place).

All men winners unless other noted as: boys, youth.

Sample

name of athlete, [Greek spelling], name of city
name of father
date, name of festival,[(source)] type/ place/score

A

Ainetos [*Αἴνετος*] of Amyklai (Lakedaimon)
und, Olympia[Moretti]

Ainias [*Αίνιας (Αίνέας, Αίνείας)*]
unc
und, ufs
Aischines [*Αίσχίνας*] of Elis (twice)
und, Olympia^Moretti
und, Olympia^Moretti
Akastidas [*Άκαστίδας*] of Thebes
182 B.C. Panathenaia^IG VII
Akmatidas [*Άκματίδας*] of Sparta
500 B.C., Olympia^Moretti (*akoniti*)
P. Albinius [*Π. Άλβίνιυς*] of Corinth
Son of Methodicus
und, Erotidia at Thespiai
systephanoi—tie
Alexibios [*Άλεξίβιος*] of Heraia°
312 B.C., Olympia^Moretti
Androbios [*Άνδρόβιος*] of Sparta
ca. 316 B.C., Lycia in Arcadia^SIG 314
Andromenês [*Άνδρομένης*] of Kos
Son of Ecarodorov
182 B.C., Kos—boys
Antiochos [*Άντίοχος*] of Lepreon
ca. 400 B.C. Nemea
" " Nemea
" " Isthmia
" " Isthmia
Ant[...] [*Άντ*...] of Assos
Son of Appolonidou
178 B.C., Kos
Apollôdorus [*Άπολλόδωρος*] of Cyme
Son of Demetriou
178 B.C., Kos—boys
Apollônios [*Άπολλωνιος*] of
Alabandeys
Son of Menophilo
1st century B.C., Pelasgiotis at Larisa—boys^IG IX
Aratos [*Άρατος*] of Sikyon
und, ufs
Arkas [*Άρκάς*] of unc
Son of Alexibios
ca. 320 B.C., Lykaia in Arcadia^SIG 314
Argeios [*Άργείος*] of Lusianactos(?)
Son of Andromachos
ca. 320 B.C., Lykaia in Arcadia^SIG 314
Aristodamos [*Άριστόδαμος*] of unc
198 B.C., Kos—boys
Aristolas [*Άριστόλας*] of Rhodes
Son of Aristandrou
230 B.C., Kos—youth
Aristolas [*Άριστόλας*] of Rhodes

1st century B.C., Isthmia
" " Nemea
Aristomêdês [*Άπριστομήδης*] of Rhodes
Son of Simou
182 B.C., Kos—boys/2nd
178 B.C., Kos—youth
Aristônymidas [*Άριστωνυμίδας*] of Kos
72 B.C., Olympia^Moretti
Harmodios [*Άρμόδιος*] of Halicarnassos
Son of Harmodios
178 B.C. Kos—youth/2nd
Harmonikos [*Άρμονικὸς*] of Lakedaimon
Son of Eydamisa
1st century B.C.Pelasgiotis at Larisa^IG IX
Aurelius Polycratês [*Αύρήελιος Πολυκράτης*] of Cibyra
A.D. 3rd c, numerous (3–0)
Automedes [*Αύτομήδης*] of Phlious
460–440 B.C.?, Nemea (3–2)

β

(Few proper names began with β in classical Greek and there were none among the 111 entries of this register)

Γ

Gorgos [*Γόργος*] of Elis
und, Olympia^Moretti
und, Olympia^Moretti
und, Olympia^Moretti
und, Olympia^Moretti
(only known 4× Olympic winner)
Gorgos [*Γόργος*] of Messene°
232 B.C., Olympia^Moretti
Aelius Granianus [*Άέλιος Γρανιανός*] of
Sikyon
A.D. 137, Olympia^Moretti
A.D. 141, Olympia^Moretti

Δ

Damiskos [*Δαμίσκος*] of Messene
368 B.C., Isthmia
365–60?, Nemea
Dêmêtrios [*Δημήτριος*] of Boiotia
194/93 B.C., Panathenaic^IG VII
Dêmêtrios [*Δημήτριος*] of Salamis
229 C.E., Olympia^Moretti
233 C.E., Olympia^Moretti
und, Koinen of Asia (3–2)
3rd century C.E., Isthmia/tie (?)

3rd century C.E., Isthmia/tie (?)
3rd century C.E., Hadrianeion at
  Anazarbos/tie (?)
3rd century C.E., Hadrianeion at
  Anazarbos/tie (?)
Demosthenês [Δημοσθένης] of unc
? C.E., Thespiai, Boiotia^{IG VII}
Diophon [Διοφών] of unc
  Son of Philon
  5th century B.C., Isthmia
  5th century B.C., Pythia

E

Emprepôn [Ἐμπρέπων] of Kos
  Son of Antiochou
  246 B.C., Kos—youth
Epainetos [Ἐπαίνετος] of unc
Epicharês [Ἐπιχάρης] of Chalcis
  Son of Diogenes
  und, Oropus
Hermias [Ἑρμίας] of Halicarnassos
  Son of Tauriscou
  182 B.C., Kos/2nd
  und, Eleusis
Euanactidas [Εὐανακτίδας] of Rhodes
  Son of Euanactida
  250 B.C., Kos—youth
Eupolemos [Εὐπόλεμος] of Elis
  398 B.C.?, Pythia
  397 B.C.?, Nemea
  394 B.C.?, Pythia
Eurybatês [Εὐρυβάτης] of Argos
  ca. 490 B.C., Nemea
Eutelidas [Εὐτελίδας] of Sparta
  628 B.C., Olympia—boys^{Moretti}
Euthyklês [Εὐθυκλῆς] of Lokris
  488 B.C., Olympia^{Moretti}

Z

Zôpuriôn [Ζωπυρίων] of Kos
  Son of Philocleus
  250 B.C., Kos—boys

H

Hêgesippos son of [...]odôros
  [Ἡγήσιππος .... οδώρου] of Kydnos
  Son of Antiocheus
  182 B.C., Kos—youth/2nd
Hêrakleitos [Ἡράκλειτος] of Kos
  Son of Simou
  214 B.C., Kos—boys

Θ

Theodôros [Θεόδωρος] of Elis
  und, Olympia^{Moretti}
Theopompos [Θεόπομπος] of Heraia°
  484 B.C., Olympia^{Moretti}
  480 B.C., Olympia^{Moretti}
Thrasumêdês [Θρασυμήδης] of Rhodes
  Son of Aristophilou
  250 B.C., Kos

I

Ia...l.ch.l.e (?) [ΙΑ...Λ.Χ.Λ.Η] of Smyrna
  Son of Amyn?
  <180 B.C., Panathenaia^{IG VII}
Hierônymos [Ἱερώνυμος] of Andros°
  492 B.C., Olympia^{Moretti} (3–2)
Ikkos [Ἴκκος] of Taras
  444 B.C., Olympia^{Moretti}

K

Kallias [Καλλίας] of Kos
  Son of Kallianactos
  246 B.C., Kos
Kallippos [Κάλλιππος] of Athens
  332 B.C., Olympia^{Moretti}
Kallônos [Κάλλωνος] of Thebes
  2nd century B.C., Basileia at Lebedeia
    in Boiotia
Kêton [Κήτων] of Lokris
  448 B.C., Olympia^{Moretti}
Klearchos [Κλέαρχος] of Elis
  und, Olympia^{Moretti}
Kleinomachos [Κλεινόμαχος] of Elis
  und, Olympia^{Moretti}
Kleon [Κλέων] of Sparta
  Son of Timarchos
  und, ufs—boys
Kratippos [Κράτιππος] of unc
  6th century B.C., Isthmia
  6th century B.C., Isthmia
  6th century B.C., Isthmia

Λ

Lampis [Λάμπις] of Sparta
  708 B.C., Olympia^{Moretti}
  [1st known Olympic winner]
Leôn [Λέων] of Messene
  194 B.C., Pythia
Lycos [Λύκος] of Messene uncertain
  und, Olympia^{Moretti}

M

Mantheos [Μάνθεος] of unc
Son of Aethus
und, ufs
Menalkês [Μενάλκης] of Elis
und, Olympia[Moretti]
Menestratos [Μενέστρατος] of
Halicarnassos
Son of Euanactos
182 B.C., Kos—youth
Aurelius Mêtrodôros [Αὐρήλιος
Μητρόδωρος] of Kyzikos
A.D. 197, Olympia[Moretti]
A.D. 2nd c, Byzantium
" " Chalcedon
" " Kyzikos
" " Nicomedia
" " Pergamum
" " Perinthus
Moschiôn [Μοσχίων] of Chalcis
Son of Ermaphlou
2nd century B.C., Euboia at Chalkis
2nd century B.C., Heracleia at Chal-
kis[IG XII]

N

Nikarchos [Νίκαρχος] of Myrina
Son of Pro[...]enou
178 B.C., Kos/2nd
Nikolaidas [Νικολαίδας] of Corinth
5th century B.C.
5th century B.C., Pythia
" " Isthmia
" " Isthmia
" " Isthmia
" " Nemea
" " Nemea
" " Nemea
" " Panathenaic
" " Phlius (3–0)
" " Pellene
" " Pellene
" " Pellene
" " Pellene
" " Lykaion
" " Lykaion
" " Tegea
" " Aigina
" " Epidauros
" " Thebes

" " Pythious
" " Megara
Nikomachos [Νικόμαχος] of Messene
(or Achaea)
Son of Leonidas
194 B.C., Pythia
190 B.C., Kos
186 B.C., Panathenaic
182 B.C., Panathenaic[IG VII]
Nikôn [Νίκων] of Thebes
Son of Nikôn
und, Oropos—boys
Nikostratos [Νικόστρατος] of Alexan-
dria
Son of Nikostratos
230 B.C., Kos—boys
Noumênios [Νουμήνιος] of Athens
Son of Eubius
<180 B.C., Panathenaia[IG VII]

Ξ

Xenôn[...] [Ξένων...] of Rhodes
Son of ?androu?
178 B.C., Kos—boys/2nd
Xenophôn [Ξενοφῶν] of Corinth
466? B.C., Isthmia
465? B.C., Nemea
464 B.C., Olympia[Moretti]
464? B.C., Isthmia

O

Onasiôn [Ονασίων] of Argos
2nd century C.E., Isthmia—youth
Oyliadis [Οὐλιάδης] of Chrysaoris
Son of Artemisius
A.D.?, Thespiai-Boiotia[IG VII]

Π

Pankratios [Παγκράτιος] of Athens
A.D. 365, Olympia[Christensen]
[last known ancient Olympic winner]
Pantaleôn [Πανταλέων] of Myndos
Son of Demophon
1st–2nd century B.C., Thespiai
Parmeniskos [Παρμενίσκος] of Kos
Son of Thearet(?)
1st century B.C., Pelasgiotis at
Larisa—youth[IG IX]
Polybios Koyarteinos [Πολύβιος
Κουάρτεινος] of unc
und, ufs

Polykrates [Πολυκράτης] of Cibyra
und, ufs—boys (3–0) akoniti
und, ufs—boys (3–0) akoniti
und, Athens—Hadrianeia
Poplios [Πόπλιος] of Antioch
Son of Ailios
2nd century C.E., Isthmia
Aulus Postumus [Αὖλος Πόστουμος
Ισιδώρου]
Son of Isidôros of Alexandria
und, Neapolis
Psychicus [Ψυχικυς] of Thebes
Son of Heracleon
und, Erotidia at Thespiai
systephanoi—tie
Publius Asklêpiadês [Πόπλιος
Ἀσκληπιάδης] of Corinth
A.D. 241, Olympia[Moretti]
Pythoklês [Πυθοκλῆς] of Elis
452 B.C., Olympia[Moretti]

Σ

Satyr [Σάτυρος] of Thebes
Son of Nikôn
und, Oropos
Sôgenês [Σωγένης] of Aegine
487 B.C., Nemea—boys
Sôtôn [Σώτων] of unc
Son of Kallikratos
2nd century B.C., Heraia at
Samos[Dunst p. 23]
Spintharos [Σπίνθαρος] of unc
und, ufs
Stomios [Στόμιος] of Elis°
376 B.C., Olympia[Moretti]
380–70?, Nemea
380–70?, Nemea
380–70?, Nemea

T

Timarchos [Τίμαρχος] of Mantinea
296 B.C., Olympia[Moretti]
Timasianax [Τιμασιάναξ] of Rhodes
Son of Timasianautos
194 B.C., Kos
182 B.C., Kos
Timochlês [Τιμοκλής] of Sikyon
Son of Charicles
166 B.C., Panathenaia[IG VII]
Timokreôn [Τιμοκρέων] of unc
und, ufs

Timôn [Τίμων] of Elis
200 B.C., Olympia[Moretti]
ca. 200 B.C., Pythia
ca. 200 B.C., Nemea
Timostratos [Τιμόστρατος] of Kos
Son of Timostratos
190 B.C., Kos—boys
Tisamenos [Τισάμενος] of Elis
492 B.C., Olympia/2nd place (2–3)

Y

Hysmon ["Υσμων] of Elis°
384 B.C., Olympia[Moretti]
365? B.C., Nemea

Φ

Phaÿllos [Φάϋλλος] of Kroton
ca. 500 B.C., Pythia
" " Pythia
Philinos [Φιλῖνος] of unc
Son of Dionuciou
2nd century B.C., Heracleia at Chalcis—youth[IG XII]
Philombrotos [Φιλόμβροτος] of
Sparta
676 B.C., Olympia[Moretti]
672 B.C., Olympia[Moretti]
668 B.C., Olympia[Moretti]
Philonicos [Φιλόνιχος] of Barces
Son of Alcimou (Ptolemy)
230 B.C., Kos

X

Chionis [Χίονις] of Sparta
656? B.C., Olympia [non winner]

Ω

Opatus [Ωρατυς] of unc
A.D. 229 or 233, Koinen of Asia/2nd
(2–3)

PARTIAL NAMES
[LISTED CHRONOLOGICALLY]

[...]amos of Miletos
472 B.C., Olympia[Moretti]
[...]s of Elidos
Son of Xenotimou Achaios
190 B.C., Kos—youth

[...]tion of Taras
468 B.C., Olympia^Moretti
[...]nomos of [...]
456 B.C., Olympia^Moretti
[...]mios of [...]
A.D. 21, Olympia^Christensen
[...]s of Elidos
Son of Xenotimou Achaios
190 B.C., Kos—youth
[...] of Kos
1st century B.C., Isthmia
1st century B.C., Nemea

Unnamed
[Listed Chronologically]

Anaxander pappos [Ἀναξάνδρου πάππος] of Sparta (grandfather of Anaxander)
b/w 576–416 B.C., Olympia^Moretti

[...] of Taras
476 B.C., Olympia^Moretti
[...] of Elis
252 B.C., Olympia^Moretti
[...] of Rhodes
Son of Klenagora
214 B.C., Kos—youth
[...] of Kos
Son of Ducaithou
198 B.C., Kos—youth
[...] of Rhodes
son of Sta[...]nos
194 B.C., Kos—youth
[...] of Korinth
127 C.E., Caesarea at Isthmia
[...] of Neikopoleites
127 C.E., Caesarea at Isthmia
Amyntoy son [Ἀμύντου υἱός] of unc
und, Panathenaic

11. Pentathlon Statues
of Ancient Greece

Winners at Olympia were given the opportunity to dedicate a statue of themselves within the sacred area of the *Altis*. Many did so, although this expensive practice waxed and waned over the centuries. Multiple winners could erect multiple statues. Families, admirers or city-states of the victors underwrote the venture. There is a wonderful tale of a presumptuous young sprinter who, after an oracle predicted his Olympic victory, had his own statue sculpted before the Games and carried it to Olympia himself. The oracle proved accurate and he dedicated his own statue to Zeus that very day.

Fewer victor monuments were set up at other Crown Games, but at Olympia the practice was prolific. It was even customary for victors to erect statues of themselves for victories at local games. But the erection of a statue in the Altis at Olympic was an honor which the Elean officers in charge of the games gave to victors to glorify their success. The first victory statues dedicated at Olympia came at the 59th Games (544 B.C.) and were made of wood. Later the cost of making, transporting and setting up the statue was considerable.

By the 2nd century A.D. the sanctuary at Olympia was almost completely filled with statues and busts of Olympic victors, eminent citizens and war heroes. It was a virtual forest of bronze and marble.[1] While traveling in the mainland of Greece at this time, during and after the reign of Hadrian, Pausanias wrote a detailed account of what he saw within the Olympia sanctuary.

Apparently the *Hellanodikai* allowed one statue for each victory. Aischines of Elis had a pair of Olympic pentathlon victories to his credit between 276 and 252 B.C. and erected a statue for each. The inscription of one has been recovered. But none of the victor statues themselves survive, either having been carried off to Italy by Roman devotees of Greek culture or destroyed by bands of invading barbarians between the 3rd and 5th centuries C.E. Yet the detailed accounts of Pausanias and the archaeological excavation of many of the base fragments give us a good idea of the number, size and shape of the statues.

Pausanias identified 192 such life-like or portrait statues (busts),[2] and W.W. Hyde estimates, given the number of surviving base fragments, that there were nearly 500 monuments within the sacred Altis in its heydey.[3]

Pentathlon winners had their share of victor statutes at Olympia. Pausanias identified "15 pentathlon victors at Olympia, who had statues erected in their honor, for 17 victories, thus giving pentathletes 6th rank there in point of number."[4] Using Hyde's figuring we can estimate that there may have been another 15 to 20 more pentathletes on display at Olympia.

Characteristics of Victor Statues

The pentathlon represented the whole physical training of Greek youths; consequently the pentathlete was looked upon as the archetypal athlete, inferior in specialty events but being superior to others in all-round ability. From all the quotations of Aristotle and Xenophon, we gather that the pentathlete's balanced muscular development made beautiful athletes, and this beauty must have been carried over into their statues.

The statues at Olympia were nearly life size, nude and many sported long hair. Pentathlon victor statues were usually represented by one of its three unique events, the jump, discus and javelin. A number of victor statues showed pentathletes holding jumping weights (*halteres*). The statutes of two Elean winners, Hysmon and Anauchidas, were displayed with halteres.[5] Over

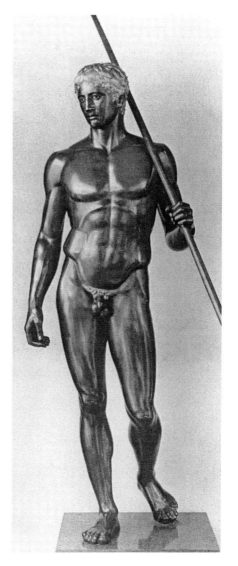

A Roman copy of the bronze *Doryphoros* (spear carrier) by Polyclitus, about 440 B.C. Found at old palaestra at Pompei, now in Naples Museum. The spear is modern. This is a modern bronze reconstruction by Georg Roemer of the original and is 2 meters (6 feet, 6¾ inches) tall. The original was formerly in the Munich Museum and was destroyed in 1944 (Foto Marburg/Art Resource, New York).

the years the type of jumping weights changed and we can safely assume that the sculptors copied the kind of jumping weights which were in use in the era of the honored athlete. The halteres made their appearance late in the sixth century B.C. and likely began to appear on pentathlon statues soon thereafter.

Discuses made of stone were replaced by metal ones around the end of the 6th century B.C. Surviving vase paintings, statues, statuettes, small bronzes and coins all illustrate the various positions in the ancient throwing technique. The most famous statues of this genre are *Standing Diskobolos* by Naukydes,[6] which dates to 420–400 B.C., and its more famous counterpart, *Diskobolos* by Myron, which dates to approximately 460–450 B.C. The former is now in the Vatican Museum while the latter original has been lost. Yet there are many copies of Myron's work from antiquity. Neither was an Olympic victory statue but both surely represented pentathletes.

The best example of a sculpture of the ancient javelin thrower is *Doryphoros* (spear bearer) produced by Polykleitos in the mid–5th century B.C. A marble *Doryphoros*, found in the Palestra at Pompeii, and now in the Naples Museum, was a copy of the original bronze. A Roman copy of *Doryphoros* was found at Olympia (1st century B.C., or 1st century C.E.). W.W. Hyde speculates that this very well could have been a pentathlon victor statue since, so highly regarded was Polykleitos that the victor could have requested it instead of a generic or personal sculpture.

In short, attaching jumping weights, disks or javelins to athletic sculptures was a likely ingredient of the pentathlete's victory statue.

Two additional comments seem warranted. First, the dimensions of the statues were likely just short of life-size. Lucian tells us that the Hellanodikai did not allow victors to erect life-size (or taller) statues at Olympia for fear of annoying the gods who were, after all, bigger than life. It would have been deemed impudent, almost disrespectful. Yet, there may have been exceptions. The *Doryphoros* of Naples measures 1.99 meters (6 feet, 6½ inches) and would surely have been much bigger than Greek athletes (perhaps many of the gods as well) of 25 centuries ago. Today a decathlete 1.99 meters tall does not seem out of place.

Second, the number of victor statues and the type of statues is of interest here. We know from Pliny that winners were allowed a statue per victory and portrait statues (busts) were deemed appropriate for multiple winners. For example, at Olympia Pausanias identified a bust of Gorgos of Elis, the only four time pentathlon champion.[7]

The number of Pentathlon victor statues was likely to be smaller at other Crown and local games and, for obvious reasons, a complete listing is unavailable. But at Olympia victory statues of famous pentathletes were erected even though a pentathlon victory did not occur there. And two of the most noteworthy pentathletes of antiquity never did have victory statues in the sacred

Altis. For example, there was a victory statue of the famous Spartan sprinter Chionis (also of 52 foot long jump fame) who won four Olympic stade crowns, but whose famous jump did not result in a pentathlon victory at Olympia. Chionis was the beneficiary of a kind of veterans' committee vote, for his statue was erected long after his final Olympic win in 656 B.C. At Olympia Chionis's statue was supplemented by a bronze tablet which listed is major career victories. And the celebrated Phaÿllos of Kroton (of 55 foot long jump fame) never won a crown at Olympia. A victory statue was erected for him at Delphi for his accomplishments at the Pythian Games. It seems, in this virtual Olympic pentathlon hall of fame, there was never any evidence, documentation, confirmation, testimony or even mention of jumps of over 50 feet.

The first Olympic pentathlon winner, Lampis of Elis, never got a victory statue. But his son, Timoptolis, for whom an honorary statue was erected at Olympia, did.[8] Eupolemos of Elis was a notable pentathlete who won several five-event crowns at Delphi. But his victory statue at Olympic represented a disputed sprint victory. Finally, one ancient pentathlete was responsible for six statues at Olympia, but they were not of the victory variety. Kallipos of Athens won the pentathlon in 332 B.C. by bribing his opponents. The fine for Kallipos was so great that the money collected (the Athenians actually paid the fine for him) was enough to erect six *Zanes*, statues to Zeus placed near the entrance of the stadium warning athletes not to cheat.

12. Extant Pentathlon Odes

In the last half of the 6th century and for a good deal of the 5th century B.C., winners at major Crown games (*Epinicia*) had odes, lengthy poems performed to music, written to celebrate their victories. Epinician odes for successful athletes formed a separate genre within Greek poetry. "These victory odes had the characteristics of a hymn in that it was often sung at a festival of a god and contains references and homage to him."[1]

Successful athletes or those associated with him, that is: family members, wealthy aristocrats or the victor's home city, commissioned these odes, usually from a famous poet, and paid a considerable sum to do so. The victory ode was an ideal way to announce to the whole Greek world the victor's accomplishments and could be far more widespread and lasting than erecting a statue. Today more odes survive than statues.

The genre of the Epinician ode flourished for only a short time and its most important poets were Simonides, Pindar and Bacchylides. By far Pindar, who wrote between 498 and 446 B.C., is the most famous poet for victory odes. Sixty Epinician odes survive in their entirety, 45 by Pindar and 15 by Bacchylides. The poems themselves do not describe the details of the contest. Rather, they provide, in disguised literary form, the name of the winner, his family and city and earlier major victories. These are woven within a history of the city or mythological tales of the gods to whom the games were dedicated.

Of the 60 preserved victory odes, three (two by Pindar and one by Bacchylides) honor pentathlon winners. This represents only 5 percent of the total.[2] In the following examples the line numbering is my own and provided for note referencing.

Pindar

Pindar was perhaps the greatest Lyric poet of ancient Greece. He was a native of Thebes in Boetia (522–ca. 443 B.C.). He wrote 45 odes for victors at the four Crown (14 for Olympian, 12 for Pythian, 11 for Nemean and 8 for Isthmian) games. Thirty-two of his odes were dedicated for combat athletes (boxing, wrestling, pankration) or charioteers. Two were written for pentathlon winners, one at Olympia and another at Nemea. Pindar's two pentathlon odes are presented here in their entirety.[3] They belong to Ernest Myers, a fellow at Wadham College, Oxford, as *The Extant Odes of Pindar* (London: Macmillan, 1904). They were among the earliest English translations of Pindaric odes.

OLYMPIAN 13: FOR XENOPHON OF CORINTH
[Winner of the Stade and the Pentathlon at Olympia, 464 B.C.]

Pindar's ode celebrates Xenophon's 464 B.C. unusual double Olympic victories in the stade and pentathlon, as well as victories by his clan, the Oligaethidae, at a variety of festivals. The ode is rife with legendary references to Corinth.

Pindar of Thebes dates from 522 to 443 B.C. His victory odes are celebrations of triumphs in Panhellenic festivals and generally celebrate athletes from aristocratic families. Olympian Ode 13 honors Xenophon of Corinth, who won the Olympic pentathlon in 446 B.C. A marble bust, Kunsthistorisches Museum, Vienna Austria (Erich Lessing/Art Resource, New York).

Thrice winner in Olympic games,
of citizens beloved, to strangers
hospitable, the house in whose praise
will I now celebrate happy Corinth
portal of Isthmian Poseidon   5
and nursery of splendid youth.
For therein dwell Order, and her sisters,
sure foundation of states,
Justice and likeminded Peace,
dispensers of wealth to men,   10
wise Themis' golden daughters.

And they are minded to keep far from them
Insolence the braggart mother of Loathing.
I have fair witness to bear of them,
and a just boldness stirreth my tongue to speak.   15
Nature inborn none shall prevail to hide.
Unto you, sons of Aletes, ofttimes
have the flowery Hours given splendor of victory,

as to men excelling in valor,
pre-eminent at the sacred games,   20
and ofttimes of old
have they put subtleties into your men's hearts
to devise; and of an inventor cometh every work.

Whence were revealed the new graces
of Dionysos with the dithyramb that winneth the ox   25
Who made new means of guidance to the harness of horses,
or on the shrines of gods
set the twin images of the king of birds
Among them thriveth the Muse of dulcet breath,
and Ares in the young men's terrible spears.   30

Sovran lord of Olympia,
be not thou jealous of my words
henceforth for ever, O father Zeus;
rule thou this folk unharmed,
and keep unchanged the favourable gale   35
of Xenophon's good hap. Welcome
from him this customary escort of his crown,
which from the plains of Pisa he is bringing,
having won with the five contests the stadion-race beside;
the like whereof never yet did mortal man.   40

Also two parsley-wreaths shadowed his head
before the people at the games of Isthmos,
nor doth Nemea tell a different tale.
And of his father Thessalos' lightning feet
is record by the streams of Alpheos,   45
and at Pytho he hath renown for the single
and for the double stadion gained both in a single day,
and in the same month at rocky Athens
a day of swiftness crowned
his hair for three illustrious deeds,   50

and the Hellotia seven times,
and at the games of Poseidon
between seas longer hymns followed
his father Ptoiodoros with Terpsias and Eritimos.
And how often ye were first at Delphi   55
or in the Pastures of the Lion,
though with full many do I match
your crowd of honors,
yet can I no more surely tell than
the tale of pebbles on the sea-shore.   60

But in everything is there due measure,
and most excellent is it to have respect
unto fitness of times.
I with your fleet sailing a privateer
will speak no lie concerning the valor of Corinth's heroes,   65
whether I proclaim the craft of her men of old

or their might in war, whether of Sisyphos
of subtlest cunning even as a god,
and Medea who made for herself a marriage
in her sire's despite,   70
saviour of the ship Argo and her crew:

or whether how of old in the struggle
before the walls of Dardanos
the sons of Corinth were deemed to turn
the issue of battle either way,   75
these with Atreus' son striving to win Helen back,
those to thrust them utterly away.
Now when Glaukos was come thither
out of Lydia the Danaoi feared him.

To them he proclaimed that in the city of Peirene   80
his sire bare rule and had rich heritage of land and palace,
even he who once, when he longed to bridle
the snaky Gorgon's son, Pegasos, at Peirene's spring,
suffered many things, until the time when maiden Pallas
brought to him a bit with head-band of gold,   85
and from a dream behold it was very deed.
For she said unto him
"Sleepest thou O Aiolid king?
Come, take this charmer of steeds, and
show it to thy father the tamer of horses,   90
with the sacrifice of a white bull."

Thus in the darkness as he slumbered
spake the maiden wielder of the shadowy aegis
—so it seemed unto him—
and he leapt up and stood upright upon his feet.   95
And he seized the wondrous bit that lay by his side,
and found with joy the prophet of the land,
and showed to him, the son of Koiranos,
the whole issue of the matter,
how on the altar of the goddess he lay all night   100
according to the word of his prophecy,
and how with her own hands the child of Zeus
whose spear is the lightning brought unto him the soul-subduing gold.

Then the seer bade him with all speed obey the vision,
and that when he should have sacrificed   105
to the wide-ruling Earth-enfolder the strong-foot beast,
he should build an altar straightway to Athene,
queen of steeds.
Now the power of Gods bringeth easily
to pass such things as make forecast forsworn.   110
Surely with zealous haste did bold Bellerophon
bind round the winged steed's jaw
the softening charm, and make him his:
then straightway he flew up
and disported him in his brazen arms.   115

In company with that horse also on a time,
from out of the bosom of the chill and desert air,
he smote the archer host of Amazons,
and slew the Solymoi, and Chimaira breathing fire.
I will keep silence touching the fate of him: 120
howbeit Pegasos hath in Olympus found a home
in the ancient stalls of Zeus.

But for me who am to hurl straight the whirling javelin
it is not meet to spend beside the mark
my store of darts with utmost force of hand: 125
for to the Muses throned in splendor
and to the Oligaithidai a willing ally came I,
at the Isthmos and again at Nemea.
In a brief word will I proclaim the host of them,
and a witness sworn and true shall be to me   130
in the sweet-tongued voice of the good herald,
heard at both places sixty times.

Now have their acts at Olympia, methinks,
been told already: of those that shall be hereafter
I will hereafter clearly speak.   135
Now I live in hope, but the end is in the hands of gods.
But if the fortune of the house fail not,
we will commit to Zeus and Enyalios
the accomplishment thereof.
Yet other glories won they, by Parnassos' brow,   140
and at Argos how many and at Thebes,
and such as nigh the Arcadians
the lordly altar of Zeus Lykaios shall attest,

and Pallene, and Sikyon, and Megara,
and the well-fenced grove of the Aiakidai,   145
and Eleusis, and lusty Marathon,
and the fair rich cities
beneath Aetna's towering crest, and Euboea.
Nay over all Hellas if thou searchest,
thou shalt find more than one sight can view.   150
O king Zeus the Accomplisher, grant them
with so light feet to move through life,
give them all honor,
and sweet hap of their goodly things.

Line Notes

1. **Thrice**: refers to the Olympic victories in the pentathlon and stade which Xeno-phon won in 464 B.C., which this ode celebrates, and another stade won by his father, Thessalos, forty years earlier, which is referred to later in line 44.

28. **king of birds**: This refers to the images of eagles which were placed on pediments by Corinthians.

42. **at the games of Isthmos** (Isthmian Games).

43. **Nemea**: Xenophon won double victories at both the Isthmian Gems in Corinth

and the Nemean Games, but it is uncertain whether they were in the stade, the pentathlon or a combination of events.

44. **Thessalos**: his father's victory at Olympia of 504 B.C. may also have been celebrated by Simonides with an ode.

56. **the Pastures of the Lion**: the Nemean games, and mythologically, the site of Heracles' first labor, the slaying of the Nemean Lion.

67. **Sisyphos**: the legendary founder of Corinth, Xenophon's hometown. Sisyphus, a noted con artist, was sentenced to perpetually push a rock up a hill.

78. The Lykians who fought under **Glaukos** on the Trojan side were of Corinthian descent.

90. **father the tamer of horses:** This refers to Poseidon.

127. The clan of the **Oligaithidai**, to which Xenophon belonged.

131. **good herald:** the herald traditionally proclaimed the name and the city of the Olympic winner.

140–145. **Parnassos' brow** and at **Argos and Thebes, Arcadia, Pallene, Sikyon, Megara,** and **Aiakidai** (island of Aegina) were all festival cities where Xenophon's family won athletic prizes.

152. **so light feet**: a compliment to the fast feet of Xenophon.

Nemean 7: For Sogenes of Aegina
[winner of the Boys' Pentathlon, (before 460 B.C.?)[4]

Pindar's 2nd and last ode to a pentathlete seems diffident. There may be more going on here than just a celebration for Sogenes. The ode seems to be more about Neoptolemus, son of Achilles and patron of Sogenes' hometown of Aegina. Pindar may have vilified the cruel Neoptolemus in an earlier ode for slaying Priam, king of Troy.

O Eileithuia that sittest
beside the deep-counselling Moirai,
child of the mighty Hera,
thou who bringest babes to the birth,
hearken unto us!   5
Without thee looked we never on the light
or on the darkness of the night,
nor came ever unto her
who is thy sister, even Hebe
of the comely limbs.   10
But we receive our breath not all for a like life;
each to his several lot is kept apart by the yoke of fate.
Now by thy grace hath Sogenes
the son of Thearion been foremost in prowess,
and his glory is sung aloud   15
among the winners of the five-game prize.

For he is a dweller in a city that loveth song,
even this city of the spear-clashing sons of Aiakos,
and exceeding fain are they to cherish
a spirit apt for the strife of the games.   20
If a man have good hap in his attempt,
he throweth into the Muses' stream

sweet cause of song:
for even deeds of might for lack of song
fall into deep darkness,   25
and in but one way have we knowledge
of a mirror for fair deeds,
if by the grace of Mnemosyne of the shining fillet
they attain unto a recompense of toils
by the sound of voice and verse.   30

Wise shipmates know that the wind
which tarrieth shall come on the third day,
nor throw away their goods through greed of more:
the rich and the poor alike fare on their way to death.
Now I have suspicion that the fame of Odysseus   35
is become greater than his toils,
through the sweet lays that Homer sang;
for over the feigning of his winged craft
something of majesty abideth,
and the excellence of his skill   40
persuadeth us to his fables unaware.

Blind hearts have the general folk of men;
for could they have discovered the truth,
never would stalwart Aias in anger
for the arms have struck   45
through his midriff the sharp sword—
even he who after Achilles
was best in battle of all men whom,
to win back his bride for fair-haired Menelaos,
the fair breeze of straight-blowing Zephyros   50
wafted in swift ships toward Ilos' town.

But to all men equally cometh the wave of death,
and falleth on the fameless and the famed:
howbeit honour ariseth for them
whose fair story God increaseth   55
to befriend them even when dead,
whoso have journeyed to the mighty
center-stone of wide-bosomed earth.
There now beneath the floor of Pytho
lieth Neoptolemos, dying there   60
when he had sacked the city of Priam
where the Danaoi toiled with him.

He sailing thence missed Skyros,
and they wandered till they came to Ephyra,
and in Molossia he was king for a little while: 65
howbeit his race held this state continually.
Then was he gone to the god's home,
carrying an offering of the chief spoils from Troy:
and there in quarrel concerning meats
a man smote him with a knife.   70

Thereat were the Delphian entertainers
of strangers grieved exceedingly:
nevertheless he but paid a debt to destiny:
for it was needful that in that most ancient grove
someone of the lords the sons of Aiakos 75
should abide within thenceforward,
beside the goodly walls of the god's house,
and that when with plenteous sacrifice
the processions do honor to the heroes,
he should keep watch that fair right be done. 80
Three words shall be enough:
when he presideth over the games
there is no lie found in his testimony thereof.
O thou Aigina, of thy children that are of Zeus

I have good courage to proclaim 85
that as of inheritance they claim the path to glory,
through splendor of their valorous deeds:
howbeit in every work a rest is sweet,
yea even of honey cometh surfeit
and of the lovely flowers of Love. 90
Now each of us is in his nature diverse,
and several are the lots of life we draw,
one this and one another:
but that one man receive perfect bliss,
this is impossible to men. 95
I cannot find to tell of any to whom Fate
hath given this award abidingly.
To thee, Thearion, she giveth fair measure of bliss,
first daring in goodly deeds,
and then understanding and sound mind. 100
Thy friend am I, and I will keep far from the man
I love the secret slander, and bring nigh
unto him praise and true glory,
as it were streams of water:
for meet is such recompense for the good. 105

If there be near me now a man of the Achaians
who dwelleth far up the Ionian sea,
he shall not upbraid me: I have faith in my proxeny:
and among the folk of my own land I look forth
with clear gaze, having done naught immoderate, 110
and having put away all violence from before my feet.
So let the life that remaineth unto me run cheerily on.
He who knoweth shall say if indeed I come
with slanderous speech upon my lips to strike a jarring note.
To thee, Sogenes of the house of the sons of Euxenos, 115
I swear that without overstepping the bound
I have sent forth the swift speech of my tongue
as it were a bronze-headed javelin,

such as saveth from the wrestling
the strong neck sweatless yet,   120
ever the limbs be plunged in the sun's fire.
If toil there were, delight more abundant followeth after.
Let be; if somewhat over far I soared when I cried aloud,
yet am I not forward, that I should deny his glory
unto one that conquereth.   125
The weaving of wreaths is an easy thing: tarry a little:
behold the Muse fasteneth together gold and white ivory,
and a lily flower withal, that she hath plucked
from beneath the deep sea's dew.

Of Zeus be mindful when thou tellest of Nemea,   130
and guide the multitudinous voices
of our song with a quiet mind:
meet is it that with gentle voice we celebrate
in this land the king of gods:
for they tell how he begat Aiakos   135
of a mortal mother,

to be for his own fortunate land a ruler of cities,
and for thee, Herakles, a loving friend and brother.
And if man receiveth aught from man,
then may we say that neighbor is to neighbor   140
a joy worth all else, if he loveth him with steadfast soul:
now if even a god will consent hereto,
then in such bond with thee,
O conqueror of the giants, is Sogenes fain to dwell
happily in the well-built sacred street of his ancestors,   145
cherishing a mind of tenderness toward his sire:
or as when four horses are yoked together in a car,
so hath he his house in the midst of thy holy places,
and goeth in unto them both
on the right hand and on the left.   150

O blessed spirit, thine is it to win hereto
the husband of Hera, and the grey-eyed maid;
and thou art able to give to mortals strength ever
and again against baffling perplexities.
Make thou to cleave to them a life of steadfast strength,   155
and wind the bliss thereof amid both youth
and a serene old age,

and may their children's children possess continually
the honors that they now have,
and greater in the time to come.   160
Never shall my heart confess
that I have outraged Neoptolemos with irreclaimable words.
But thrice and four times to tell over the same tale
is emptiness in the end thereof, even as he of the proverb
that babbleth among children   165
how that Korinthos was the son of Zeus

Line Notes

1. **Eileithuia**: the goddess of childbirth. Professor Richard Stoneman believes that Pindar is indicating that Thearion was blessed with a son, Sogones, very late in life. It was Thearion who commissioned Pindar for an ode to his son, and if paid piece-meal (by the word or by the line) cost Thearion dearly. Line 62 refers to Pindar as Thearion's guest.

9. **Hebe** was the goddess of youth and beauty and was often invoked for winners of boys' events.

50. **fair breeze of straight-blowing Zephyros**, the West Wind. Wind-aided.

98. **Thearion** was the father of Sogones.

60 and 162. **Neoptolemus** was the mythical son of Achilles, and, in a sense, an early war criminal who provoked the wrath of Apollo, who caused his death at Delphi. Neoptolemus was a resident and patron of Sogones' hometown in Aegina, and became, in spite of the vindictive wishes of Apollo, a patron at Delphi where the Pythian Games were held.

118–121. **bronze-headed javelin ... saveth from the wrestling**, Pindar implies that Sogones won the javelin and it saved him from having to wrestle under the hot sun. Yet Pindar likely makes a mistake by referring to the javelin as bronze-headed (bronze tipped). There is no evidence that competition javelins, unlike their warrior counterparts, had a metallic tip. This is likely just a figure of speech.

129. **deep sea's dew**, Myers translates this to mean coral, while later interpretations refer to it as a wave.

144. **conqueror of giants** refers to Herakles.

150. Pindar seems to be implying with **hath he his house** that Sogones was a neighbor of Herakles.

152. **grey-eyed maid** refers to Athena.

155. **cleave to them** refers to both Sogones and his father, Thearion.

Bacchylides

The Greek poet Bacchylides, who lived from 518 to 438 B.C., was a contemporary of the slightly older Pindar, but is often characterized as less talented. The remains of his poetry were not known until 1896, when a text of a papyrus from Egypt reached the British Museum in London. There are fewer versions of his work than that of Pindar, but 15 odes survive and his 9th was dedicated to Automedes, winner of the pentathlon at Nemea. Because of mutilations of the papyrus, there are frequent gaps in the text. But most of the text for this pentathlon ode survives. Presented here is Sir Richard C. Jebb's 1905 translation, still one of the most authoritative (*Bacchylides: The Poems and Fragments*, by Sir Richard C. Jebb, Cambridge University Press, 1905, pp. 301–313).

9TH: FOR AUTOMEDES OF PHLIUS
[Winner of the Pentathlon at Nemea, About 450 B.C.?][5]

Graces of the golden distaff, may ye grant the charm that
Wins mortal ears; for the inspired prophet of the violet-eyed
Muses is ready to sing Phlius and the verdure–clad domain of
Nemean Zeus; where white-armed Hera nourishd the deep-

voiced lion, slayer of sheep, first of the foes on whom Heracles   5
was to win renown.

> There, the heros with red shields
> The flower of the Argives, held the earliest games,
> in memory of Archemorus,
> who was slain in his sleep by the huge dragon   10
> With fiery eyes, an omen of slaughter to come. Ah, fate of
> mighty power! The son of Oicles could not persuade them
> to return to the streets of the good city. Hope robs men of
> prudent thoughts,—

she who then sent Adrastus, son of Talaüs   15
to Thebes, as patron of the exile Polyneices.
> Illustrious are the mortals who, from those famous contests
> at Nemea, crown golden hair with the triennial wreathe. To
> Automedes the god has now given it for his victory.

For he shone among his rivals in the pentathlon as the   20
brilliant moon of the mid-month night makes the rays of the
stars seem pale beside her own. Even thus, amidst the vast
concourse of the Greeks, showed he his wondrous form, as he
threw the round quoit, and roused the shouts of the people
when he sped the branch of the dark-leaved elder tree from his   25
hand to the high heaven,

or put forth his flashing swiftness of movement of the wrestling
match at the end. Such was the mighty spirit and strength
with which he brought stalwart forms to earth, ere he returned
to the Asopus with dark-eddying tide; that river whose fame   30
has gone out into all lands, even to the uttermost regions of
the Nile.
> Yea, the maidens who dwell by the fast-flowing stream of
> Thermodon, the skilled spear-women, daughters of horse-urging
> Ares,   35
have tasted the valour of thy descendants, O thrice-glorious lord
of streams: Troy also has known it, city of lofty gates.
> The vast fame of thy children goes forth on a wide path in
> every land,—those bright-girdled daughters whom the gods
> established with happy fortunes, as ancestral heroines of cities   40
> which should defy the spoiler.
> Who does not know the well-built town of dark-haired Thebe?
Or Aegina of glorious name, who in wedlock with mighty Zeus
Bore the hero (Aeacus)?
....   45

....

fair-robed Clione,
and Peirene with diadem on her brows, and all those other
gracious daughters of the ancient river god, lord of sounding
waters, who became the illustrious brides of gods.   50
[Verses 66–81 partially restored] Now is the ancient city of

Asopus filled with revelry for victory, and with the blended strains of
flutes and lyres.... It is meet to hymn first the majesty of great Zeus
and Hera;
then also to praise Hebe, daughter of mighty Zeus, maiden divinely   55
fair, with violet locks,—and the mother of the pitiless Loves....
    Automedes we have brought thee the song of the island Muse
Which shall remain for thee in thy life and after thy death, for endless
Years, to tell all generations of thy victory at Nemea.
    A goodly deed that has won the strains of a true poet is laid   60
up on high with the gods. When mortal lips give honest praise,
there is a glory that survives death in song the joy of the
[glorious] Muses
    *[In Jebb's interpretation the general sense is fairly clear: the details
are partly conjectural]*
    There are many paths for excellences
of men; but it is the counsel of the gods that decides what is   65
veiled in the gloom of night. [The weaker man and the stronger are
alike led on their way by the doom of Zeus the thunderer. Who is to put
forth high deeds, and who is to fail, is a secret, till they come to the
trial;] and to few mortals have the Fates granted the gift of conjecturing
the future.   70
    To you (of Phlius), for the sake of Demeter and of Dionysus, the son
of Cronus has granted to dwell in a god-honoured city, unravaged and
prosperous. When a man wins a meed of honour from golden-sceptred
Zeus, let us all give praise;—attend ye with festal songs on the son of
Timoxenus, for his victory in the pentathlon.   75

Line Notes

    3–4. **domain of Nemean Zeus**—three columns of the temple of Zeus at Nemea still
stand today.
    5. **first of the foes**, slaying the Nemean Lion was the first of the 12 Labors of Heracles.
    23. **his wondrous form, round quoit**, it is entirely possible that Bacchylides refers to
the technique in throwing the discus (quoit) and not the thrower's physique.
    Different translations of Bacchylides offer different interpretations of the poet's intent.
If one examines, for example, the line 23 the reader comes away with a certain impression
of the pentathlon winner, Automedes. Yet another version, provided by H.A. Harris in 1966,
without the use of reference or citation, leaves little doubt that his sentiment for Automedes
is mostly physical—*radiance of the stars, lovely body, Lithe movements.*
    Harris' version:

> He shone among the other pentathletes as the bright moon in the middle of the month
> dims the radiance of the stars: even thus he showed his lovely body to the great ring
> of watching Greeks, as he threw the round discus and hurled the shaft of black leaved
> elder [javelin] from his grasp to the steep heights of heaven, and roused the cheers
> of the spectators by his lithe movements in the wrestling at the end–[*Bacchylides* as
> offered by H.A. Harris, 1966].[6]

Even Harris' numbering is incorrect since he claims this is the "8th" ode of Bacchylides.
Whether Harris simply copied an earlier Bacchylides translation or altered the description
himself cannot be determined. But it is quite evident that his version differs substantially
in meaning from the more standard translation of Jebb which is offered here.
    23–27. it is inferred here that, because the discus, javelin and wrestling are mentioned,

Automedes must have won these events and thus did not win the jump nor the sprint. Since the pentathlon went to the final event, the final score must have been 3–2 in favor of Automedes.

25. **branch of the dark-leaved elder tree**, the javelin. There also seems to be a difference of opinion on the type of tree from which the javelin was fashioned, elder (Sambucus nigra) or elm (Ulmus campestris). Any arborist will tell you that an elm tree and an elder tree are different species. Why Harris changed Automedes' javelin from elm to elder is anyone's guess. Later scholars use elm. Unfortunately the Harris version has made its way into modern decathlon literature without any critical assessment. For example, McNab simply reproduces the Harris version and connotation without examination.[7]

34–35. **skilled spear women, Ares**—Amazon women who worshipped the god of war.

Simonides

Simonides, the uncle of Bacchylides, was born on the island of Ceos around 556 B.C. The Epinician ode, familiar to us because of Pindar, seems to have owed much to Simonides. Because of the increasing prestige of athletic victories in the 6th century, an era when the Pythian, Isthmian and Nemean games were founded, the victory ode becomes important. We have evidence that Simonides was writing victory odes as early as 520 B.C.[8] Unfortunately none of his odes survive in their entirety. Some scholars suggest that an entire book by Simonides, entitled *Pentathletes*, included only victory odes for pentathletes.[9] All that has survived is one small fragment. We know that Simonides wrote the following for some victor in the pentathlon[10]:

> As when in a winter month Zeus makes fourteen days of calm—
> men on earth call it the holy season,
> which forgets the winds and nurses the young of the pied halcyon.

Scholars normally interpret this simile, although we do not know its context, as a sudden of unexpected victory, in this case, in the pentathlon.

13. Rewards for
Pentathlon Victors

In the Archaic age (before 6th–8th century B.C.) rewards for athletic success, for example, at funeral games, was nonstandard. In Homer's meticulous *Iliad* account of the funeral games for Patroclus, noble participants received valued objects (tripods and cauldrons), animals (horses, cattle) or women as prizes. They are trophies, spoils of war. When athletic contests became institutionalized (in approximately the 6th century B.C.), so did the commensurate rewards for victors.

For virtually the entire history of sacred Crown Games—Olympia, Delphi, Corinth and Nemea—the rewards for a pentathlon or any other event, victory was purely symbolic, that is a wreath. Yet throughout antiquity athletic champions, including pentathlon victors could be expected to harvest sizeable rewards.

For Greeks, the overriding athletics emphasis was on the victory and the accompanying fame. Greek athletes from all classes (i.e., noblemen, the working or lower classes and the strictly professionals) accepted prizes for athletic victories without any criticism from society. The Greek term *athlon* means a prize and an "athlete" is one who competes for a prize. There was never any disapproval that men made a living from athletic skills. This does not mean that all ancient athletes were basically professional. Many did not dedicate all of their time and their entire youth preparing for games. Some were wealthy enough and did not need to make a living from athletics. But all were in it for the glory and the prizes could be considerable.

H.W. Pleket tells us that in 17th and 18th century England the landowning aristocracy had no objection to participating in contests with "professionals" or to competing for money prizes. Only in the 19th century was money and sport separated. The 19th and 20th century anti-pro ideology has no predecessor in antiquity. The modern Coubertinian belief that participation was just as important as victory would have been nonsense to the Greeks.[1]

At the crown games of Olympia, Delphi, Corinth and Nemea, the pentathlon winners received only a wreath. But later rewards could be substantial. Panathenaic shaped amphora, late 6th century B.C. British Museum (*Greek Athletic Sports and Festivals*, 1910).

And what type of prizes awaited pentathlon winners? The answer depended upon the nature of the specific festival. There were different categories of festivals, but to make it simple, and to the chagrin of some scholars, we shall use just two classifications of athletic contests, the sacred crown games and the more localized money-prize games.[2] Until Roman times this classification is adequate for our purposes.

Sacred Crown Games

The first, the sacred crown games, or *periodes*, were universally recognized as the premier religious athletic festivals. These festivals were officially announced by organizing cities (Olympia, Delphi, Corinth and Nemea) and kings dispatched official representatives to the organizing city. There was so much prestige attached to these festivals that the reward of a wreath was deemed sufficient. This was a symbolic honor. Branches from a tree considered sacred to each specific festival were cut and fashioned into wreaths. At Olympia this was an olive tree; in Delphi a laurel tree; in Isthmia fresh celery and later the pine tree; and in Nemea, ivy.[3]

If a pentathlete won, for example, at Olympia, he was set for life, what Pindar called "sweet, smooth sailing." He came home to a magnificent reception. The victor received considerable material benefits. Some rewards were universally practiced while others were locally specific. In the former category one includes an extravagant parade, a pile of cash, invitations to all great banquets and a place of honor at the theater. In the latter category we find tax immunity, pensions, free villas, and free meals for life at the town's expense. The latter was an Athenian custom and Socrates groused at this claiming that the privilege should have been extended to him instead.[4] Proud cities might even stamp a winner's profile on coins.

In the mid–6th century B.C. the Athenian lawmaker Solon had decreed that winners from his city would be handsomely rewarded with cash: 100 drachma for a win at Delphi and 500 drachma for an Olympic victory. Numerous other cities were just as or even more generous. Yet as magnanimous as it appears, this may have been a grandstand play by Solon, for our surviving Olympic victor lists find few Athenians.[5]

So too, the winning athlete would have reciprocated. On occasion winning pentathletes commissioned a ceremonial discus and dedicated it to the gods. There is a fine example of a ceremonial discus found at Olympia engraved with images of a javelin thrower on one side and a long jumper on the reverse. As well he might dedicate his sports accessories (for pentathletes this would include haltere, javelins and disci) to the gods and leave them in the temple. There is a modern but unintentional corollary here. In 1976 Olympic decathlon champion Bruce Jenner left his encased vaulting poles in a Montreal Stadium tunnel. This was no dedication to the gods. Instantly retiring, Jenner simply no longer had a need for vaulting poles. "They're yours," he told anyone who would listen. Two years later they showed up at his California home. Postage due.

Local Festivals

At local games, including the innumerable funeral games and games in honor of local heroes and gods, were not announced to the world at large and organizers could decide if they were open to citizens only or to foreigners as well. We know from passages in Pindar that, by 500 B.C., there were as many as 30 of the latter type games in the Greek world. Approximately 120 years later, in the first half of the 5th century B.C., the boxer-pankrationist Theogenes of Thasos is said to have won 1300 times. Doubtless, most of his victories came at these local games.

By the 2nd century C.E. it is estimated that this list exceeded 300 (and perhaps approached 500) annual, biannual or quadrennial games in the Greco-Roman world. And all sported a reward system. In the pre-monetary era prizes would, also, have been tangible assets. Some evidence of the value of prizes from these local games survives, and it is by looking at the pentathlon rewards that we glean a better appreciation of the Greek pentathlete in his day.

It should be remembered that coinage made its debut in the late 7th century B.C. in Lydia in Asia Minor, and by the 550 B.C. the practice of striking coins was established in all important trading cities throughout the Greek world. The standard unit of account within Greece during the Roman period was the silver Roman denarius (plural denarii), and Biblical references indicate that in early Christian times a denarius represented a day's wage. In the United States at the beginning of the 21st century this would represent, at a minimum, approximately $100.00.[6]

We are fortunate in having a number of descriptions from the unimportant city of Aphrodisias in Asia Minor enumerating the prizes in the games there early in the Christian era. The list is noteworthy since it illustrates the relative popularity of the different events. These are the prizes in the men's competitions:

Pankration	3000 denarii	Dolichos	1000 denarii
Boxing	2000	Long-distance race	750
Wrestling	2000	Pentathlon	500
Stade	1250	Race in armor	500[7]

The pentathlete's prize of 500 denarii would amount to approximately $10,500 today.[8] The games at Aphrodisias had three divisions: adult men, youths (often called beardless youths, referring to boys 20–21 years of age) and boys (teenagers). From the above amounts the monetary prizes were roughly two-thirds for the youths' and one-third for the boys' classifications.

More importantly we have a clear indication of the value of prizes in the mid–4th century B.C. at the Panathenaic Games, the greatest of all local festivals, and one so celebrated that it nearly rivaled the sacred crown games. A surviving epigram was uncovered and translated in the 1980s and lists many of the Panathenaic winners and the value of their prizes which, like at Nemea, Isthmia and Delphi, were given for three age categories: boys, beardless youths and men. At Athens, prizes were also given for second place, and the ratio of first to second place awards was 5 to 1. Understandably, the prizes for youths were slightly greater than those for boys.[9]

The prizes for the athletic contests at Athens were jars of choice olive oil which came in fine-looking jars or *amphoras*. Stephen Tracy indicates that on the front of each was depicted an armed Athena, *Athena Promachos*, with an inscription, "From the contests in Athens." And on the back was a depiction of the event in which the prize was won. There are a long series of these *amphorai* stretching from the archaic and classical periods into Roman times.

There is no complete tabulation, but the events depicted are those known from the inscriptions: footraces, the events of the pentathlon, wrestling, boxing, pankration, apobatai, races on horseback, and chariot races. These amphorai and the oil in them were highly prized; the vases were cherished symbols of victory in the great games. They were clearly kept as heirlooms and treasured the way an Olympic gold medal is today.[10] Modern museums now display any number of the prize amphorai with pentathlon scenes.

Pentathlon champions were awarded 60 amphorai filled with olive oil. Second placers won 12

The most lucrative of the major non-crown festivals was the Panathenaic Festival in Athens. First and second place finishers received valuable amphorae filled with olive oil. The vessel itself depicted the winner's event on one side and the festival's patron, Athena, on the other. It typically featured black figures on a red background and was valued as a keepsake, much like Olympic medals today (Metropolitan Museum of Art, New York, 1914).

amphorai of oil. The Panathenian amphora contained one *metretes* which amounted to 39.39 liters or 10.4 gallons. The price of one *metretes* ranged between 11 and 55 drachmas and about 17 drachmas was normal in the Classical era. Young has used a conservative estimate of 12 drachmas per amphora, and I'll do so as well.

It has been regularly reported at this time that one drachma per day was the working man's normal daily wage. Young used, because of ancient Greek inflation in the Classical age, 1.417 drachmas per day as an average wage. The average daily wage of an American working man in 2009 was $164.96.[11] So winning pentathletes in Athens would earn a prize worth about 12 drachmas x 60 amphora or 720 drachmas. This can be translated, although it is a delicate procedure, to about $83,800 2009 dollars. This is a conservative estimate. Young has presented some insight into the value of these prizes.

Value of Pentathlon Prizes[12]

	# of amphorae	value in drachmas	value (at 1.417d/day) in # of working days	value in years at full employment (300 days)
Pentathlon 1st place	60	720	508	1.69 years
" 2nd place	12	144	102	.34 years

The pentathlon victor's 720 drachmas, from selling his prize amphoras, was worth—on the low side—the wages of at least 508 working-man days (720d/1.417). That's about 19 months' (1.69 years) earnings of a skilled worker. The table above offers commensurate values for the pentathlon runner-up. Alternatively, the value of money is what it can buy. The winning pentathlete's earning in 350 B.C. could purchase 4 slaves or 60 sheep or 2 homes. The conclusion is clear. The pentathlon victor earned a considerable sum.

Using a similar process, we can attach the Panathenaic prizes for all pentathlon winners and runners-up.

Modern Value of Pentathlon Prizes at Panathenaic Games

		amphorae	drachmas	2009 $
Men	1st	60	720	$83,800
	2nd	12	144	16,825
Youths	1st	40	480	53,310
	2nd	8	96	11,060
Boys	1st	30	360	41,900
	2nd	6	72	8,380

But why settle for cash prizes or jars of tradable oil? Numerous scholars maintain that Olympia was a perfect springboard for a career change. Olympic champions could and did become legislators, priests, military leaders, judges and ambassadors. For example, after his chariot win in 416 B.C., Alciabiades landed a plum military command in the invasion of Sicily. The great Theagenes of Thasos became a politician, styling himself as the "Son of Hercules." In the Roman era one Marcus Aurelius Asclepiades became a senator in Athens. Other victors were even hired as the emperor's personal trainer.[13]

It is little different in modern times. America has had twelve different modern-day Olympic decathlon champions since Jim Thorpe won the initial contest in 1912. All found the title "Olympic decathlon champion" more than a little rewarding. The last two winners are still active. Of the remaining ten, three—Thorpe, Jim Bausch (1932), Glenn Morris (1936)—went on to play in the National Football League. Thorpe, in fact, became the league's first president. One, Harold Osborn (1924), went to medical school and another, Bob Mathias (1948, 1952), moved on to politics, serving six terms as a member of the U.S. House of Representatives. Milt Campbell (1956) used his Olympic win to embark of a career as a motivational speaker while Rafer Johnson (1960) dedicated his life to youth and Special Olympics programs. Bill Toomey (1968) went into broadcasting while Bruce Jenner (1976) appeared in a few badly made movies but spent most of his professional life as a "celebrity." His name is still one of the most recognizable in the history of his sport. Only one modern Olympic champion, Dan O'Brien (1996), has made a career of coaching. All, in their lifetime, were household names. And so it must have been with ancient pentathlon winners. We know they were well compensated for their efforts.

Just as the fortunes of the ancient victor rose, the prospects for the defeated plummeted. Yet few pentathletes ever got as far as the Olympic Games without having some success along the way. Losing at Olympia brought humiliation. Non-winners would return to the training regimen and wait for the next crown games. There would always be the opportunity to win cash prizes at local games, a sort of redemption for their recent loss. Except in Athens, there were no second place prizes. Sportsmanship was almost non-existent and, while champions were being feted by dignitaries and fans, the humiliated non-winners slipped away quietly. Their homecoming might be met with disgrace, dishonor and, at times, public mockery. But there was always the next festival. At ancient games the stakes, in terms of reputation and pride, were high.

14. Return of the Ancient Pentathlon[1]

In the early days of the 6th century C.E., after a run of twelve centuries of religious-athletic festivals which normally included the pentathlon, the event faded into history. Yet the idea of the versatile, all-around performer was so ingrained in sporting consciousness of Western man that, when formal sporting events returned in the modern era, the pentathlon or its relatives, like a Phoenix, resurfaced.

The first time the term "pentathlon" was regularly used in modern times occurred in late 18th century Germany when it was applied to a set exercises for youth. The celebrated Dessau Pentathlon, conducted at the educational reform Philanthropinum of Basedow (now Germany) and founded in 1774, consisted of running, jumping, climbing and balancing exercises and carrying weights. It was conducted for pupils in an attempt to make gymnastics part of the educational curriculum and was technically not a sporting event.

Combined events first made their reappearance, not in Germany or Greece, but in the Scottish Highlands. By the 1820s Highland festivals with their running, leaping and especially heavy throwing contests were gaining in popularity. The Scots, who exported their culture to America, combined many of the contests to establish all-(a)round champions.[2] There is evidence that *mano-a-mano* all-round contests were discussed by Boston Caledonian clubs as early as 1857 and, when he authored his memoirs after an extensive career, the great Donald Dinnie recalled winning an all-round competition in Coatbridge, Scotland, in the early 1860s. He even remembered the score, 31–28.

In an early Olympic revival attempt William Penney Brooks added a pentathlon to his Much Wenlock Games in Shropshire, England, in 1868.[3] His eclectic combination of high jump, long jump, two-handed weight throw, rope climb and an 880 yard hurdle race disquieted onlookers, yet his pentathlon was popular for a few years before disappearing. It would be another 60 years before England even saw another combined-event competition.

147

1896–1906 Athens Stadium. The first Olympic pentathlon of the modern era was conducted at the 1906 Intercalated (10th anniversary) Games in Athens. The Athens Stadium was restored in 1895. Swede Hjalmar Mellander won the scoring-convoluted pentathlon with 24 points (Alinari/Art Resource, New York).

The idea of combined events received a boost from the touring Caledonian professionals in America who did much to popularize all-round meetings. By the 1870s many Caledonian Games were offering all-round or general medals for the most versatile athlete. Beginning in 1884 the American amateur movement adopted and standardized the all-around event into a one day, 10 event contest. It was the AAU all-around which evolved into the modern decathlon at the beginning of the next century. But, until the last decade of the 19th century, the term pentathlon was rarely used.

The Return of the Pentathlon

By the reincarnation of the modern Olympic Games in 1896, nine nations were actively practicing athletic combined events to some degree. In North America both Canada and the United States had been producing versatile all-around champions and conducting combined event meetings for a generation.

The American amateur all-around already sported a rich history and was using a stylish scoring table. In the British Isles the English had not seen a combined event contest for nearly thirty years, but the Scots continued to offer all-round or general medals at Highland Games while the Irish had gone in for the all-round in a big way. The world's best combined eventer was Irishman Tom Kiely, a Tipperary farmer who, no matter how Irish organizers altered its all-round program, could and would not be beaten.

Combined events were a sporadic experiment in Germany but found an incubator in Scandinavia. Norway (1891) was the first to offer annual pentathlons (*funkamps*), based on the ancient Greek model, wrestling and all.[4] Sweden soon followed. Finland was a hotbed of combined event action in the last decade of the 19th century, yet nothing became standard. Interestingly, Norway, in an attempt to be historically accurate, soon began to include a triple jump in its pentathlons, since the state of modern day research suggested that the Greeks had used a triple jump.[5] Meanwhile Denmark would soon adopt the American AAU all-around, eventually using the term *tikamp* (ten event contest).

The story of the athletics program at the revival Olympic Games in Athens is a lengthy tale. At the time the sport of athletics was a combination of events with either Highland or Classical credentials. There was considerable support to include a pentathlon in the 1896 program to give the revival of the Games an ancient flavor. It made it to the planning stage but was apparently dropped by the Baron de Coubertin in early 1895 and replaced with a marathon.[6]

The 1900 Olympic Games were conducted in Paris, where a pentathlon was listed on the official program. But it was never contested.[7] By 1904 the Olympic movement had not gained the worldwide approval of later years. The games were held in St. Louis that year and even its modern founder, the Baron de Coubertin, did not attend. The 1904 program was planned by James E. Sullivan, the secretary of the U.S. Amateur Athletic Union (AAU). There is a romantic yet erroneous belief that the AAU all-around, held on July 4, 1904, in St. Louis, was part of the Olympic track and field program. Unfortunately this has no basis in fact, since the athletic portion of the St. Louis Games was held two months later. Sullivan may have thought that since the standard AAU all-around was also held in St Louis, the Olympic program needed no combined event.

In 1904 Irishman Tom Kiely traveled to America on his own and won the AAU all-around in St. Louis. Kiely left America with a standard AAU medal and the understanding that he had won America's annual affair, to which Sullivan had attached the appellation "World's Championship." Incidentally, in 1904 Ireland was not part of the Olympic movement and Kiely's participation in the games would have had to be as an Englishman, something he abhorred. Years after Kiely's death, in 1951, an energetic Irish journalist agitated the

International Olympic Committee (IOC) to recognize Kiely as an Olympic champion. Without evidence the IOC swallowed the idea and today Kiely is listed as the first modern Olympic combined event champion. Nothing is further from the truth. It is a fact, however, that no athlete ever needed the "Olympic champion" label less than Tom Kiely, who was universally acknowledged as the world's finest athlete of his age.

The Ancient Pentathlon of 1906

With the Olympic movement on wobbly legs, a 10th anniversary (of 1896) games was planned for Athens in 1906, later referred to by historians as "the Intercalated Games." It was here that the ancient pentathlon made its modern international appearance.

The contest, an attempt to recreate the ancient counterpart (sometimes referred to as "Pentathlum") drew 26 competitors from 11 nations. Half came from America and Scandinavia, and predictably no one from Britain.[8] Organizers wished to recreate the ancient pentathlon, yet the state of Classical sporting scholarship was in its infancy in 1906 and the only certainty was that wrestling had been the final ancient sub-event. But the remaining order and how events were conducted was unknown to both scholars and Greek organizers, who did a lot of guessing in their conduct of the event. To determine a winner, the *triad* notion was scrapped in favor of a successive elimination (devil-take-the-hindmost) and a simple point system in which athletes earned 1 point for first place, 2 points for second place and so on, low tally wins. It was not a confusing system, but without knowledge of how the real ancient pentathlon was conducted or a scoring table, the first international pentathlon in 14 centuries resulted in the damnedest finale imaginable. What is more surprising is that it was not controversial at the time.

The scheduled order of events read: standing long jump, discus, 192m sprint, javelin and wrestling, and the pre-meet favorites were American Martin Sheridan and Swede Erik Lemming. The former, a 25-year-old New York City policeman who had emigrated from County Mayo, Ireland, was the American all-around champion and record holder and, more notably, the reigning Olympic champion and world record holder in the discus event. The latter, 26, from Göteborg, had made a reputation competing in numerous combined events meetings in his homeland but was better known as the javelin's world record holder. Most of the attention in Athens was on the pair of strapping specimens, either of whom could have posed for Myron or Polykreitos two millennia earlier.[9]

So highly regarded was Sheridan (6'4", 212) that USA coaches entered him in an ungodly 10 events in Athens! He competed in seven and, amazingly, medaled in five and earlier had won a 2nd discus crown. The mustachioed

Lemming (6'3", 194) too had already won the Athens javelin event with a world record to boot. All 26 entrants competed in the first three events. But the strain of too many competitions played on the Irishman. Although placing 3rd, he injured himself in the jump and limped away. Sheridan's injury opened the door to Lemming, Swedish teammate Hjalmer Mellander and bulky Hungarian István Mudin.

The standing jump went to speedy American Lawson Robertson (29.55cm/ 10 feet, 2 inches) earning him one point. But he was a feeble thrower and soon fell out of contention. The discus, thrown Greek-style from a sloping pedestal, went to the huge Hungarian (6'3", 220) with a toss of 32.64m/108 feet, 9 inches.[10] He had placed 4th behind Sheridan in the open discus 5 days earlier. Lemming was 2nd and Mellander 5th. Predictably, Lemming easily won the javelin.

After three events all but the top eight scorers were dropped. Under the ancient rules only the individual event winners (in this case Robertson, Mudin and Lemming) would have advanced to the sprint. Robertson, a small man (5'11", 150), who later became a well known coach, won the 192 meter sprint while Mudin lumbered in last. At the end of four events the score stood:

Mellander	SWE	21 points
Mudin	HUN	24 points
Lemming	SWE	25 points

The top six now advanced to the skamma to wrestle.

The huge Mudin was a certain winner here, and his one point was sure to make his final tally 25 points. Lemming, who already had 25 points and could not win the overall title, was ironically paired with Mellander in his last wrestling match, which would determine 3rd and 4th place. Close observers may have noticed that the taller and stronger Lemming did not seem to try very hard and the bout went to his 25-year-old Swedish teammate. Mellander thus earned three points for third place and won the ancient pentathlon, its first Olympic victor in 14 centuries. Final scores were:

Hjalmer Mellander	SWE	24 points
István Mudin	HUN	25 points
Erik Lemming	SWE	29 points

A year later Lemming revealed that he had deliberately lost the wrestling contest to Mellander. Magazine accounts reported that the pair of Swedes faked the final wrestling match to allow Mellander to win.[11]

The 1906 Olympic pentathlon is instructive in that it shows that different winners would result depending upon the scoring system used. Given the ancient system presented and defended in this volume (*triad*), Lemming would likely have been the winner since he, Robertson and Mudin, each with one event victory, would have advanced to the sprint. Robertson won the sprint gaining two wins and Lemming and Mudin would have had to contest a *stade repêchage* and the right to advance to the wrestling final. Lemming would have been heavily favored here. And the results tell us that Lemming, with a 44 pound weight advantage on Mellander, was a far superior wrestler. Indeed, Robertson, realizing he had no chance in the wrestling event, withdrew after 4 events. Yet, by using Harris' disputed scheme of a wrestling repêchage, Mudin likely would have won the overall title on the basis of strength alone, gaining his triad with a victory in discus and two in wrestling.

But the title went to the consistent Hjalmer Mellander, who placed no worse than 7th in any individual contest. In 1906 the actions of Lemming and Mellander never became an issue. Neither was seen as a modern day Kallippos. There were no charges of chicanery, no investigation, no hearings, no disqualification, no fines, no *Zanes*. No big deal. Olympic historians, perhaps unwilling or unable to unravel the scoring morass, appear to be completely unaware of the issue. For his part Lemming may have been lauded (at least in Sweden) for his sportsmanship; 1906 was a different era. Identical actions today would create a furor.

When the Games returned to their quadrennial cycle in 1908, London served as host and set records for bickering. But no combined event, pentathlon or otherwise, could be found on the festival program.

Yet 1908 was not without a superlative pentathlon. Just days after he won a 3rd consecutive Olympic discus crown, Martin Sheridan (making his Olympic career haul nine medals) announced that he would spend a few days visiting his family in Bohola, County Mayo, Ireland. An Irish promoter, Frank B. Dineen, contacted Tom Kiely and arranged a five event, points-for-place contest between the two all-around champions. Billed as the "greatest individual athletic contest in Irish history," the match of five throwing events was, in effect, a forerunner of the popular "throwers pentathlon."

Sheridan, 27, was at his athletic peak while Kiely was nine days shy of his 39th birthday. They had never met on the track. Both claimed undefeated all-around careers. Irish railroad companies ran special trains in Dungarvan in County Waterford on the southern coast. Thousands watched the two giants compete and the finish was both storybook and anti-climactic. With the score two wins apiece, both athletes fouled on all three attempts in the last event. Confused, officials, unsure what to do, huddled with the athletes, then declared a tie. Thus both finished their all-around careers undefeated.

More Olympic Pentathlons

The next Olympic Games were awarded to Stockholm, and in 1910 Swedish organizers requested that two combined event contests, a pentathlon and decathlon, be added to the program. No one objected since Sweden had been conducting *fenkamps* (5 event meets) and *tiokampfs* (ten event contests) since 1893 and 1903 respectively. To prevent any future controversy, the Swedes replaced the pentathlon wrestling event with an endurance race, the 1500 meters. As well they brought the ancient event up to date by sensibly adopting a *running* long jump, used a standard 200 meter race distance and dismissed the sloping discus platform. Although the decathlon adopted a scoring table to decide its winner, the pentathlon continued to use a points-for-place system of 1906. The scoring tables would be used for the pentathlon only in the case of a tie.

For the 1912 Olympic pentathlon and decathlon it made absolutely no difference how the winner was determined, so dominant was the victor. An American Indian, Jim Thorpe, won both in a convincing fashion: a world record score in the decathlon six days after recording a near perfect pentathlon score of 7. A perfect score would have been 5. So dominant was Thorpe that he won three of the first four events, and under ancient rules, his triad would have allowed him to win akoniti.

The 1912 Olympic pentathlon contained a scoring oddity. For combined events, the tale is in the details. The official score sheets for the 1912 games are housed at the National Archives in Stockholm. I've had a look at them and they indeed reveal an unprepared situation. The Swedes had substituted the 1500 meters run for wrestling to eliminate the Lemming-Mellander temptation. But they were unprepared for what to do when athletes did not finish an event. One of the seven athletes who advanced to the 1500 meters, a chubby American from Chicago named Avery Brundage, simply walked off the track during the race. He just quit. Uncertain how to score the "effort," officials noted on his card that he "did not finish" but awarded him the 7 points he would have earned had he finished and been last. The decision allowed Brundage to be ranked 6th overall. It was not a glaring officiating error and is a scoring conundrum since athletes are required to "make an attempt" at each event.

But Brundage became a notable figure in the sporting world. Four decades later he became the president of the International Olympic Committee (IOC), and for the next twenty years reminded everyone within shouting distance that he had placed 6th at the 1912 Olympic pentathlon. And he is still listed as such. In fact, he never finished the event.

Thorpe's story, well worn, is less complex. In 1909 Jim had left Carlisle with no intention of returning. He played minor league baseball in North Carolina for two seasons before being talked back to school by the Carlisle coach, Pop Warner.[12] Jim had used his own name, although it was standard practice for collegians to play summer ball under an assumed name. The thought never occurred to Jim to use another name. When a Massachusetts newspaper revealed Jim's open secret in January 1913, Pop Warner wrote Jim's confession,

James Sullivan removed Jim's name from the record books and the Olympic medals and prizes were returned. The pentathlon medal was offered to the Stockholm runner-up, Norwegian Ferdinand Bie, who refused to accept it, claiming that Thorpe had earned it and Thorpe should keep it. The medal was donated to a museum, later stolen and never recovered. Jim and his relatives spent the next 70 years attempting to clear his name and get the medals back. In 1982, 29 years after Jim's death, the IOC restored Jim's name to the record books and returned facsimiles of the original medals.

In 1913 the pentathlon became major collegiate event in America when Robertson, now coach at the University of Pennsylvania, gave it "Championship of America" status and added to the popular Penn Relays program. Robertson was the last great pentathlon holdout of modern times, frequently claiming, well after the event had been superseded by the decathlon, that five events were plenty to determine a champion of athletic versatility. It took a dozen years before the pentathlon was replaced by the decathlon at the Penn Relays.

The pentathlon continued as an Olympic event. The 1916 Games of Berlin were cancelled due to World War I, and a Finn, Eero Lehtonen (1898–1959), won both the 1920 pentathlon in Antwerp and the 1924 affair in Paris. Both pentathlons contained scoring curiosities involving an American, Robert LeGendre. In Antwerp LeGendre missed placing 4th, and thus the bronze medal outright, in the 1500 meters by half a step to Helge Lovland of Norway. The American's 5 event points gave him a total of 26, the same number as Finn Hugo Lahtinen. The Finn was a controversial figure who was allowed to compete under the protest of several nations claiming he possessed a well known professional reputation. When the decathlon scoring tables were consulted to break the deadlock it was found that Lahtinen had earned third by a few points. Four years later LeGendre, in the very first event, broke the open record for the long jump with an extraordinary leap of 7.765m/25 feet, 5½ inches. For this momentous effort he earned the ordinal one point. At the end of the competition Legendre's 18 points was good for third place behind Lehtonen's winning score of 14 points. Had the scoring tables been in use, Legendre's leap would have been justly rewarded with a cardinal score and he would have won the gold medal.

Soon thereafter Olympic officials dropped the pentathlon from the men's program, claiming that the ordinal point-for-place system was inadequate in determining the finish order. Besides, two combined event competitions were redundant. The more popular decathlon, with its scoring tables, survived. The pentathlon, on the other hand, was banished to Limbo.

It has never returned as part of the men's program, but when the women's Olympic program was expanded in 1964, a pentathlon was added (100m hurdles, high jump, shot put, long jump, 800 meters). The first female pentathlon champion was 25-year-old Irina Press of the Soviet Union.[13] Throughout much

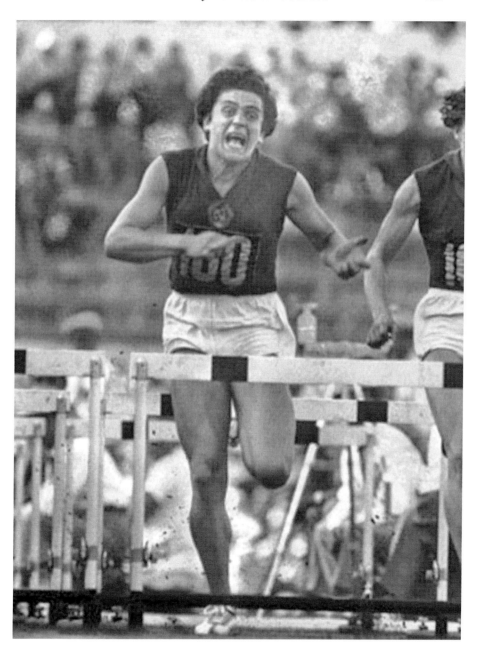

Irina Press, 25, won the first female Olympic track and field pentathlon at the 1964 Games in Tokyo. Press, a Ukrainian who competed for the Soviet Union, and her sister Tamara, set 26 world records in the 1960s before gender verification tests became a mandatory part of the sport (author's collection).

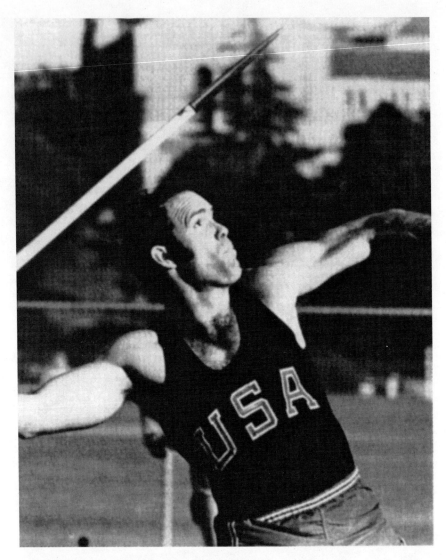

Bill Toomey, the 1968 Olympic decathlon champion, still holds the world pentathlon record (4282 points). The event seemed to be tailored to his skills. The International Association of Athletics Federation (IAAF) still maintains rules and records for the event, which is held infrequently (author's collection).

of her career Irina and her sister Tamara, the Olympic shot put champion, faced widespread speculation that they were taking male hormones or that they were actually men, which would make Irina the last male, not Eero Lehtonen, to win Olympic pentathlon gold. In 1966 the International Amateur Athletic Federation (IAAF) announced that they would conduct sex tests at the upcoming European championships. Both sisters withdrew and immediately retired (incidentally, at very young competitive ages).

The women's pentathlon made its last visit to the Olympic athletics schedule at the games in Moscow in 1980 and was eventually replaced by a two-day, seven-event heptathlon. Two years earlier, in a housekeeping maneuver, the new American track and field federation, The Athletics Congress (TAC), eliminated numerous events including the men's pentathlon, from its championship program. Until then the men's pentathlon had served as a cult event and decathlon stepping stone. The 1967 world record by American Bill Toomey (4282 points) still stands. The mark is still listed on the record books and pentathlon regulations remain in rulebooks.

The ancient pentathlon lasted for over 1200 years, but its modern counterpart was on the world stage for less than 20. It made a lively, dramatic, if truncated comeback, from 1906 to 1924. Today combined events abound in track and field but pentathlons take a back seat to their elongated counterparts, the decathlon and heptathlon. On the men's side outdoor pentathlons are rare and indoor affairs occasional. The women's indoor pentathlon is a championship event. Veterans, youths and throwers conduct pentathlons.

15. Why the Ancient Pentathlon Matters

We have already answered many of the longstanding questions about the ancient pentathlon: how it was conducted, the order of events and how the victor was determined. Also addressed throughout the book are questions about the importance of the pentathlon to the Greeks themselves and why it lasted as long as it did. Yet, in a broader sense other questions linger. For example: what is the relevance of the ancient pentathlon to modern sport; why did its modern reincarnation last only a few years, and why should we care? The interrelated answers are provided in this chapter.

Importance to Modern Sport

The legacy of the ancient pentathlon is that it allowed the Greeks, by combining disciplines, a formal way to judge athletic talent. By combining events the ancient Greeks introduced sport to the importance of versatility. They demonstrated that the multi-talented or all-around competitor was just as good an athlete, perhaps even better, than the specialist. Athletic ability was, in a sense, redefined. The adaptable, resourceful athlete became as important and appreciated to the Greeks as the athlete with high quality, individual talent. The concept alerted observers, from philosophers to fans, that an athlete who could demonstrate a combination of skills, even if individually they were not as proficient as those of a specialist, was a superior athlete. The Greeks introduced the idea. The athletes, from Gorgos of Elis to Thorpe of Carlisle, did the rest.

Of course, everyone is not convinced. A long-time idea suggests that specialists in a competitive sporting event are the better athlete. That is, the one who demonstrates outstanding specialized flair should be rated higher than the athlete who displays a range of ability. Some may insist, for example, that ancient fighter Myron of Kroton or Michael Jordan today had been the greatest athletes of their age. There is no doubt that, in their long careers, both Myron and Jordan displayed specific, dominant skills, were well compensated and well liked. Yet popularity and versatility should not be confused. Other authorities rejoin that Myron's opinion of his own strength or Jordan's inability to hit a curveball is evidence enough.[1]

The Failure of the Pentathlon

The ancient pentathlon had simple rules and was offered in a Spartan (no pun intended) era. Its longevity was a function of its clear, straightforward procedure in determining a victor. It applied neither measurements nor clocked times. The triad, with its standardized order of events, was enough for the Greeks to select a victor at a specific time and place.

When the pentathlon was reintroduced in the late 19th and early 20th centuries a more contemporary system was devised to select the winner. Scoring tables, although available, were not used except to break ties. Instead successive rounds of eliminations and a points-for-place (low score wins) procedure were included to replicate the ancient victor scheme. Measurements of field events and timed races were incorporated into the system. Yet this new arrangement, seemingly uncomplicated on the surface, created its own anomalies and problems. We have already seen that the selection of three different victor procedures would have produced three different winners at the 1906 ancient "pentathlum." The story of an inadequate points-for-place scoring system used in the early 20th century is in the details. Here are some of the knotty problems of the "modern" ancient pentathlon:

1. The inclusion of a wrestling match at the end of the pentathlon not only led to potential chicanery in close matches (remember Athens in 1906) but did not sit well with purists who felt that any sporting effort that could not be measured or timed did not belong in a track and field meet. They felt that wrestling just did not fit in. In fact the spinoff of wrestling into a discrete sport did not occur until the final quarter of the 19th century. For example, Highland Games programs regularly incorporated wrestling into its athletics and track and field program.
2. The subjective selection of the five pentathlon events went a long way in determining the winners, especially in small fields. Which events to include was a critical question. To be true to its ancient heritage, the discus, long jump, javelin and sprint were incorporated into the program. In 708 B.C. these four contests made up virtually the entire list of track and field events.

By the turn of the 20th century track and field could claim more than two dozen running, jumping and throwing contests. Those athletes whose skills lay in the ancient events held an advantage. Others, who could, say, high jump, throw the shot or hammer, pole vault or hurdle, were out of luck when it came to the pentathlon. No better example is needed than the very first American pentathlon. At the 1912 U.S. Olympic Mid-western pentathlon trials (curiously held on a Thursday morning by the sponsoring club, the Chicago AA), only two athletes appeared. One, University of Chicago undergraduate J. Austin Menaul, a 5'9", 155 pound bundle of energy, was simultaneously the Big Ten Conference high jump and shot put champion. But neither of his specialties were on the card. Had they been, his opponent, the slowish Avery Brundage, would have been reduced to a historical footnote.

3. When fields were small the final scores were predictable. Again, the aforementioned 1912 U.S. Olympic Trials bear out the point. While Brundage was a notable thrower, Menual was also a well known runner. Since the pentathlon included a pair of throws and a pair of races, the pentathlon winner was literally predetermined by who won the long jump, the very first event. Within five minutes, when Brundage won the long jump by a few inches, the pentathlon was, de facto, over. Brundage won the two throws (although one was very close) while Menaul easily won the two races. The final score was a predictable 7–8 in favor of Brundage. In fact, using a points-for-place system with only two athletes, there are only three possible final scores: 5–10, 6–9 and 7–8. Predictable outcomes make very poor sporting events. Later the application of scoring tables would have made Menaul an easy winner.

4. The successive elimination process, that is, a paring of the field after three and then four events, made the order of events critical in determining the winner. Those whose favorite events came early in the program were likely to make the cut. Those whose best events were late in the program, for example, the javelin and 1500 meters, were out of luck, unlikely to advance. A modern parallel, at least in terms notoriety, is provided by the 1984 Olympic decathlon. The first two events, the 100 meters and long jump, were won by Daley Thompson of Great Britain, who remained with the leaders throughout the entire contest that he eventually won. Yet a 31-year-old Austrian, Georg Werthner, whose specialties were the final two events, the javelin and 1500 meters, both of which he won, was hardly noticed over the two days. A "reverse decathlon" would have made him much more prominent. In fact, the javelin and 1500 meters were the final two events of the reincarnated 20th century pentathlon and those with "Werthner skills" never had a chance using a points-for-place scoring scheme.

The moral is clear. The size of the field, the selection of contests and their order had an awful lot to say about who won pentathlons.

5. Without scoring tables the pentathlon did not reward great efforts. We have already mentioned the long jump (a world record) by Robert LeGendre in 1924 which simply earned him an ordinal one. Without scoring tables all pentathlon numbers were ordinal. With scoring tables the cardinal values more justly reflect performance. A points-for-place scoring system gives no indication of the quality of the performances. A winning score of 5 told one nothing about the worth of the competition, weak or strong, only that an individual won each of the five events. The scores were not comparable and could never be extended beyond a particular meet.[2]

6. At times a points-for-place system did not encourage an athlete to do their level best. Rather they just encouraged them to simply win events. Good runners could

Because the Greeks combined individual (and popular) contests, they introduced the concept of versatility and created a fresh and different way to evaluate sporting ability. The selection of events and the determination of the winner was never an issue for them. Amphora in British Museum shows, left to right, a coach, discus thrower and another athlete (*Journal of Hellenic Studies*, 1907).

    ease up at the finish and good jumpers and throwers often did not take second or third attempts. If the event was already won it did not pay to push oneself. The result would be the same, one point for the win. In terms of spectatorship this can be disappointing.

7. When ties for any place occurred (and this was frequent) the decathlon scoring tables were used to break the tie. Many wondered why the scoring tables were not used in the first place. The answer may lie in the attempt to be historically consistent, that is, to simulate, to the degree possible, the ancient victor scheme.

    During antiquity the simplicity of relying only on event wins made the pentathlon successful. In a world without measurement, stop watches or scoring tables, this up-front and clear-cut approach worked. And it worked for more than 1200 years. The view that a system of event victories did not provide absolute evidence of talent was discarded by the Greeks. To them the relative evidence, which is, winning at a particular time and place, was paramount.

    A criticism of the ancient pentathlon has always been that it may have attracted some specialists who would keep solid non-specialists from advancing through the elimination process. The slap against its modern version was that five events may not be enough to demonstrate versatility. The sporty Scots, Turners and Celts added many useful and popular events. It was ultimately a practical issue. The American all-around had demonstrated that ten events could be conducted, with adroit scheduling and officiating, in one day. And two days would certainly be long enough to comfortably handle large fields. Given that a wider range of skills could be demonstrated and verified and the event could be administered without difficulty, it is no wonder that the decathlon pushed the pentathlon from the program card.

While ancient pentathlon and its modern counterpart applied to a particular day or meeting, the use of scoring tables made its successor apply more universally. And so the decathlon ameliorated many of the concerns about the contemporary pentathlon. The growth of sport itself, technical improvements in equipment, measuring and timing devices and the numerous available events to test versatility made the adoption of the decathlon inevitable. When the cost of using the pentathlon as an all-around test, in terms of conceptual or scoring problems, became too high, the IAAF eliminated the pentathlon from major competition. The 1924 Olympic pentathlon in Paris was the last major pentathlon held in modern times. Today the IAAF relies solely on the decathlon as its all-around test for men. And, after a 16 year experiment with the pentathlon for women, the IAAF replaced it after the 1980 Moscow Olympic Games with a seven event heptathlon. The men's decathlon and women's heptathlon have held the combined events center stage since and both are seen as adequate, objective measures of athletic talent.

The Relevance of the Pentathlon

We care about the ancient pentathlon because it was the first combined events contest. Although the pentathlon has virtually disappeared, the concept it introduced, that of demonstrated versatility, has not. Today, within the world of athletics, that idea continues in the form of the popular decathlon and a variety of other "thlons." And combined events grace many other modern sports. No matter what we call them: all-arounds or triathlons, pentathlons or heptathlons, decathlons or anythlons, we can trace their heritage to the ancient Greek pentathlon. The Greeks were the first to devise, promote and appreciate the all-around or balanced athlete.

Today many individual sports include a combined events contest as a way to judge its most versatile, balanced athlete. Track and field is the most notable and some of its combined events have spawned entire families. Track and field's decathlon, with its relatives of a different number of events, now includes indoor and outdoor events for men, women, double decathlons and time constrained decathlons lasting 30 minutes, 60 minutes and one hour.[3]

But track and field is hardly alone. Combined event contests abound in other sports; for example, gymnastics, rodeo, Nordic skiing, lumberjacking and weightlifting. Some combined event contests even blend sports. For example, the modern pentathlon requires training in pistol shooting, fencing, riding, swimming and cross-country running. And the popular triathlon combines endurance skills from swimming, biking and running.

And it does not end there. Archery, skateboarding, billiards, dressage, show jumping, trampoline, parachuting, alpine skiing, piloting, and target shooting all have all-around champions. Non-athletics all-around contests are conducted for artists, dancers, cooks, singers, and even dogs (best of show).

The concept of the all-around performer is now so ingrained in sporting consciousness that it is simply taken for granted. It all began with the ancient Greek pentathlon, whose life expired in the 6th century C.E.and, like a Phoenix, resurfaced in the modern era.

Why is the pentathlon important? It left us with a formal, objective way to judge athletic talent. All other measures are, in a sense, subjective or skewed by personal opinion. An objective test, although not perfect, helps us define modern sport. The Greeks didn't just create another sporting event (for example: change the distance, put up barriers, use a series of leaps), they created a different kind of event. The lesson is clear. The combined event nature of the ancient pentathlon "defined" what a superior athlete was. Even more so, it piqued our imagination, and lives today in the form of its champions: Jim Thorpe, Rafer Johnson, Daley Thompson, Jackie Joyner-Kersee, Roman Sebrle, Carolina Kluft, Bryan Clay, Trey Hardee and Ashton Eaton.[4]

Appendix A: Order of Events in Ancient Pentathlon by a Sampling of Modern Writers

Author	Date	1	2	3	4	5
Gardner	1880	Jump	Discus	Jav	Run	Wrestling
Myers	1881	Jump	Discus	Jav	Run	Wrestling
Marquardt	1886	Run	Jump	Discus	Jav	Wrestling
Fedde	1888	Run	Discus	Jump	Jav	Wrestling
Faber	1891	Jump	Run	Discus	Jav	Wrestling
Henrich	1892	Run	Jump	Jav	Discus	Wrestling
Gardiner	1904	-1st four make no difference-				Wrestling
Alexander	1925	Run	Discus	Jav	Jump	Wrestling
Gardiner	1925	Run	Jump	Discus	Jav	Wrestling
Maroti	1944	Run	?	?	Discus	Wrestling

The order of events of the pentathlon has only been an issue of modern scholars. Most likely those events common to the pentathlon came early in the contest. Shown in this drawing from a lekythos (oil flask) in the British Museum are two pentathletes. On left an athlete holds two javelins and a halter. The middle athlete holds a discus in front of a coach or official on the right (*Journal of Hellenic Studies*, 1907).

Author	Date	1	2	3	4	5
Bean	1956	-no opinion, no one can know the order-				
Highmore	1956	Jump	Discus	Jav	Run	Wrestling
Ebert	1963	-1st 3 uncertain-			Run	Wrestling
Harris	1964	Jump	Discus	Jav	Run	Wrestling
Schöbel	1965	Discus	Jump	Jav	Run	Wrestling
Barazanic	1970	Run	Jump	Discus	Jav	Wrestling
Segal	1971	Run	Discus	Jump	Jav	Wrestling
Ebert	1974	Discus	Jump	Jav	Run	Wrestling
Swaddling	1980	Discus	Jump	Jav	Run	Wrestling
Sweet	1983	-1st four make no difference-				Wrestling
Casson	1984	Jump	Discus	Jav	Run	Wrestling
Romano	1993	Run	Jump	Discus	Jav	Wrestling
Matthews	1994	Discus	Jump	Jav	Run	Wrestling
Pissanos	2002	Jump	Discus	Jav	Run	Wrestling
Palaeologos	2003	Jump	Discus	Run	Jav	Wrestling
Spivey	2006	Run	Discus	Jump	Jav	Wrestling
Valavanis	2004	Jump	-uncertain-		Run	Wrestling
Perrotte	2004	Discus	Jav	Jump	Run	Wrestling
Kyle	2007	Discus	Jump	Jav	Run	Wrestling

Note: A number of authors present still different orders of events, but some cannot be taken seriously. For example, E.S. Mildner (1930) writes a fanciful story about the conduct of a pentathlon in the *American Journal of Nursing*, maintaining that the order was: run, jump, wrestling, javelin, discus.

Appendix B:
Order of Modern Track
and Field Combined Events

Men's Combined Events

All-Around—10 events, began in 1884, ended 1978
  100yd (run), SP (throw), HJ (jump), 880walk (run), hammer (throw), PV (jump), 120ydH (run), 56lbwt (throw), LJ (jump), Mile (run)

Irish International All-Round—12 events, offered in 1888
  56lbwt (throw), HJ (jump), 100yds (run), hammer (throw), LJ (jump), 120ydH (run), SP (throw), st LJ (jump), 440yds (run), 28lbs (throw), st HSJ (jump), Mile (run)

Modern Ancient Pentathlon—5 events, offered only at 1906 Olympic Games
  St LJ (jump), Discus (throw), 192m (run), Jav (throw), Wrestling

Decathlon—10 events, began in 1911, 2 days
  Day 1: 100m (run), LJ (jump), SP (throw), HJ (jump), 400m (run). Day 2: 110mH (run), Discus (throw), PV (jump), Jav (throw), 1500m (run)

Pentathlon—5 events, began in 1912, Olympic event through 1924
  LJ (jump), Jav (throw), 200m (run), Discus (throw), 1500m (run)

Indoor Pentathlon—5 events, begun in 1971
  60mH (run), LJ (jump), SP (throw), HJ (jump), 1000m (run)

Indoor Heptathlon—7 events, begun in 1984, 2 days
  Day 1: 60m (run), LJ (jump), SP (throw), HJ (jump). Day 2: 60mH (run), PV (jump), 1000m (run)

Women's Combined Events

Pentathlon—5 events, began in 1951, Olympic Games 1964–1980
  100mH (run), HJ (jump), SP (throw), LJ (jump), 800m (run)

Heptathlon—7 events, begun in 1980, Olympic Games 1984 to present, 2 days
  Day 1: 110mH (run), HJ (jump), SP (throw), 200m (run). Day 2: LJ (jump), Jav (throw), 800m (run)

Decathlon—10 events, begun in 1970s, IAAF approved in 2002, 2 days
  Day 1: 100m (run), Discus (throw), PV (jump), Jav (throw), 400m (run). Day 2: 100mH (run), LJ (jump), SP (throw), HJ (jump), 1500m (run)

Indoor Pentathlon—5 events, begun in 1970s, IAAF indoor championship event
60mH (run), HJ (jump), SP (throw), LJ (jump), 800m (run)

Legend

60mH	60-meter hurdle
100mH	100-meter hurdle
110mH	110-meter hurdle
120ydH	120-yard hurdle
880walk	880-yard race walk
100yds	100-yard race
400yds	400-yard race
100m	100-meter race
192m	192-meter race
200m	200-meter race
400m	400-meter race
800m	800-meter race
1,000m	1,000-meter race
1,500m	1,500-meter race
Mile	Mile race
PV	Pole vault
HJ	High jump
LJ	Long jump
St LJ	Standing long jump
St HSJ	Standing hop-step-jump
SP	Shot put
Discus	Discus throw
Jav	Javelin throw
hammer	Hammer throw
28lbs	28-pound throw
56lbwt	56-pound weight throw

Appendix C: Summary of Modern Scholars' Opinions on How the Winner Was Determined

This appendix contains 31 theories, arranged chronologically

Pinder (1867): At each step the number of athletes is reduced until only two remain. They wrestle. Jump is first and only first five are allowed to continue.
It's possible one could win first 4 events but lose wrestling and thus lose pentathlon. Large fields a problem.

Gardner (1880): Competition conducted à la tournament with athletes arranged in pairs, each pair contesting each other in all five events.
Unbelievably convoluted. Time consuming and byes are possible. The accepted wisdom in England in the 19th century.

Myers (1881): Athletes would be drawn in pairs after each event.
See comments on Gardner. With large fields this would be a circus, an administrative nightmare.

Holwerda (1881): Only those who won any of the first 4 events advanced to wrestling.
Problem of what to do if one had two wins and two had one win.

Marquardt (1886): Total points. Top 5 in run advance to wrestling semifinals with a bye. Preliminary sections in each event. Athletes are drawn by lot.
The most problematical system imaginable. Imaginative.

Fedde (1888): A field of 24 required and athletes would be divided into 8 groups of 3.
Believed all pentathlon fields had 24 competitors because there are 24 letters in Greek alphabet. I won't go any further.

Faber (1891): A maximum field of 12 accepted and all those who met a certain pre-determined standard would advance to wrestling.
Obviously influenced by pre–1891 AAU all-around rules. This would be time consuming to administer since measurements would be required and lots of passing in field events. It's no wonder the AAU banished it after 1892 and replaced it with scoring tables.

Gardiner (1903): Triad necessary but 2nd and 3rd places counted and used if no triad winner developed.

169

An illogical and bizarre system using comparative victories. Lack of track and field background noticeable.

Pihkala (1925): Absolute wins unimportant. Relative victories important. Three comparative wins necessary.

Very intricate and would require a CPA to straighten it out (not a few minutes by means of a simple scoring sheet) and it is still possible that no winner would emerge. No system would have recommended itself to the Greeks which required paper and pencil.

Gardiner/Pihkala (1925): Places in first four events determined who advanced to wrestling final. Three comparative victories, not outright wins necessary. Pihkala system adopted by Gardiner.

Needlessly complicated and requires that every attempt be measured so that places could be determined and assumes that judges could accurately pick lower places in the run.

Raubitschek (1956): All competitors 1st or 2nd in initial triad were admitted to footrace, which would have 2 to 6 participants. Those first or second in foot race advanced to wrestling (called the "Fourth Theory").

An athlete could win pentathlon having won a single event, wrestling.

Moretti (1956): Ranked (ordinal) results where athletes earn a system of points. First place system secures *n* points, 2nd place *n*-1. Points system was applied if there was no clear winner of 3 after 4 events.

The pentathlon winner did not need to win any individual event. Needlessly complicated and requires everything to be measured. From a spectator's standpoint, no one could keep track.

Bean A (1956): A series of successive reductions to 2 athletes, 2nd and 3rd places were important.

Possible that athletes still would not have the prerequisite wins for triad.

Bean B (1956): Reduction of competitors in three stages: triad of field events; running; wrestling. Same as Bean A but one had to win an event to advance to running.

Doesn't provide details but it's the first reasonable theory and has Plutarch confirmation about letter "A."

Bean C (1956): Similar to B, but when each field event had an individual winner, then two races (*stade* = ca. 200 meters and *diaulos* = ca. 400m) were run and the two winners advanced to wrestling. (called the "Third Theory").

In effect five events are increased to six.

Bean D (1956): Similar to Raubitschek but an athlete had to win at least one first place or two 2nd places to advance to the footrace. First and second advance to wrestling (called "Fifth Theory").

Here one could win pentathlon à la Peleus. Same objection as original Raubitschek.

Kalfarentzos (1962): Ties were not only possible but likely so there is likelihood of no winner.

Suggests that ties are the reason we do not know the names of many ancient pentathlon winners. Implausible.

Ebert (1963): Relative victories are important.

Elimination came when athletes were shown to be inferior 3 times. Rather naïve; see objections for Moretti, Pihkila.

Harris (1966): Triad, used wrestling as a semi-final to obtain two finalists.

This would be destroyed in an Athens minute by the first heavy athlete who would recognize that all he needed was a discus win and a semi-final wrestling win to advance to final wrestling, likely as the favorite. Sweet dismisses him for this over-

sight. The fact that there are no reported wrestlers-pentathlon double winners at Olympia is evidence enough that this system was not used.

Maroti (1968): Footrace came first, javelin 4th (Lee, p. 41, "Yet Another...." Nikephorus

Bazanic (1970): Has no clear cut opinion. Reviews everyone else.
Difficult to critique.

Merkelbach (1973): First and second place counted, field was narrowed before final event.
Again, difficult to keep track of places beyond first.

Sweet (1983): Everyone advances to run, but if no triad, drawing by lot for 2nd try at random events.
Unbelievably complicated and confusing for athletes and spectators. Second places could advance and win. Some events would be done over by matching. This could take a great deal of time.

Langdon (1989): Buys into the Harris system even though he realizes that the method of victory used attracts certain types of athletes.
The Greeks would have understood this and not invented a game where the winner was pre-ordained. The Greeks recognized what made competition interesting was that the outcome was in doubt. What Harris never understood was that the type of athlete who tries these combined events is determined by the rules (in modern times, the scoring tables) and those who promote and devise them must be careful (by selection of events, order, and manner of victory) not to skew them in favor of certain types.

Kyle (1990): Triad. If there are more than 2 individual winners after 4 events, a semifinal run used.
The most logical theory yet, for no "type" of athlete would have an advantage.

Waddell (1990): First and 2nd place finishes counted in advancing to wrestling.
Not as confusing as Gardiner but still requires judges to determine 2nd places in field events, which could require measurements. Messy. Spectators would be confused.

Lee (1991): Provides no new evidence and lumps Kyle and Sweet positions and supports Harris's notion that a *repêchage* of wrestling was used when necessary.
There is no new evidence, just the support of the Harris approach on spectatorship only grounds.

Jackson (1991): Progressive eliminations. Last man was dropped after each event.
Definitional problems. No indication if "last" meant last in that event (meaning measurements would be required of everyone) or "last after that event" with no indication on how that would be calculated.

Lee (1995): Uses a combination of relative and absolute victories. Also claims that the method of scoring may have evolved and may have varied from place to place.
There are conceptual problems and would not work in a large meet. As to his claims: both are very doubtful. Of course there may have been some minor differences in how the pentathlon was conducted, but changing what it took to win is unlikely.

Valvanis (2004): It is unclear. He provides no details.
Impossible to critique.

Tyrrell (2004): Summarizes other theories but offers no solution or opinion.
Makes very general observations, not inclined to go into details.

Appendix D: Number of Possible Ancient Pentathlons

The traditional date of the first ancient pentathlon is 708 B.C. The final pentathlon was likely held at the isolympic games of Antioch (in what is now Syria) in the early 6th century C.E.[1] In the 12 centuries in between, there may have been nearly a quarter of a million festivals which conducted the pentathlon (see table below). A broad agonistic infrastructure was in place from the 5th century B.C. onwards. It included the major or sacred crown games, upgraded local games such as those designated isolympic, isopythic and so on, and a very large number of local prize games. Much of the wide dissemination of Greek athletic festivals in the ancient world can be traced to the military and political victories of Alexander the Great and the keen interest taken later by Roman emperors.[2]

The number of concurrent local festivals probably reached a peak in the 2nd century C.E. H.A. Harris maintained that there were over 300 festivals in the first century of the Roman Empire.[3] His maps show the distribution of athletic festivals. He reminds the reader that some cities on his list of Greek colonies, from Adana to Zeugma, were held annually, some (like the Crown Games) were biennial or held every fourth year. On the other hand, Wolfgang Leschhorn says that at least 400 agones are recorded on coins and there were probably 500.[4] The numbers of opportunities for competing athletes were so numerous that calendar organizers made it easy for athletes to compete in nearby cities.[5] The athletes were constantly traveling.

We also have a good idea as to how long many of these festivals lasted. The Games at Olympia now appears to have lasted into the 5th century C.E. We also know that the Nemean Games went into the mid–3rd, the Isthmian Games survived into the 4th, and the Panatheniac Games in the early 5th century (410 C.E.).[6]

We also know than many of the festivals conducted pentathlon for various age groups, usually including categories for boys (*paides* = παιδας), beardless youths (*ageneiois* = αγενίεους) and men (*andres* = ανδρας). Olympia was atypical in this respect since, with one exception, only a pentathlon for men was conducted.

In an effort to estimate the number of pentathlon contests held in antiquity, I have prepared the table below and assumed the following:

1. Festivals were held as scheduled, that is, an Olympic Games every 4th year, and Nemean Games every 2nd year. In fact, most local festivals were annual.
2. Conservative is the word. Even though we are reasonably certain, for example, that there were as many as 500 annual athletic festivals in the 2nd century A.D., I've used a figure of 400 to be on the low side.

The final tally for the number of ancient pentathlons is staggering: nearly a quarter of a million. And many of the festivals held pentathlons for more than one age category. It is likely that there were more than half a million pentathlon winners.

Number of Possible Ancient Pentathlons

Date	Crown Games[1]	Iso Games[2]	Local Games[3] × years	Total Games
708–600 B.C.	28	0	20 × 100	2,028
599–500	126	0	50 × 100	5,126
499–400	150	0	100 × 100	10,150
399–300	150	0	150 × 100	15,150
299–200	150	0	200 × 100	20,150
199–100	150	0	200 × 100	20,150
99–1	150	6 × 25	250 × 100	25,300
1–99 C.E.	150	20 × 25	250 x 100	25,650
100–199	150	50 × 25	400 × 100	41,400
200–299	150	40 × 25	400 × 100	41,150
300–399	130	15 × 25	300 × 100	30,505
400–499	8	2 × 25	80 × 100	8,058
>500	0	6	10 × 20	206
	1492	3331	240,200	245,023

Legend:
1—Includes Olympic, Pythian, Isthmian and Nemean Games. From 5th century B.C. to 3rd century A.D. 150, Crown Games were held every century (Olympic and Pythian Games every 4th year, Isthmian and Nemean games every other year).
2—Iso or franchised games for a century. We know, for example that scholars have identified as many as 25 isolympic and 27 isopythian Games in the 1st century A.D.
3—to put this on a century basis I've estimated number of local, annual games and multiplied by 100 years. For example, in the 3rd century B.C. we assume that on average about 200 Greek cities held annual athletic festivals each year for 100 years, then for the century, there were 20,000 games.

Appendix E:
Odysseus the Athlete

Odysseus is not only a figure of poetic inspiration. Tennyson makes him the modern hero ... to strive, to never say die. Some see the *Odyssey* as a metaphor for the journey of life and Odysseus is its hero. He is *polymetus* (versatile), long enduring, and resourceful while managing to survive, the very characteristics of the modern decathlete. The following is a description of what his athletic career would look like if it was prepared by a modern day track statistician. As well, Odysseus may be considered a double decathlete: 10 years of war, 10 years of journey home.

Athletic Career of Odysseus

Date	Event	Meet/Venue	Opponent	Outcome	Mark	Prize	Source
Pre-fall/ Troy	Sprint	FG/ Patroclus*	Ajax	w**	nm	silver mixing bowl	*Iliad*
"	Wrestling	FG/ Patroclus*	Ajax	tie	-	tripod	*Iliad*
"	Javelin	FG/ Patroclus*	Agamennon	pass	-	cauldron	*Iliad*
Post-fall/ Troy	Jump	Phaecia	Phaeacians	pass	-	-	*Odyssey*
"	Discus	Phaecia	Phaeacians	w	nm	-	*Odyssey*

*Funeral Games of Patroclus, (**deity aided [Athena], Results from Book 23, *Iliad* and Book 8 *Odyssey*)

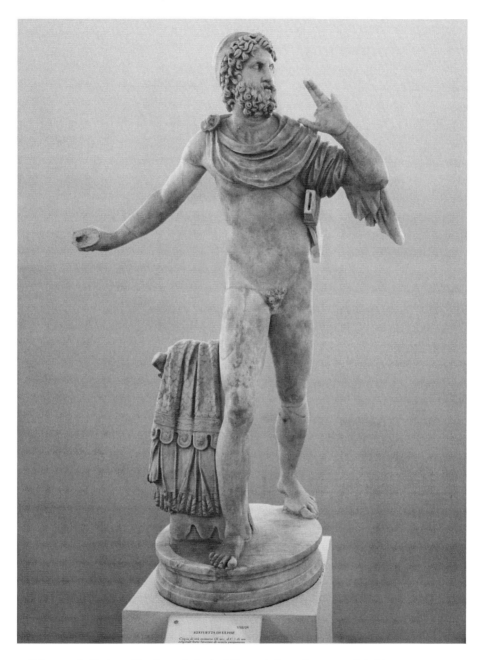

Odysseus is the lone Greek mythological figure to have been associated in some way (through passages in the *Iliad* and *Odyssey*) with all five pentathlon events. Marble Roman copy of 3rd century B.C. Hellenistic original (Archaeological Museum of Venice Vanni/Art Resource, New York).

Appendix F: Pentathlon Victor Statues at Olympia[1]

Athlete	City	Date	Sculptor	Notes
Stomios	Elis	376 B.C.		later a cavalry general who challenged the enemy to a duel and was slain.
Antiochus	Lepreon	400 B.C.	Nikodamos	won OG pankration and pent 2× at Isthmus and 2× at Nemea.
Hysmon	Elis	384 B.C.	Kleon	muscle disease as a boy and took up pent to become sound and healthy. His statue has jumping weights.
Theopompos	Heraia	484–480 B.C.	Eutelidas of Argos	his father and his son (another Theopompos) were also Olympic champions
Ikkos	Tarantine	444 B.C.		became top trainer (coach) of his age.
Gorgos	Messene	232 B.C.	Theron	son of Eukles (who won pent? Gorgos or of Boiotia Eukles?).
Hieronymos	Andros	492 B.C.	Stomois	beat Tisamenos/Elis, who was later a prophet for the Greeks against Mardonio and the Persians at Plataia.
Aischines	Elis	unknown		2× pentathlon winner and has two statues.
Kleinomachos	Elis	unknown		
Eutelidas	Sparta	628 B.C.		won 1st and only boys' pent, was also 2× boys' champ at wrestling. This was the oldest statue Pausanias saw at Olympia, and at the time was 800 years old.
Gorgos	Elis	unknown		4× winner, and also won double stade and race in armor
Timon	Elis	200 B.C.		won all crown games but

By the 2nd century A.D. there may have been as many as 35 statues of Olympic pentathlon winners. Pentathlete statues in the sacred Altis at Olympia were rarely as elaborate as this mid 2nd century B.C. bronze statue of a javelin carrier. It was inspired by
a statue of Alexander the Great by Lysippus and is now housed in the Museo Nazionale
Romano in Rome (Vanni/Art Resource, NY).

Athlete	City	Date	Sculptor	Notes
				Isthmus (where all Eleans were barred) and took part in Aitolian campaign against Thessaly, and he commanded a garrison at Naupaktos.
Menalkes	Elis	unknown		
Theodoros	Elis	unknown		
Klearetos	Elis			
		unknown		
Alexibios	Heraia in Arkadia	312 B.C.	Akestor	

Additional Pentathlon Statues

Chionis	Sparta	668, 664, 660, 656	-	a tablet was also on display next to his statue, which was erected long after his death. He was an OG runner winner, not pent, and who long jumped 52 feet.
Eupolemos	Elis	396 B.C.	-	Daidalos of Sikyon won for running at Olympia but also won pentathlon 2× at Pythian Games and another at Nemea. His sprint win was disputed.
Lampis	Sparta	708 B.C.	-	his son, Timoptolis, has a statue, not Lampis himself.

15 statues of 14 winners of pentathlon at Olympia (excluding boys' pentathlon).

Glossary of Terms

ageneiois (pl. ageneioi)   an age category for young men between *paides* and *andres*. Literally, "beardless youth." Specific age limits varies from place to place but the category was used at Pythian, Isthmian and Nemean Games, but never at Olympia, which used just two categories, *paides* (youth) and *andres* (men).

akon (or akontion)   the javelin or light spear used in athletic competition. It differed in weight and length from the military or hunting counterpart.

akoniti   literally, "without dust," and applies, for our purposes, to the pentathlete who won the overall contest without having to contest the wrestling event. Wrestlers had to "dust up" or powder their bodies with dust before competing. The final *akoniti* tally was either 3–0 (an athlete having won the first three events) or 3–1 (having won three of the first four events).

Altis   a sacred grove at Olympia, west of the stadium, wherein the temple of Zeus was located.

alytes   officials within the stadium who administered floggings after false starts.

Amphoras, amphorai   decorated jars used for the storing and transportation of products like olive oil. Specifically, they were highly valued prizes at the Panathenaia festival in Athens.

andres   men. The oldest competitive category at ancient festivals.

ankyle   a leather thong or strap wrapped around the center of gravity of the javelin to aid in the accuracy and distance of the throw (*amentum* in Latin).

athlon   a prize given at a contest (*athlete* is one who competes for a prize) (*athlos*—contest).

aulos   a flute, *auletes* (the flute player).

balbis   a starting line for runners. Often used as the throwing area for the discus.

basileis   upper or ruling class

bater   specifically used to designate the take-off spot for the *halma* (jump). More generally, it has also been used to identify the starting line for races.

combined events   any all-around athletic competition with more than one contest. In modern athletics this has included all-arounds, pentathlons, heptathlons and decathlons.

Crown Games   sacred Panhellenic festivals. They included Olympic, Pythian, Isthmian and Nemean Games.

denarius (pl. denarii)   a small silver coin in ancient Rome.

diaulos   a footrace twice the length of the *stade*. The closest modern equivalent would be 400 meters.

Discobolos   generically, a discus thrower. Specifically, the most famous sculpture of antiquity, by Myron, ca. 450 B.C.

diskos (pl. discoi) an elliptical throwing implement, initially made of stone, later metal and today of metal and wood. An event in which the implement is thrown for distance.

dolichos a distance race. We are uncertain of its length but likely in the area of 5000 meters or 3 miles.

Doryphoros "the spear bearer," famous sculpture (by Polykleitos), 450–400 B.C.E.

drachma an ancient Greek silver coin, equivalent to six obols.

ephebos a young man who had reached the age of training (normally 18) for citizenship (some of which was physical). His training was called *ephebic*.

epigram a short, often satirical poem.

epigram an engraved inscription.

fillet a ribbon, usually of wool, given to the winner of an Olympic event and usually worn around the head until the final awards ceremony.

gymnasion (Latin: gymnasium) the nude place. A place for nude exercise. It often consisted of a covered practice track, one *stade* long, and an open air space for running and for throwing the discus and javelin.

halma the long jump of the pentathlon. Ancient jumpers were accompanied by music from an *aulos* and carried jumping weights called *halteres*.

halter (pl. haltere) a hand held weight used in the pentathlon jump.

Hellanodikai a judge or meet official. After 472 B.C. there were three hellandikai for the pentathlon.

Hellanodikaion a place for the judges (Hellanodikai), often a building.

hoplitodromos a footrace in military armor (helmet, shin greaves—later dropped—and shield), otherwise nude. Usually the length of the *diaulos*, or two *stades*.

hysplex a mechanism for starting a footrace where a rope or gate drops as a starting signal, possibly used for the pentathlon *stade*.

isolympia a designation for a festival that was modeled after the Olympic Games, including the event program (including the pentathlon). Cities paid a franchise fee to Eleans for the use of the term. In a sense, a franchised Olympic Games.

isonemean a designation for festivals that were modeled after the Nemean Games. See *isOlympia*.

isopythian a designation for festivals that were modeled after the Pythian Games. See *isOlympia*.

Isthmian Games one of the four original Panhellenic Crown Games where only a branch of fresh celery (and later pine) was used to honor winners. Held every other year in Corinth.

kanon often referred to as a measuring rod. But more likely a rod used to help pentathletes get steps in the *halma* or *akon*.

Magna Gracea western Greece, usually refers to the Greek colonies and settlements in Italy and Sicily.

metretes a measure of liquids, equivalent to almost 39 liters.

Nemean Games one of the four original Panhellenic crown games where only an ivy branch was given to victors. Held in Nemea.

Olympia the site of the sanctuary of Zeus and of the ancient Olympic games, in the northwest Peloponnese, with Pisa as the nearest settlement.

Olympic Games the original Panhellenic Crown Games, held every fourth year at Olympia.

paides (s. pais) boys, usually under 17 or 18. The term was used to designate the youngest category of boys who were allowed to exercise in the *gymnasion* or compete in athletic contests.

palaistra (Latin: palaestra) "the wrestling place." Usually a building attached to the gymnasion where wrestling was taught or practiced.

pale the wrestling event, either open or as part of and final event of the pentathlon.

Panathenaia Festival a popular, major annual athletic festival held in Athens with enhanced emphasis every fourth year.

Panhellenic athletic festivals open to all free males of the Greek world, as opposed to local games.

pankration a brutal combat contest, a combination of wrestling and boxing with few rules.

pentathlon a competition with five sub-events: *diskos, halma, javelin, stade* and *pale*, in that order. The competition ended when one athlete had won three of the events.

periodes a circuit comprising of four Panhellenic festivals: Olympia, Delphi, Nemea and Corinth.

periodonikes one who won at each of the periodes, the circuit.

poda para poda a call by officials for the athletes to ready for the *stade*. Literally "foot by foot," meaning get your feet set in the *balbis*. Akin to the modern call of "on your marks."

Pythian Games one of the four original Panhellenic crown games where only a laurel branch was given to victors. Held at the Sanctuary to Apollo in Delphi.

repêchages a rerun or second chance. For the pentathlon a second sprint race to determine who would advance to the wrestling event. In modern days, competition within a "losers' bracket."

semeion (pl. semeia) pegs or markers used to indicate the length of the throws or jumps in the pentathlon.

skamma an area of softened earth used for both the pentathlon jump and for wrestling bouts. Literally "the dug up area."

stade, stadion the shortest of the Greek races, a sprint one length of the stadion. Originally a unit of measurement of 600 ancient feet, although a "foot" varied from place to place. Eventually it came to mean the site of the race itself, the stadium.

stele a block or slab of stone, often a pillar.

strigil a curved cleansing tool used to scrape the sweat, dirt and oil form one's body after competition or exercise.

systasis the starting position for wrestling, appearing much like the pointed rafters of a roof.

Tailteaan Games concurrent ancient athletic festival, held from early in the second millennium in what is now Ireland. Originally pre–Celtic. Discontinued in early 2nd millennium C.E. No evidence of cross-pollination between Olympian and Tailteaan cults. A different set of jumping and throwing contests was used.

terma often used to designate the finish line of a race.

triad the winner of three sub–events in the pentathlon, and therefore the overall crown.

triakter winner of three falls in wrestling and therefore the bout.

xystarches the leader of an athletic guild or union.

Zanes statues set up at the entrance to the stadium at Olympia warning competitors not to cheat. Paid for with fines levied on cheaters and bribers.

Glossary of Greek Writers

Aristotle (Ἀριστοτέλης)   A student of Plato and mentor to the young Alexander the Great. Aristotle was one of the founding fathers of Western Philosophy. He wrote on many subjects including an update of Olympic victor lists.

Bacchylides (Βακχυλίδης)   A lyric poet from the 5th century B.C., noted for his clear expression. His career benefited from the reputation of his uncle, Simonides, who introduced Baccylides to wealthy patron families. Sometimes he has been unfavorably compared to Pindar. One ode to a pentathlete survives.

Hippias (Ἱππίας)   A Sophist lecturer, statesman and philosopher from Elis (approximately 460–400 B.C.) who created the initial Olympic victor lists. Described by Plato as a superficial blowhard. Modern scholars have expressed misgivings about the reliability of his victor lists.

Homer (Ὅμηρος)   The author of the *Iliad* and *Odyssey*, which have some of the earliest descriptions of athletic events. He is recognized as the greatest ancient Greek epic poet. He is dated approximately to the 8th century B.C.

Pausanias (Πίνδρος)   A Greek traveler and geographer from Lydia, from the 3rd century C.E. A contemporary of Roman emperor Hadrian, Pausanias, in his *Description of Greece*, gave a first hand, accurate, detailed and reliable account of the sanctuary at Olympia.

Philostratus (Φιλόστρατος)   A Greek sophist who studied and taught in Athens, and is dated to approximately 172–250 C.E. He authored *Gymnasticus* in approximately 220 A.D., which, according to modern scholars, is a less than reliable account of the Olympic Games and athletics in general.

Pindar (Πίνδαρος)   An elegant Ancient Greek lyric poet who wrote numerous victory odes about Crown Games winners. Two of his victory odes to pentathletes survive. We date him to about 522–443 B.C. A rival and contemporary of Bacchylides.

Simonides (Σιμωνίδης)   A Greek lyric poet (556–468 B.C.) from the island of Ceos who wrote numerous victory odes, none of which survive in their entirety. One modern scholar suggests that Simonides wrote an entire book of victory odes about pentathletes. Nothing survives. Uncle of Bacchylides.

Xenophon (Ξενοφῶν)   A Greek soldier, philosopher and military historian from Athens, dated to 430–354 B.C., making him a contemporary of Socrates. His reliable accounts occasionally touched on Olympia. Not to be confused with the Corinthian pentathlete by the same name.

Notes

Preface

1. The most recent decathlon record set in Götzis was 9026 points in 2001 by Czech Roman Sebrle, an event I juried.

2. Frank Zarnowski, *Decathlon: A Colorful History of Track and Field's Most Challenging Event*. Champaign, IL: Leisure Press, 1989.

3. Frank Zarnowski. *All-Around Men: A History of a Forgotten Sport*. Lanham, MD: Scarecrow Press, 2004.

4. E.N. Gardiner, "Throwing the Discus," *The Journal of Hellenic Studies*, Vol. 27, 1907, pp. 1–36.

Chapter 1

1. Maria Koursi, ed., *The Olympic Games in Ancient Greece*, Athens: Ekdotike Athenon, 2003, p. 222. The pentathlon winner Perseus was the father of Achilles, the warrior hero of the Trojan War. In Book 8 of the *Iliad*, Homer describes the funeral games for Patroclus, arranged by his friend Achilles. These games offered only single events but no pentathlon. Perhaps Perseus neglected to tell his son about the pentathlon. In fact, the pentathlon was unknown at the time of the writing of Homer's epic.

2. Today the people of Lemnos claim that they are descendants of Jason and the pentathlon was born on their island. See http://www.lemnos.gr/eng/lemnos/history/pentathlo.htm.

3. The pentathlon's creation must have happened during the latter stages, perhaps on the return leg, of the Argo. The expedition had included a who's who of mythical heroes. Hercules, for example, had joined the expedition at the start but left the Argo before the Fleece was "rescued." One can only wonder how Hercules, the ultimate warrior-athlete, would have fared in this "first" pentathlon? Screenwriters for the 1997 animated Disney movie *Hercules* inserted a scene in which the hero trained for the decathlon.

4. Historians have used a convenient categorization of ancient athletic festivals. So great was the prestige of the sacred Crown Games (Olympic, Pythian, Isthmian and Nemean) that only a symbolic wreath was awarded to winners. In Prize Games, money or merchandise was commonly bestowed.

5. M.I. Finley and H.W. Pleket, *The Olympic Games: The First Thousand Years*, New York: Viking, 1972, p. 56.

6. Ibid., pp. 56–57.

7. Waddell is one of the few scholars who ask this pointed question. See Gene Waddell, "The Greek Pentathlon," *Greek Vases in the J. Paul Getty Museum*, The Museum, Malibu, CA, Vol. 5, 1990, p. 99.

8. W.T. Stace, *A Critical History of Greek Philosophy*, New York: Macmillan, 1928, p. 318.

9. Gene Waddell, "The Greek Pentathlon," *Greek Vases in the J. Paul Getty Museum*, Vol. 5, 1990, pp. 99–101.

10. The original has been lost but and what we have today are mostly Roman reproductions. There may be as many as a million copies today. Chionis, a seventh century Olympic victor and pentathlete from Sparta, was commemorated in an idealized bronze by Myron.

11. Ludwig Drees, *Olympia: Gods, Artists and Athletes*, New York: Praeger, 1968, p. 24.

12. Drees, p.24. Drees says that among these references we find *Lucian* and *Anecdotae Graecae*.

13. The funeral games for Patroclus, staged by his grieving friend Achilles, offer contests in wrestling, javelin, and foot racing, among others, in Book 23 of Homer's *Iliad*. Jumping and discus throwing appear as part of other funeral games and contests in the Book 8 of Homer's *Odyssey*.

14. Steve Craig, *Sports and Games of the Ancients*, Westport, CT: Greenwood, 2002, p. 86.

15. Wolfgang Decker, *Sports and Games of Ancient Egypt*, New Haven: Yale University Press, 1992, p. 67.

16. See Thorsten Veblen, *The Theory of the Leisure Class: An Economic Study of Institutions*, New York: Macmillan, 1912. In particular, see Chapter 9, "The Conservation of Archaic Traits."

17. Drees, p. 31. Wrestling was also added as an individual contest in 708 B.C. Drees tells us that wrestling and the events of the pentathlon came directly from funeral games of Pelops.

18. The 8th book of the *Odyssey* tells a tale of five events being conducted by the Phaeacians which look suspiciously like the ancient pentathlon and in which Odysseus wins the discus. One internet reviewer, N.S. Gill (About. Com/Classical History), incorrectly refers to this as a formal pentathlon event, further confusing the issue.

19. To add an event or sport to the summer Olympic program today takes a considerable amount of debate and effort. Generally, once a sport has gone through preliminary steps as an exhibition or demonstration event and has at least 50 member nations sponsoring it as a national championship, it can apply for inclusion into the program. Conversely, sports/ events may be dropped from the Olympic program. In more recent years this has been the fate of baseball, softball and wrestling.

20. See H.A. Harris, *Greek Athletics and Athletes*, Bloomington: University of Indiana Press, 1966. When Harris claims that "today field events are often less highly esteemed than those on the track, and a similar attitude among the Greeks may have been partly responsible for the grouping" (p. 77), we get a faulty look at the basis of the pentathlon. When he further states, "If it is strange that the pentathlon should have been invented, it is even more remarkable that it should have lasted so long" (p. 77), the reader begins to understand why his understanding and conclusions about the pentathlon cannot be taken seriously.

21. Even today Herakles is used as a sporting image. For example, David P. Willoughby used his own watercolor of the 11 foot statue of Herakles (The Farnese Hercules, Museo Archeologico Nazionale, Naples, Italy) as a frontispiece for his *The Super Athletes*, South Brunswick and New York: A.S. Barnes, 1970. In 1997 I served as an adviser to the Disney animated feature *Hercules*. In it actor Danny DeVito reminded a young Hercules that "he

was not training for some minor league decathlon."

22. In 1999 Modern Library named Joyce's *Ulysses* as the top rated English novel of the 20th century. For more on the athletic career of John S. Joyce, see Catherine and Colm Murphy, *The College Sports: The University Sports, Cork, 1869–1914*, Cork: Queens College, 1999.

23. A 1996 suggestion by the American representative to the International Amateur Athletics Federation (IAAF) Technical Committee that the decathlon order of events be changed was met with so many objections and such vehemence that the individual narrowly escaped with his life.

24. There have been six different official IAAF scoring tables (1912A, 1912B, 1934, 1950/ 51, 1962, 1985) for modern combined events.

25. The Greek acrophonic numbering system had a special symbol for 5. This is not surprising and presumably arises from counting on fingers.

26. No scholars raise the obvious question of why five events are configured and not, for example, four or six or some other figure? Modern coaches, administrators and athletes would question the number of events yet modern scholars do not seem to have done so. The explanation is that these are distinct groups. The answer is that five was simply a practical, serviceable number adequate to prove the point of versatility.

27. The ancient Greeks did not high jump, pole vault, triple jump, hurdle, or toss the hammer. Yet there is substantial evidence that a concurrent sporting culture did practice many of these events. The Celts of Ireland in the annual (and older than the ancient Olympic Games) fertility Tailteaan Games, on the hill of Tara, were known to conduct running, jumping and throwing contests. There may have been some Greek contact with Celtic culture but not much. As far as I know there have been no studies attempting to link the pair of ancient games, although there is documentation that Greek navigators reached the Irish Sea in the 4th century B.C. See, for example, Barry Cunliffe, *The Extraordinary Voyage of Pytheas the Greek*, New York: Penguin, 2002.

28. Reginald E. Allen, ed., *Greek Philosophy: Thales to Aristotle*, New York: Free Press, 1966, p. 38.

Chapter 2

1. Terrell, William Blake, *The Smell of Sweat: Greek Athletics, Olympics and Culture*, Wauconda, Ill., Bolchazy-Carducci, 2004, p. 216.

2. Hugh M. Lee, "Some Changes in the Olympic Program and Schedule," *Proceedings of an International Symposium on the Olympic Games*, Athens, 1992, pp. 105–11 (William Coulson and Helmut Kyrieleis, eds.), Athens, 1992.

3. Frank, Zarnowski, *How to Organize and Run a Decathlon*, Tucson: United States Track and Field Federation, 1972.

4. Modern track and field rules require a 30 minute break between the finish of a preceding event and the start of the next event. Spectators spend a good deal of time watching athletes rest. The amount of time allowed to rest within combined events has evolved. For example, beginning in 1885 the N4A (the national governing body for track and field in athletics before being replaced by the AAU in 1888) allowed only a 5 minute break between events for their standard and annual combined event championships, the one-day, ten event All-Around. The shorter the rest time, the more endurance becomes a factor in determining the winner.

5. Lee, p. 109.

6. 5! = $5 \times 4 \times 3 \times 2 \times 1 = 120$.

7. E. Norman Gardiner (1903) and Waldo Sweet (1983).

8. Joachim Ebert (1963) and Donald Kyle (1990).

9. See Gene Waddell, "The Greek Pentathlon," *Greek Vases in the J. Paul Getty Museum*, Santa Monica, CA, Vol. 5, 1990, pp. 99–106.

10. Stephen G. Miller, *Arete: Ancient Writers, Papyri, and Inscriptions on the History and Ideals of Greek Athletics and Games*, Chicago: Ares, 1979, p. 35, and Kyle, Donald G, "Winning and Watching the Greek Pentathlon," *Journal of Sport History*, Vol. 17, No. 3 (Winter), 1990, p. 293.

11. See, for example Stephen G. Miller, *Ancient Greek Athletics*, New Haven: Yale University Press, pp. 241–252, whose detailed glossary simply ignores the *kanon*.

12. Waldo E. Sweet, *Sport and Recreation of Ancient Greece: A Sourcebook*, New York: Oxford University Press, 1987, p. 38.

13. Ludwig, Drees, *Olympia: Gods, Artists and Athletes*, New York: Praeger, 1968 (trans. G. Ohn), p. 72.

14. George Highmore, "The Victor of the Greek Pentathlon," *Folklore*, Vol. 67, No. 3, September 1956, pp. 129–141.

15. Here I ignore events of more modern origin like hurdles, walks or relays.

16. For the development of modern combined events, see Frank Zarnowski, *All-Around Men: Heroes of a Forgotten Sport*, Scarecrow Press, Chapter 3, "The All-Around and the Evolution of Modern Combined Events," pp. 25–26.

17. Here I am referring to the Pastime AC, designer and host of the first amateur all-around in 1884, the New York Athletic Club which took over the event a year later and made alterations in the events themselves without ever sacrificing the alternating principle, the National Association of Amateur Athletes of America (N4A) and by 1888, the Amateur Athletic Union (AAU), both of which were federations that sanctioned the all-around.

18. Sweet, p. 214.

19. Nigel B. Crowther, "Numbers of Contestants in Greek Athletic Contests," *Nikephoros*, No. 6, 1996, p. 40.

20. See Tony Perrotte, *The Naked Olympics*, New York: Random House, 2004, p. 105. Twenty athletes would require 300 throws and jumps in the first three events alone. Assuming no rest between events, this would have taken a minimum of five hours and seem endless to spectators. This estimate is appallingly high.

21. Ibid., pp. 50–52.

Chapter 3

1. See Donald G. Kyle, "Winning at Olympia," *Archaeology*, April 2004, http://www.archaeology.org/online/features/olympics/index.html.

2. The ancient pentathlon dates to the end of the Greek Dark Ages where there is no surviving evidence of the use of writing. The palaces of an earlier Mycenae civilization used an administrative sort of writing called Linear B which had disappeared by the time the pentathlon was invented. And since, in the first millennium B.C., the Greeks used an acrophonic numbering system (the symbol for the numbers was based on the first letter of the number name), no formal numbering system was yet available at the time of the pentathlon's invention.

3. Donald G. Kyle, "Winning and Watching the Greek Pentathlon," *Journal of Sport History*, Vol. 17, No. 3, Winter 1990, pp. 295.

4. See Allen Guttman, *From Ritual to Record: The Nature of Modern Sport*, New York: Columbia University Press, 1978, pp. 16–55.

5. See Victor Matthews, "The Greek Pentathlon Again," *Zeitschrift für Papyrologie und Epigraphik*, Vol. 100, 1994, p. 133.

6. E.M. Gardiner, "The Method of Deciding the Pentathlon," *Journal of Hellenic Studies*, Vol. 23, 1903, pp. 54.

7. The first British nationals, the AAA

Championships for the Decathlon, were held on the July 6–7, 1928, at Stamford Bridge. The event was then discontinued until 1936, held in 1936, 1937, 1938, and discontinued again until 1947. It has been held continuously from 1947 onwards.

8. For a complete list of all competitors in the modern Olympic Games combined events until 1988, see Frank Zarnowski, *The Decathlon: A Colorful History of Track and Field's Most Challenging Event*, Champaign, IL, Leisure Press, 1989, Olympic section and index of Olympic competitors.

9. See David C. Young, "How the Amateurs Won the Olympics," in Wendy J. Raschke, ed., *The Archaeology of the Olympics: The Olympics and Other Festivals in Antiquity*, Madison, University of Wisconsin Press, 1988, p. 69. For a defense of or explanation for many of Gardiner's faux pas see Donald G. Kyle, "E. Norman Gardiner: Historian of Ancient Sport," *International Journal of the History of Sport*, Vol. 8, No. 1, 1991, pp. 28–55.

10. See L. Pihkala and E.N. Gardiner, "The System of Pentathlon," *Journal of Hellenic Studies*, Vol. 45, 1925, p. 134. As for his part, Pihkala had an undistinguished athletic career. He is listed as a competitor in two Olympic Games, with substandard results at best. In 1908 he was unable to throw 30 meters (98–5½) in the discus trials, one of 30 athletes who did not advance to the finals. In the high jump he cleared 1.67m/5–5½, good for a tie for 16th in the 22 man field. In 1912 he did not complete his event. He is not remembered in Finland for his athletic accomplishments but is better remembered as the inventor of a Finnish version of baseball.

11. See George E. Bean, "Victory in the Pentathlon," *American Journal of Archaeology*, Vol. 60, No. 4, October 1956, pp. 361–368.

12. See Joachim Ebert, *Zum Pentathlon Der Antike*, Berlin, Akademie-Verlag, 1963. In his lengthy manuscript Ebert spends a considerable amount of time critiquing all other victor schemes.

13. See E.A. Harris and H.A. Harris, "The Method of deciding Victory in the Pentathlon," *Greece and Rome*, Vol. 19, No. 1, April 1972, pp. 60–64. He was a senior lecturer at St. David's College, Wales, and a cricket devotee. His annoying analogy that the ancient pentathlon was like a five set tennis match reveals his lack of understanding of either sport. A careful reading of his descriptions of athletic technique make the reader wonder if he was familiar with athletics meetings. He died suddenly in 1974.

14. This is exactly what the Scots did with early 19th century all-rounds. Virtually all the events were heavy throws and all-round champions were burly and broad shouldered athletes like Donald Dinnie.

15. See H.M. Lee, "Wrestling in the *Repêchage* of the Ancient Pentathlon," *Journal of Sport History*, Vol. 20, 1991, pp. 277–79.

16. Kyle, p. 297. Kyle is referring to Sweet's very successful and generally helpful sourcebook which will be used for years to come. See Waldo E. Sweet, *Sport and Recreation in Ancient Greece: A Sourcebook with Translations*, New York, Oxford University Press, 1987.

17. Kyle, 1990.

18. Having been a combined events athlete, a distance runner, a competitor in modern pentathlon and having wrestled formally, I can tell you that nothing would be more ill-advised than to place a skill, agility, speed or technical event after an endurance event. Athletes could conceivably compete in sprinting, jumping and throwing events when tired, but what would be the point? Although this is a matter of degree, when you are exhausted there can be no legitimate exercise.

19. Russ Hodge and Dick Emberger each scored exactly 7728 points (1962 IAAF tables) at the second 1964 U.S. Olympic Team decathlon trials in Los Angeles.

Chapter 4

1. The first copy of this famous sculpture to have been discovered was found in Rome in 1781 and was called *Discobolus Palombara*. It is a first century copy of Myron's original. In 1937 Adolf Hitler negotiated to buy it, offering five million (prewar) lire, and succeeded in 1938. It was returned in 1948 and is now housed in the National Museum of Rome.

2. H.A. Harris, *Sport in Greece and Rome*, Cornell University Press, Ithaca, NY, 1972, p. 38.

3. Heinz Schöbel, *The Ancient Games*, Princeton: Van Nostrand, 1965, p. 88.

4. Harris, p. 38.

5. Of the 17 most important surviving amphora depicting the ancient discus, all from the 4th to 6th century B.C., six are housed at the J. Paul Getty Museum in Los Angeles and the remainder are spread among museums in Athens, Amsterdam, Berlin, London, Naples, Tarquinia, Rome, The Vatican, and Wurzburg. All show large, flat discs.

6. Stephen G. Miller, *Ancient Greek Athletics*, New Haven, Yale University Press, 2004, p. 61.

7. Tony Perrottet, *The Naked Olympics,* New York, Random House, 2004, pp. 107–08.

8. J. Kenneth Doherty, *Modern Track and Field*, Prentice Hall, New Jersey, 1963, p. 364.

9. William Blake Tyrrell, *The Smell of Sweat: Greek Athletics, Olympics and Culture*, Wauconda, Illinois, Bolchazy-Carducci, 2004, p. 207.

10. Panos Valavanis, (trans. David Hardy), *Games and Sanctuaries in Ancient Greece*, Los Angeles, Getty, 2004, p. 420.

11. Harris, p. 37.

12. E.K. Brothwick, "The Gymnasium of Bromius," *Journal of Hellenic Studies*, Vol. 84, 1964, p. 50, fn 11.

13. Paul Tasch, "Quantitative Measurements and the Greek Atomists," *Isis*, Vol. 38, No. 3/4 (February 1948), pp. 185–189. Tasch (1910–2001), an inquisitive and creative scientist, philosopher and historian, published 150 scientific papers on a variety of subjects.

14. See Ernest W. Adams, "On the Nature and Purpose of Measurement," *Synthese*, Vol. 16, No. 2, Symposium on the Nature of Measurement (November 1966), pp. 126–27.

15. "Effect of Wind and Altitude," *The Big Gold Book*, Mountain View, CA: Tafnews Press, 2005, pp. 136–144.

16. Wendy J. Raschke, ed., *The Archaeology of the Olympics: The Olympics and Other Festivals in Antiquity*, Madison, University of Wisconsin Press, 2002, pp. 185–186.

17. Tyrrell, p. 210.

18. Nigel B. Crowther, "Number of Contestants in Greek Athletic Contests," *Nikephoros*, Vol. 6, 1993, p. 48.

19. E.N. Gardiner, "Throwing the Discus," *The Journal of Hellenic Studies*, Vol. 27, 1907, pp. 1–36.

20. In fact Gardiner had both unfamiliarity with and a dislike for the modern discus event. In his seminal article he claims that the modern discus event is a variation of the hammer throw using 2 or 3 turns (p. 11) before release. The number is 1½. He also claims that the modern discus is a thick, clumsy object, inferior to its ancient counterpart. "There is no authority for it whatsoever" (p. 7).

21. It is hard to be impartial here but there are just too many mistakes in the description. See H.A. Harris, *Sport in Greece and Rome*, Cornell University Press, Ithaca, NY, 1972, p. 38.

22. Harris, pp. 38–39.

23. Judith Swaddling, *The Ancient Olympic Games*, Austin, University of Texas Press, 1999, p. 66.

24. Tyrrell, pp. 208–210.

Chapter 5

1. William Blake Tyrrell, *The Smell of Sweat: Greek Athletics, Olympics and Culture*, Wauconda, Illinois, Bolchazy-Carducci, 2004, p. 212.

2. In modern times nine different types of leaps have been official in the sense that they were part of major sporting events (e.g. Olympic Games, national championships) and for which records were maintained. They are running and standing long jumps, triple jumps, high jumps and pole vaults for height and distance and the hitch and kick.

3. One scholar has even concluded that the Greek jump was a quadruple one, yet this cannot be taken seriously. See R.K. Barney, "The Ancient Greek Pentathlon Jump: A Preliminary Reinterpretive Examination," in *Philosophy, Theology and History of Sport and of Physical Activity*, Book 8, published by Symposia Specialists, Miami, FL, 1978, pp. 279–288.

4. H.A. Harris, *Greek Athletes and Athletics*, Westport, CT, Greenwood Press, 1964, p. 165.

5. Tyrrell, p. 211.

6. The Rhodes inscription, discovered in 1956, can be found in numerous texts about the ancient Olympics. It is the best evidence we have on the number of attempts. Some early classical scholars simply assumed that "3" was handed down from Mount Olympus.

7. Stephen G. Miller, *Ancient Greek Athletics*, New Haven, Yale University Press, 2004, p. 64.

8. Those who have made the mistake of assuming a modern practice, the Greek use of sand in the long jump area, include Harris (1960, 1964, 1972), Schöebel (1965), Swaddling (1980, 1999), Tyrrell (2004) and Valavanis (2004).

9. There are any number of reasons why this makes little sense. First, just try it. Even the Greeks did not call their own fouls.

10. The earliest reference to drawing a line in the earth to mark the jump comes from P. Gardner, "The Pentathlon of the Greeks," *Journal of Hellenic Studies*, Vol. 1, 1880, p. 213.

11. This black figure amphora is now located at the British Museum in London.

12. See Nigel Crowther, "Second Place Finishes and Lower in Greek Athletics (Including Pentathlon)," *Zeitschrift für Papyrologie und Epigraphik*, Vol. 90, 2001, p. 102.

13. Incidentally, this is not allowed today. The IAAF, USATF, NCAA (and any other modern governing body) prohibit the placement of markers in the landing area.

14. See Tony Perrottet, *The Naked Olym-*

pics, New York, Random House, 2004, p. 113. He is influenced by a passing reference in Waldo E. Sweet, *Sport and Recreation in Ancient Greece: A Sourcebook with Translations*, New York, Oxford University Press, 1987, p. 46, that a *kanon* measured the jump. This is hardly reassuring.

15. Sweet, pp. 46–47.

16. An extensive examination of surviving *haltere* can be found in Julius Jüthner, *Über Antike Turngeräthe*, Vienna, Hölder, 1896, pp. 3–13.

17. Miller (2004), p. 64.

18. The number of scholars who have insisted that the jump used the *balbis* as a toe board is too numerous to recount.

19. Sweet (1987), p. 228. (Philostratos, *On Athletics*, was written around 200 CE).

20. Christine, Alexander, *Greek Athletics*, New York, Metropolitan Museum of Art, 1925, p. 12. This thin but enlightening booklet clearly shows jumpers landing on their feet.

21. In Roman Sebrle's 2001 world decathlon record his 8.11m/26–7¼ long jump was measured from the final mark in the Götzis, Austria, pit. The indentation was made by the back of his right shoulder.

22. Miller, 2004, p. 67. There are some minor technique problems with body posture at the take-off and landing. Beyond that these drawing by Reuben Santos are a very good representation on what the Greek jump must have looked like.

23. Examples of this flaw can be found in Harris (1960), Perrotte (2004) and Valvanis (2004). One writer, H.A. Harris, *Greek Athletes and Athletics*, Westport, CT, Greenwood Press, 1964, contends that music cannot possibly be useful in performing the jump. This, of course, is nonsense.

24. Miller, 2004, p. 84. Pythokritos is one of just a few musicians from antiquity whose name is known.

25. The major international invitational decathlons/heptathlons are conducted annually in Götzis, Austria; DeSanzano, Italy; Ratingen, Germany; and Talence, France. A popular international decathlon formerly conducted annually at Stanford University was called DecaJam, where music and athletics shared equal billing. In the past two decades only a single decathlete of international stature, American Sheldon Blockburger, asked meet officials and spectators for silence during his long jump attempts, preferring to concentrate on his technique internally.

26. Tyrell has confused his accomplishments, giving Phaÿllos two *stade* victories and one pentathlon win at Delphi.

27. See, for example, H.A. Harris, "An Olympic Epigram: The Athletic Feats of Phaÿllos," *Greece and Rome*, Vol. 7, No. 1, March 1960, pp. 3–8. This is pure fiction.

28. In 1994 Visa and USA Track and Field conducted a camp and clinic in San Diego for potential decathletes and, among others, invited the 1984 Olympic triple jump champion (whose lifetime triple jump best was just over 55 feet). But when he had trouble handling the unfamiliar discus, his training partners created a modern day Phaÿllos on the spot by proclaiming "here's [ ] whose jump and discus PRs are both 55 feet."

29. Naismith Hall of Fame candidate Jim Phelan, who won 820 games at Mount St. Mary's College, frequently complained of too many Janes.

30. Tyrrell, 2004, p. 212.

31. I realize that today many track coaches have to deal with apathetic sports information directors, but waiting 600 years to report a 55 foot long jump must itself be a record.

32. See Tom McNab, "The Ancient Pentathlon," *Decathlon*, London, British Amateur Athletic Board, 1972, p. 6.

33. Stephen G. Miller, "Turns and Lanes in the Ancient Stadium," *American Journal of Archaeology*, Vol. 84, p. 159.

34. Ebert (1973) carries the conversion to five decimal places—0.32045 meters—but it makes in infinitesimal difference.

35. Heinz Schöbel, *The Ancient Games*, Princeton: Van Nostrand, 1965, p. 89.

36. See, for example, Judith Swaddling, *The Ancient Olympic Games*, London, British Museum, 1980 (1st edition), and Judith Swaddling, *The Ancient Olympic Games*, 2nd ed., Austin, University of Texas Press, 1999. In the first edition (p. 56), she simply copies Schoebel's error. In the second edition (p. 71), she compounds the errors by rounding up to 16.30m and 16.70m. This is sloppy research and the moral may be that the Greeks have much to teach us about mathematics.

Chapter 6

1. Steve G. Bazarnic, "The Ancient Pentathlon and Aspects of the Greek Ideal," unpublished master's thesis, Penn State University, 1970, p. 55.

2. Some scholars have erroneously concluded that each athlete was allowed three throws because a vase painting depicts an athlete carrying three javelins (see, for example, Gardiner, Drees and Bazarnic). This can hardly be called conclusive, for other vase paintings show athletes carrying one, two and four javelins. Five throws was standard.

3. Barzanic, p. 55.

4. E. Norman Gardiner, "Throwing the Javelin," *Journal of Hellenic Studies*, Vol. 27, 1907, p. 252.

5. H.A. Harris, *Sport in Greece and Rome*, Ithaca: Cornell University Press, 1972, p. 36.

6. William Blake Tyrrell, *The Smell of Sweat: Greek Athletics, Olympics and Culture*, Wauconda, Illinois, Bolchazy-Carducci, p. 213.

7. Ibid., p. 214. Normally accurate in his technical descriptions of pentathlon field events, in this case Tyrrell has it backwards when he says, "In pentathlon, accuracy could be sacrificed in quest for distance."

8. See, for example, the IAAF, USATF or NCAA rule books on the layout of the javelin sector. All use a 26 degree angle to determine sector lines for the legal landing area.

9. Stephen Miller, *Ancient Greek Athletics*, New Haven: Yale University Press, 2004, p. 69.

10. Ulrich Sim, *Olympia: Cult, Sport and Ancient Festival* (trans. Thomas Thornton), 2000, Princeton, Markus Wiener, p. 6. A description of the ancient javelin throw and the *ankyle* can be found in any number of texts. More modern texts accept carte blanche earlier descriptions. For example, a note-by-note paraphrasing on the ancient javelin by Harris (1966), see Swaddling, Judith, *The Ancient Olympic Games*, London, British Museum, 1980, pp. 52–54.

11. Tyrrell, pp. 214–216.

12. Although there seems to be an understanding among scholars as to how the ancient javelin was performed, nonetheless, this has not prevented a certain amount of carping within the literature. See, for example, H.A. Harris, "Greek Javelin Throwing," *Greece and Rome*, 2nd series, Vol. 10, No. 1, March 1963, p. 30, who groused about other writers on the subject, "Neither Jüthner nor Gardiner appears ever to have thrown a javelin himself, with or without a thong."

13. In the 65 reviewed articles or chapters by modern scholars about the ancient javelin throw, not a single author even mentions the function of the left arm (for right-handed throwers) in creating force for the throw. This is partly due to ancient amphorae depicting only early stages of the throw and the inability of ancient artists to capture the motion of the throw. Many illustrate preparation, fixing or holding the *ankyle* or *amentum* taut, but none shows body position at the release of the javelin. Without mentioning what happens at the time of release, only half of the technique story of the javelin is told.

14. Modern coaches would argue that there

is no optimal angle of release. It all depends upon conditions. A range of 25 to 35 degrees is seen as standard. See, for example, Ken Doherty, *Track and Field Omnibook*, Los Altos, CA: Track and Field News, 1985, p. 253.

15. See Heinz Schöbel, *The Ancient Games*, Princeton: Van Nostrand, 1965, p. 90, for this inaccurate description.

16. Harris, p. 36. Once again Harris understands little of the physics of motion, leading him to offer a half explanation for the purpose of the *ankyle/amentum*. He claims, among other things, that the *ankyle/amentum* increased the probability of the javelin landing on its point. That would be determined by the force and angle at release, and the center of gravity of the implement.

17. H.A. Harris, *Greek Athletes and Athletics*, Bloomington, Indiana University Press, 1966, pp. 93–95.

18. See Robert Bittlestone, et al., *Odysseus Unbound: The Search for Homer's Ithaca*, Cambridge University Press, 2005, p. 198, where a reference to Statius (describing in the *Thebaid*) obliquely claims, in effect, that a hippodrome was four times the length of a javelin throw.

19. Between 1920 and 1950 the world javelin record floated between 66.10m/ 216-10 and 78.10m/258-2. Often Finns would use the *ankyle* in local competitions, of which there are literally hundreds each summer in *Soumi*. Invariably statisticians had a difficult time sorting out the reported marks made with and without the *ankyle*. No modern writer has even mentioned the long throws achieved by the Finns. Again, it seems that athletics people and Classical scholars are discrete groups.

20. See Ulrich Sinn, *Olympia: Cult, Sport and Ancient Festival* (trans. Thomas Thornton), 2000, Princeton, Markus Wiener, p. 6.

21. Both H.A. Harris and Norman E. Gardiner were erroneous on this point. The former concluded that the athletic javelin was sharpened at its forward end. Gardiner insisted that athletic javelins had a metallic tip. Neither was correct.

Chapter 7

1. Joachim Ebert, *Zum Pentathlon Der Antike*, Berlin, Akademie-Verlag, 1963.

2. Only Nigel B. Crowther, a Classicist from the University of Western Ontario, who has researched race issues like number of competitors, qualifying, rounds, draws, byes, walkovers, ties and the sprint finish in a series of journal articles published between 1988 and 2001, and Stephen G. Miller, University of

California, who has researched lane preparation, have delved into these ancient running
issues.

3. A noteworthy modern illustration with
11 pentathlon sprinters would never have happened. It is found in David Kennett, *Olympia:
Warrior Athletes of Ancient Greece (Illustrations)*, Walker and Co., New York, 2002, p. 32.

4. Statius, *Thebaid*, Vol. II, Book 6 of the
Loeb Classical Library (trans. J. N. Mosley),
Cambridge, MA: Harvard University Press,
1962, 6.591–617.

5. Note the use of lower case "g," referring to all Greek games, not just those at
Olympia.

6. Waldo E. Sweet, *Sport and Recreation
in Ancient Greece*, New York: Oxford University Press, 1987, p. 30.

7. References to the runners leaning so far
forward that they were nearly horizontal to the
ground should be ignored.

8. Ludwig Drees, *Olympia: Gods, Artists
and Athletes*, New York: Praeger, 1968. (trans.
G. Ohn), p. 79.

9. E.N. Gardiner, "Note on the Greek
Foot-Race," *Journal of Hellenic Studies*, Vol.
24, 1903, p. 271.

10. The annual AAU rule books limited dis-
qualifications for decathletes, but punished
them by having them move one yard back for
every false start.

11. Eric Segal, *The Ancient Games*, Xerox
Educational Group, 1971, Executive Producer
Roone Arledge, Director Lou Volpicelli, Pro-
ducer Dick Ebersol.

12. Frank Zarnowski, *The Decathlon: A
Colorful History of Track and Field's Most
Challenging Event*, Champaign: Leisure Press,
1989, p. 21.

13. Drees, p. 79. This may be a bit misleading since the contests did not start until the 4th
century B.C.

14. German scholar Joachim Ebert has
maintained that the pentathlon running event
was 5 lengths of the stadium, approximately
1000 meters, and that it would proceed the
wrestling match. Ebert's contention was that
there was magic in the number 5, and the
Greeks would have required pentathletes to
run a distance five times the length of the
stade. Not only is there no evidence for this
conjecture but scheduling a distance race before a wrestling match would humble even the
best of athletes. This notion is to be ignored.
For an explanation of Ebert's position, see
H.M. Lee, "Wrestling in the Repêchage of the
Ancient Pentathlon," *Journal of Sport History*,
Vol. 20, 1991, pp. 277–79.

15. The Iron-Man triathlon is a late 20th
century invention. In 2000 a triathlon (1500

meter swim, 40km bike race and 10km footrace) was added to the Olympic program. The
double decathlon is a Finnish concoction in
which the athlete must contest every single
track and field event, 20 of them, in two days.
The current world record (14,571 points) holder
is Joe Detmer, Lodi, Wisconsin, who is a world
class decathlete with distance running skills.
Detmer claims that in his 12 year athlete career,
completing (and winning) the world double in
2010 in Lynchburg, Virginia, was the hardest
thing he'd ever done and he concluded that
he'd never attempt it again.

16. Harris, for example, claims the surface
was dressed in sand and possibly rolled, as if
this were the truth. This mistake has been repeated in print frequently as if it were an as-
certained fact. Nothing could be further from
the truth. See H.A. Harris, *Greek Athletes and
Athletics*, Bloomington: University of Indiana
Press, p. 64. See footnote 13. The amount of
sand necessary to accomplish this would be
truly colossal.

17. Stephen G. Miller, "Turns and Lanes in
the Ancient Stadium," *American Journal of
Archaeology*, Vol. 84, pp. 164.

18. The floor of the stadium at Olympia
measured 212 meters by 32 meters. Converting
to imperial measurements this amounts to
73,038 square feet. One quarter inch of sand
covering this surface would require 1,521.62
cubic feet of sand. The standard weight of a
cubic foot of dry sand is 100 pounds requiring
152,162 pounds or 76.08 tons. It is perplexing
that some modern scholars have claimed that
the Olympic track was sanded and rolled.

19. The surface of a modern day track (400
meters × 8 lanes of 4 feet each) is a bit more
complicated but it works out to approximately
46,000 square feet. Using a 9 lane straight-
away and some runoff this works to approximately 49,000 square feet. Thus the surface of
the ancient stadium was nearly 50 percent
larger.

20. Sweet, p. 87.

21. Miller, p. 166.

22. See, for example, E.N. Gardiner, *Greek
Athletic Sports and Festivals*, London: Macmillan, 1910, p. 226, and H.A. Harris, "Stadia
and Starting Grooves," *Greece and Rome*, Vol.
7, 1960, p. 30. Neither considers the time consumed in roping a lane 200 meters long, nor
how much rope would have been required to
do so at Olympia, where there were 21 starting
positions. This would require over 2½ miles
of rope and organizers would have run into the
same problems modern organizers have of
worker rope games. Having participated in the
famous Fairfield, PA "brick-pulling contest,"
where competitors are required to pull a brick,

attached to one mile of rope, the problem is not the weight of the brick. It is, conversely, how much a mile of rope weighs. Gardiner and Harris obviously had no experience marking out more than two miles of roped lanes.

23. Initially the *cathedra* held about 10 or 12 chairs on a raised platform. Subsequently it was fitted with several rows of stone seats for more than 100 judges and guests. In the later Roman stadium the *cathedra* accommodated 500 people.

24. Nigel B. Crowther, "Resolving an Impasse: Draws, Dead Heats and Similar Decisions in Greek Athletics," *Nikephoros*, Vol. 13, 2000, p. 134.

25. The major proponents here are H.A. Harris and, more recently, Donald F. Jackson. See, for example, Harris, "The Method of Deciding Victory in the Pentathlon," *Greece and Rome*, Vol. 19, No. 1, April 1972, pp. 60–64, and Donald F. Jackson, "Philostratos and the Pentathlon," *Journal of Hellenic Studies*, Vol. 111, 1991, pp. 178–181.

26. Donald G. Kyle, *Sport and Spectacle in the Ancient World*, 2007, Malden, MA, Blackwell, p. 123.

27. This is a distinct possibility but one that has never shown up in the literature.

Chapter 8

1. Kl Palaeologos, in Maria Koursi, ed., *The Olympic Games in Ancient Greece*, Athens, Ekdotike Athenon, 2003, p. 211.

2. Waldo E. Sweet, *Sport and Rrecreation in Ancient Greece: A Sourcebook with Translations*, New York, Oxford University Press, 1987, p. 22.

3. Ludwig Drees, *Olympia: Gods, Artists and Athletes*, New York: Praeger, 1968 (trans. G. Ohn), p. 72.

4. Ibid., pp. 279–80.

5. The *skamma* had no standard size but also accommodated the boxers and pankrationists.

6. See, for example, Steve G. Bazarnic, "The Ancient Pentathlon and Aspects of the Greek Ideal," unpublished master's thesis, Penn State University, 1970, p. 65.

7. Sweet, p. 38.

8. The combat sports at Olympia were boxing, wrestling and the pankration, a sort of no holds barred melee.

9. See W.W. Hyde, *Olympic Victor Monuments and Greek Athletic Art*, Washington: Carnegie Institute, 1921, p. 361. Hyde suggests that the Altis was always crowded, ultimately reaching about 500 monuments, statues or busts.

10. Stephen G Miller, *Ancient Greek Athletics*, New Haven, Yale University Press, 2004, p. 47.

11. Ibid., pp. 218–19.

12. The 2000 USA Olympic Track and Field Trials in Sacramento provided an accommodating example. Dan Steele, now the track and field coach at the University of Northern Iowa and then a terrific decathlete, was virtually tied with one Kip Janvrin, Warrensburg, MO, whose endurance skills were legendary. "All I had to do to make the U.S. Olympic team was beat Kip ... no way.... I faced an impossible task," he would say right after the final event. He didn't. It must have been much the same in ancient Greece when pentathletes came up against champion wrestlers to win the overall title.

13. Sweet, *Sourcebook*, pp. 56.

14. Donald G. Kyle, "Winning and Watching the Greek Pentathlon," *Journal of Sport History*, Vol. 17, No. 3 (Winter 1990), p. 305.

Chapter 9

1. Scholars of ancient history conventionally end the Archaic period and begin the Classical period with the second Persian invasion (480 B.C.). The Classical Period ends with the death of Alexander the Great (323 B.C.) while the Hellenistic period is usually terminated with the Roman sack and burning of Corinth in 146 B.C. The short period called Greco-Roman begins here and ends in 27 B.C. with the emergence of Caesar Augustus as emperor of Rome, which starts the Roman Empire or Imperial period. The fact is that the pentathlon even outlasted Imperial Rome.

2. The legendary founding date of the city of Rome is 753 B.C., about the same time we are told the pentathlon was created. Greece ceased to be a major player in the Roman world in the 2nd century B.C., and the (western) Roman Empire fell in A.D. 476. We know that Greek athletic festivals were still in existence in the early part of the 6th century A.D.

3. See Peter Levi (trans.), *Pausanias: Guide to Greece*, Vol. 2 (Southern Greece), New York: Penguin Books, 1971.

4. See, for example, http://timeline.com/list events.php?subjid153&title=Greece 9/26/09.

5. See Paul Christesen, *Olympic Victor Lists and Ancient Greek History*, Cambridge, Cambridge University Press, 2007, pp. 50, 72, 159–60, 479–80.

6. See Cleanthis Paleologos, *Olympic Review*, Legends of Olympia VI (series), "Philombrotos of Sparta the Pentathlist," 1974, No. 74, pp. 39–43.

7. The statue of Eutelidas could have been as much as 700 years old when Pausanias saw it in the early part of the 2nd century A.D.

8. This does not apply to the javelin which, as far as we know, remained wooden throughout antiquity. Nor do we maintain that stone implements disappeared. We have plenty of artistic evidence that stone *haltere* were in use during the 5th century.

9. See Paul Christesen, "The Transformation of Athletics in Sixth-Century Greece," in Gerald P. Schuaus and Stephen R. Wenn, eds., *Onward to the Olympics: Historical Perspectives on the Olympic Games*: Toronto: Laurier Press, 2007, p. 63.

10. Ibid., pp. 63–64.

11. Only one modern scholar, Victor Matthews, has suggested that Hieronymous won only one of the first three events, another unknown athlete won another and then both reached the *stade* and lost to Tisamenos. He posits that Hieronymous then won a semi-final wrestling bout and then the overall pentathlon by winning the wrestling final. As we have shown earlier, this could not have happened. For Matthews see "The Greek Pentathlon Again," *Zeitschrift für Papyrologie und Epigraphik* Vol. 100, 1994, p. 135.

12. See David C. Young, *The Olympic Myth of Greek Amateur Athletics*, Chicago, Ares, 1984, p. 12.

13. Ibid., p. 12. One can also consult H.A. Harris, *Sport in Greece and Rome*, Cornell University Press, Ithaca, NY, 1972.

14. Harris' understanding of track and field was rather weak and his observations on biomechanics were as unconvincing as the fiction of a 55 foot leap.

15. See David G. Romano, *Athletics and Mathematics in Ancient Corinth: The Origins of the Greek Stadium*, Philadelphia: American Philosophical Society, 1993, pp. 17–33. In this work Romano tells us that he literally counted the number of spaces at various stadiums, including those at Olympic and Corinth.

16. See Rudolf Knab, *Die Periodoniken: in Beitrag zur Gestchicte der gymnischen Agone an den 4 griechischen Hauptfesten*, Chicago, Ares, 1934.

17. See Reinhold Merkelbach,"Der Fünfkämpfer Nikoladas," *Zeitschrift für Papyrologie und Epigraphik*, Bd. 67 (1987), pp. 293–295, published by Dr. Rudolf Habelt GmbH, Bonn, Germany.

18. See Chapter 13 for a monetary evaluation of the prizes at Athens.

19. See Victor Matthews, "The Greek Pentathlon Again," *Zeitschrift für Papyrologie und Epigraphik*, Vol. 100, 1994, pp. 134–35.

20. This is the 9th of the 15 surviving odes

of Baccylides. For all of his works see Robert Fagles, trans., *Bacchylides, Complete Poems*, New Haven: Yale University Press, 1961, pp. 25.

21. Matthew Dillon, *Girls and Women in Classical Greek Religion*, London, Routledge, 2002, p. 200–201.

22. There are excellent marble copies of *Doryphoros* at the National Museum in Naples and the Uffizi Gallery at Florence.

23. The 42 foot statue was completed about 435 B.C. and depicted Zeus seated on a huge throne. A 1958 excavation uncovered Phidias's workshop at Olympia. A drinking cup found there was inscribed with the words "I belong to Phidias."

24. See Paul Pissanos, *448 B.C. Olympiad*, Arcadia Group, Athens, 2003. There is a 90 minute English version DVD which re-enacts the 448 B.C. Games.

25. David Greenburg, *The Construction of Homosexuality*, Chicago, University of Chicago Press, 1988, p. 145. The issue of homosexuality in athletics is dealt with in "Judaism and Homosexuality: A New Response for a New Reality," by Bradley Shavit Artson, *Tikkun*, March-April 1988, pp. 52–54.

26. See Cleanthis Paleologos, *Olympic Review*, Legends of Olympia IX (series), "Hysmon of Elis Pentathlist," No. 80, 1974, pp. 358–362.

27. Mark Golden, *Sport in the Ancient World from A to Z*, London, Routledge, 2004 , p. 159.

28. Victor lists for the previous century reveal that athletes from Elis won 19 Olympic titles in a dozen different events (three in the pentathlon). For the next 56 years Eleans won only 5 Olympic wreaths, all in boxing: Asamon in 340, Satyron, 332, Pyttalos, 320, Choirilos, 316, and Theotimos, 308. See Nicolaos Yalouris, *The Eternal Olympics: The Art and History of Sport*, New Rochelle, Caratzas Brothers, 1979, pp. 289–296.

29. See, for example *The Economy of Ancient Greece*, by Darel Tai Engen, California State University–San Marcos, http://eh.net/encyclopedia/article/engren.greece (October 19, 2009).

30. Hyperides (2009), Encyclopædia Britannica. Retrieved October 23, 2009, from *Encyclopædia Britannica Online*: http://www.britannica.com/EBchecked/topic/279598/Hyperides.

31. See Lynn E. Roller, "Funeral Games for Historical Persons," *Stadion*, Vol. 7, 1981, p. 9.

32. See Mark Golden, *Sport in the Ancient World from A to Z*, London, Routledge, 2004, p. 72.

33. In describing the types of statues at Olympia, Hyde tells us that before the 5th century statues were "types," that is, clones, like Hermes or Herakles, with distinguishing features representing various contests, for example, helmet, halters or disci. See Walter Woodburn Hyde, *Olympic Victor Monuments and Greek Athletic Art*, Washington, D.C.: Carnegie Institution of Washington, 1921 pentathlon, pp. 210–214.

34. For a discussion of the epigram in question and the mistaken interpretation by Harris, see H.A. Harris, "Notes on Three Athletic Inscriptions," *The Journal of Hellenic Studies*, Vol. 82 (1962), pp. 19–24.

35. See Mark Golden, *Sport in the Ancient World from A to Z*, London, Routledge, 2004, p. 50.

36. See H.W. Pleket, "Mass-Sport and Local Infrastructure in the Greek Cities of Roman Asia Minor," *Stadion*, Vol. 24, No. 1, 1998, p. 155.

37. See Onno van Nijf, "Athletics and *Paideia*: Festivals and Physical Education in the World of the Second Sophistic," in *The World of the Second Sophistic*, Barbara Borg, ed., Berlin: Walter de Gruyter, 2004, pp. 203–228.

38. See, for example, Barbara Schrodt, "Sports in the Byzantine Empire," *Journal of Sport History*, Vol. 9, No. 3, 1981, pp. 40–59. Schrodt suggests that athletics festivals were not eliminated in 393. Meets were still held into the 6th century C.E. The Justinian code of 528 still carried a regulation that exempted from civil obligations those athletes who had won at least three wreaths at a sacred festival (p. 55).

39. The number five is used here as a matter of convenience and is useful since I try not to overstate the case. I have assumed that the ancient pentathlon field was typically small, five athletes. It is likely that the average field was larger, especially at the numerically dominant local games. If it was as high as, say, ten, my final estimates would double to one million athletes. I also assume that the typical career pentathlete's career was five meets, which is what is it is for modern day decathletes. Our 5/5 assumption then makes the number of ancient competitions and the number of athletes the same.

40. There are several "Olympic" references in the New Testament, mostly in the letters from Paul, who was educated and wrote in Greek.

41. See Mark Golden, *Sport in the Ancient World from A to Z*, London: Routledge, p. 62.

42. See Matthew Dillon and Lynda Garland, *Ancient Greece: Social and Historical Documents: From Archaic Times to the Death of Alexander the Great*, 3rd ed., London: Routledge, 2010, p. 57.

43. See Labib Boutros, *Phoenician Sport: Its Influence on the Origin of the Olympic Games*, Amsterdam: J.C. Gieben,, 1981, pp. 120–121.

44. If one examines the athletic careers of both Owens and Lewis one finds that there were both outstanding "multiple-event" athletes but not "combined event" athletes. In fact neither, in their rather lengthy careers, ever competed in a combined event (decathlon, heptathlon, pentathlon, any 'athlon") meet. See career biographies: Tony Gentry, *Jesse Owens: Champion Athlete*. New York: Chelsea House Publishers, 1990; or Jacqueline Edmondson, *Jesse Owens: A Biography*, Santa Barbara, CA, Greenwood, 2007; and Carl Lewis and Jeffrey Marx, *Inside Track: My Professional Life in Amateur Track and Field*. New York: Simon and Schuster, 1990.

45. The issue of pentathlete "type" is brought up often in scholarly writing. See, for example, Victor Matthews, "The Greek Pentathlon Again," *Zeitschrift für Papyrologie und Epigraphik*, Vol. 100, 1994, pp. 134–135.

Chapter 10

1. The appropriate professional groups are the international Association of Track and Field Statisticians (ATFS) and the American Federation of American Statisticians of Track (FAST).

2. Even though most winners came from Kos or local areas like Rhodes or Halicarnassus.

3. There may be no better modern example of local bias than the 1904 Olympic Games in St. Louis where, of the 112 athletes who competed, 85 were Americans, who won 61 (93 percent) of the 65 medals in athletics. The view that American athletes dominate the modern Games is still skewed by these numbers.

4. See, for example, Hans van Kuijen series, Combined Events Annuals (1993 to 2009), Helmond, NED.

5. See annuals provided by ATFS, FAST or van Kuijen.

6. For example, we know that Hieronymous of Andros defeated Tisamenos of Elis, three events to two at Olympia in 492 B.C.

7. The "reported" long jump marks of Phayllos of Croton and Chionis of Sparta are disregarded as highly unreliable.

8. See Rudolph Knab, *Die Periodoniken*, Chicago, Ares, 1934. Knab established that no

evidence shows any ancient pentathlete won crowns at all four ancient festivals (Olympic, Pythian, Isthmian, Nemean).

9. For the issue of Greek record keeping, see M.N. Tod, "Greek Record Keeping and Record Breaking," *Classical Quarterly*, Vol. 43, 1949, pp. 105–112, and David Young, "First with the Most: Greek Athletic Records and "Specialization," *Nikephoros* 9, 1996, pp. 175–197. The most recent discussion on Greek athletic record keeping is provided in Paul Christesen, *Olympic Victor Lists and Ancient Greek History*, Cambridge, Cambridge University Press, 2007, pp. 50, 72, 94, 108–183.

10. Most of the Isthmian victor lists can be found in Vol. 8 of the Corinth excavation reports (8.1 #14–20 and 8.3 #223, #228). Two others have been published separately in Hesperia 28 (1959): 324 and 39 (1970): 79–93. David Jordan has recently published lead tablets from Isthmia dating to the Roman era that contain judges' votes on the eligibility of contestants (Jordan, 1994).

Chapter 11

1. Some of the earliest statues were wood carvings and have not survived.

2. Pausanias, *Guide to Greece*, Vol. 2, translated by Peter Levi, New York: Penguin, 1971.

3. W.W. Hyde, *Olympic Victor Monuments and Greek Athletic Art*, Washington, D.C.: Carnegie Institute, 1921, p. 361. After interpolation of 494 monuments, Hyde suggests that this "number cannot be far from the actual number of victor statues adorning the Altis."

4. Ibid., p. 210.

5. Pausanias describes the statue of Hysmon, so we know it carried jumping weights. But he does not identify the statue of Anauchidas and it is uncertain why Hyde knows that it bore the weights. See Hyde, p. 214 and fn. 6.

6. Standing discus thrower *Discobolos* by Naukydes, circa 420–400 B.C. It was found in 1771 by David Hamilton in the "Galliens-Villa" on the Appian Way. It is now located in the Vatican Museum, Rome, Italy.

7. Hyde, p. 55. Unfortunately Hyde identifies Gorgos as a four time *pankration* winner (fn. 6 on p. 55), but is correct that Gorgos also won the hoplite race and another unknown running event at Olympia.

8. See reference to same statue in chapter 9. Also, see Pausanias, *Guide to Greece*, Vol. 2, translated by Peter Levi, New York: Penguin, 1971.

Chapter 12

1. C.M. Bowra, *Greek Lyric Poetry: From Alcman to Simonides*, Oxford: Clarendon Press, 1961, p. 9.

2. For a full treatment on the importance and development of the victory ode see Mary R. Lefkowitz, *The Victory Ode: An Introduction*, Park Ridge, NJ: Noyes Press, 1976.

3. The two Pindaric odes presented here were translated and published by Ernest Myers, a fellow at Wadham College, Oxford, as *The Extant Odes of Pindar*, London: Macmillan, 1904. They were among the earliest English translations of Pindaric odes. The first edition appeared in 1874 and was reprinted with corrections in 1884, 1888, 1892, 1895, 1899, and 1904. The translations come from Project Gutenberg e-book *The Extant Odes of Pindar*.

4. Ibid., pp. 233–244. The date of Pindar's 7th Nemean Ode is not certain. Conway suggests it may have been as early as 485 B.C. and as late as approximately 460 B.C. See Geoffrey S. Conway, trans., *The Odes of Pindar*, London, J.M. Dent, pp. xxx, 201–209.

5. Robert Fagles, trans., *Bacchylides, Complete Poems*, New Haven: Yale University Press, 1961, pp. 23–26.

6. H.A. Harris, *Greek Athletes and Athletics*, Bloomington, IN: University of Indiana Press, 1966, p. 79.

7. Tom McNab, *Decathlon*, London: British Amateur Athletic Board, 1972, p. 6.

8. Bowra, pp. 310–312.

9. See, for example, Deborah Boedeker and David Sider, eds., *Simonides: Context of Praise and Desire*, Oxford: Oxford University Press, 2001, p. 76.

10. Ibid., pp. 315–16.

Chapter 13

1. H.W. Pleket, "Games, Prizes, Athletes and Ideology: Some Aspects of the History of Sport in the Greco-Roman World," *Stadion*, Vol. 1, No. 1, 1975, p. 79.

2. The classification of Greek games is a knotty semantic problem that should not worry us here. For a good, brief description see H.W. Pleket, "Games, Prizes, Athletes and Ideology," *Stadion*, Vol. 1, No. 1, 1975, pp. 49–89.

3. Ulrich Sinn, *Olympia: Cult, Sport and Ancient Festival*, Markus Wiener, Princeton, 2000, trans. Thomas Thornton, p. 9. Sinn's universally accepted list of wreaths differs from that of one writer who claims that a branch of dried celery was the prize at Nemea. See Judith Swaddling, *The Ancient Olympic*

Games, 2nd ed., Austin, University of Texas Press, 1999, p. 94.

4. Ludwig Drees, *Olympia: Gods, Artists and Athletes*, New York, Praeger, 1968, p. 106.

5. Although the Olympic victor lists are spotty, Athenians won but 14 times in the 300 year period, from 600 to 300 B.C., about once every 20 years. In the later 600-plus year period (296 B.C. to A.D. 369), the surviving (remember: very incomplete) victor lists identify only two Olympic winners from Athens. Solon's law was hardly a tax burden on Athenian citizens.

6. If one assumes 250 working days per year (5 day per week for 5 weeks, two weeks' vacation), and a day laborer in the USA in 2000 earns $25,000 per annum, then a denari in today's terms is worth, at a minimum, $100.00.

7. H.A. Harris, *Greek Athletes and Athletics*, Westport, CT, Greenwood Press, 1964, p. 42.

8. I am using a value of $21 per denarius, a very conservative estimate. Classical historians regularly say that in the early days of the Roman Empire the daily wage for an unskilled laborer and common soldier was 1 denarius without tax, or about $21 in 2009 dollars. A reminder: it is always awkward to give even ballpark comparative values for money from before the 20th century.

9. Donald G. Kyle, *Athletics in Ancient Athens*, Leiden, E.J. Brill, 1987, p. 37.

10. Stephen V. Tracy, "The Panathenaic Festival and Games: An Epigraphic Inquiry," *Nikephoros*, Vol. 4, 1991, p. 143. p. 182.

11. Bureau of Labor Statistics, U.S. Dept. of Labor, www.bea/gov.Table 1. Summary: Mean hourly earnings (1) and weekly hours for selected worker and establishment characteristics. July 2009.

12. See David C. Young, *The Olympic Myth of Greek Amateur Athletics*, Chicago, Ares, 1984, pp. 115–127, for estimates of the value of prizes for all Panathenaic events.

13. For a good description and examples of career changes, see Tony Perrottet, *The Naked Olympics*, New York, Random House, 2004.

Chapter 14

1. Much of this chapter is adapted from two sources, both written by the author. See *Decathlon: A Colorful History of Track and Field's Most Challenging Event*, Champaign, Leisure Press, 1989, Chapters 2 and 3, and *All-Around Men: A History of a Forgotten Sport*, Lanham, Scarecrow, 2005. The reader is particularly directed to the first three chapters of

the latter volume, which covers the early modern history of track and field and the development of combined events.

2. Before the 1880s the common spelling of these tests of versatility was the adjective "all-round." Americans turned it into a noun, the "all-around."

3. It is often reported that the first modern combined event was the "general competition" or "pentathlon" concocted by Brookes. In fact Highland and German experiments preceded it. So did an 1866 offering by London's National Olympian Association. See *Bell's Life of London* and *Sporting Life* (London), both Aug. 4, 1866. The event ended in a tie, apparently with no procedure to break it. What is more interesting is the selection of Brooke's events. The long jump had a Classical Greek heritage. The 32 pound shot (one toss with each hand, distances summed) and high jump can be traced to the Scots. The rope climb was a favorite event of the German Turner movement and English rural festivals. There seems to be no explanation for the 880 yard hurdles race. See Sam Mullins, *British Olympians: William Penny Brookes and the Wenlock Games*, Birmingham, British Olympic Association, 1992, pp. 17–21, and David Young, *The Modern Olympics: A Struggle for Revival*, Baltimore, Johns Hopkins University Press, 1996, p. 198.

4. I am indebted to Rooney Magnusson's combined events research, which tells us that the first "modern" ancient pentathlon was held on June 14, 1891, on the bicycle course at Bygdoy in Oslo (then called Kristiana), Norway. The events were the long jump, javelin, 100 (yds/m?) shot put and wrestling. The shot put replaced the discus, which was unknown in Norway at that time. A year later 200m replaced the 100m, and discus replaced the shot put, putting in place all the ancient components. A Swede, Harald Andersson, won all events. This affair became a national championship from 1896 to 1905.

5. This was obviously influenced by scholars attempting to explain the 55 foot jump by Phayllos. See Chapter 5.

6. See David Young, *The Modern Olympics: A Struggle for Revival*, Baltimore, Johns Hopkins University Press, 1996, p. 216.

7. See Frank Zarnowski, "Early Olympic Games" section of Chapter 3 of *The Decathlon: A Colorful History of Track and Field's Most Challenging Event*, Champaign, Leisure Press, 1989, pp. 31–32. The Paris pentathlon was actually a four event contest and athletes were to have a choice of events as follows: 100 or 400 meters; 800 or 1500 meters; high jump, pole vault or long jump; shot put or discus. Scoring is uncertain.

8. In 1906 all Irish athletes, from a nation yet to gain independence from Britain, had the choice of wearing the Union Jack of Britain or not competing. Most chose not to compete. The world's best known all-around athlete at the time was still Kiely, who found it inconceivable to represent Britain.

9. It is now common knowledge that the headless nude statue of the perfect male which now stands in front of the Los Angeles Coliseum (built in 1922) is that of Sheridan.

10. The accepted wisdom of the day was that the ancient Greeks had thrown the discus from a sloping (toward the landing area) platform. Young has shown this notion to be the result of faulty scholarship and no such pedestal was ever used in ancient Greece. Nevertheless, for the 1906 and 1908 Olympic Games, a "Greek-style" discus was offered both as an open event and as part of the pentathlon.

11. I am indebted to Swedish expert Rooney Magnusson for his research on the Mellander-Lemming issue and for providing documentation from Swedish magazine sources which quoted Lemming as saying, "I let myself be defeated (in the final wrestling match) to arrange the gold medal for Sweden."

12. In 1909 there were 35 minor leagues operating in the United States and well over 4000 minor league players. Any collegian who wanted to get lost in the system could.

13. Irina and Tamara were Ukrainian athletes. Irina joined the KGB upon retirement and became an officer in the border troops. She died in 2004.

Chapter 15

1. Legend has it that Myron's opinion of his own strength led to his death. As the story goes, he freed an animal trapped in a split tree which snapped back on him and he was unable to escape. Trapped, he was eaten by animals. Jordan's decision to switch to baseball in the middle of a successful basketball career illustrated that his specific basketball skills were not transferable to baseball.

2. At times, pre–1920, the *Philadelphia Inquirer* would claim that the winner of the Penn Relays pentathlon had scored a record "5 points" and mistakenly compared it with Jim Thorpe's 1912 winning Olympic score of 7. Using this system, in fact, no scores are comparable.

3. The technical difference between the 60 minute decathlon and the one hour decathlon depends on its conduct and the order of events. In all "timed" decathlons the final event must be started (not completed) within a certain time.

4. All modern day Olympic decathlon or heptathlon champions.

Appendix D

1. See, for example Panos Valavanis (trans. David Hardy), *Games and Sanctuaries in Ancient Greece*, Los Angeles, Getty, 2004, p. 406. Valavanis tells us that Antioch paid a hefty franchise fee to the Eleans in A.D. 124 for the right to celebrate a isolympian games (which included a pentathlon). Antioch was a large and wealthy pagan city and the people of Antioch refused to abandon their festival when other pagan sanctuaries were closed down. They had paid a considerable sum for the rights to hold their festival. Byzantine emperors found their argument reasonable and were unwilling to risk the city ire. Thus, we do not know the last pentathlete of antiquity, but we do know that he was a pagan. The end came in A.D. 520 with a decree by Justin I ending all things pagan.

2. The pentathlon spread to Rome during the days of the Empire. We know that the pentathlon was part of, for example, the Sebasta (in honor of Augustus) isolympic games in the second century A.D. And, in 86 B.C. Domitian founded the Capitoleia in Rome which continued until the beginning of the 4th century A.D. Yet the number of Greek style games remained relatively small in the west. The great explosion of Greek festivals came in the east.

3. See H.A. Harris, *Greek Athletes and Athletics*, Westport, CT, Greenwood Press, 1964, Map 4, unpaged.

4. See Wolfgang Leschhorn, *Die kaiserzeitliche Muenzpraegung in Phrygien*, Munich, 1997.

5. See, for example, H.W. Pleket, "Mass-Sport and Local Infrastructure in the Greek Cities of Roman Asia Minor," *Stadion*, Vol. 24, No. 1, 1998, pp. 151–172.

6. For an excellent description of the reach of crown and local games, see Valavanis, pp. 286–409.

Appendix F

1. Pausanias, *Guide to Greece*, Vol. 2, translated by Peter Levi, New York: Penguin, 1971, pp. 290–337. Described by Pausanias. Page number listed on left. By my count Pausanias describes 17 victors who won a total of 21 pentathlons at Olympia (15/19). This list includes Eutelidas, who won the only boys' pentathlon at Olympia in 628 B.C.

Bibliography

With the exception of the "General" and "Specific" categories, this bibliography, organized by topic, is either distinctive or related to the ancient pentathlon and lists all of the research used by the author. There are, of course, other thorough reviews of the literature on ancient athletics, and three that I recommend are:

Crowther, Nigel B. "Studies in Greek Athletics," *The Classical World*, Vol. 79, No. 2, 1985.
Robinson, Rachel S. *Sources for the History of Greek Athletics in English Translation*, Chicago: Ares, 1927.
Scanlon, Thomas F. *Greek and Roman Athletics: A Bibliography*. Chicago, Ares, 1984.

General Works

Barnes, Ian. "Mapping History," *Ancient World*. London: Cartographica, 2007.
Cahill, Thomas. *Sailing the Wine Dark Sea*. New York: Anchor Books, Random House, 2004.
Cartledge, Paul. *Thermpolae: The Battle That Changed the World*. New York: Vintage Books, Random House, 2006.
Dillon, Matthew. *Girls and Women in Classical Greek Religion*. London: Routledge, 2002.
Feeney, Dennis. *Caesar's Calendar: Ancient Time and the Beginning of History*. Berkeley: University of California Press, 2007.
Fox, Robin Lane. *Traveling Heroes in the Epic Age of Homer*. New York: Knopf, 2009.
Hodkinson, Stephen, and Anton Powell. *Sparta: New Perspectives*. Classical Press of Wales, 2009.
Matyszak, Philip. *Ancient Athens on Five Drachmas a Day*. New York: Thames and Hudson, 2008.
Roberts, J.M. *A Short History of the World*. New York: Oxford University Press, 1993.
Warner, Rex (trans.). *Thucydides: History of the Peloponnesian Wars*. New York: Penguin, 1954.

General Works on Ancient Sport

Andronicos, Manolis. *Olympia*. Athens: Ekdotike Athenon S.A., 1983.
Boutros, Labib. *Phoenician Sport: Its Influence on the Origin of the Olympic Games*. Amsterdam: J.C. Gieben, 1981.
Christesen, Paul. *Olympic Victor Lists and Ancient Greek History*. Cambridge: Cambridge University Press, 2007.
Coulsen, William, et al., eds. *Proceedings of an International Symposium on the Olympic Games*. Athens, 1992.
Cousineau, Phil. *The Olympic Odyssey: Rekindling the True Spirit of the Great Games*. Wheaton, IL: Theosophical Society, 2003.
Craig, Steve. *Sports and Games of the Ancients*. Westport, CT: Greenwood Press, 2002.
Diem, Carl. *Weltgeschichte des Sports*, Book 1. Stuttgart: Cotta Verlag, 1867.
Drees, Ludwig. G. Ohn, trans. *Olympia: Gods, Artists and Athletes*. New York: Praeger, 1968.
Durantez, Conrado. "The Games of Antiquity Face Up to History: Part I, Olympia Under Roman Law." http://www.la84foundation.org/OlympicInformationCenter/OlympicReview/1989/ore255/ore255z.pdf.

Finley, M.I., and H.W. Pleket. *The Olympic Games: The First Thousand Years*. New York: Viking, 1976.
Gardiner, E.N. *Athletics of the Ancient World*. Oxford: Clarendon, 1930.
Gardiner, Norman. *Greek Athletic Sports and Festivals*. London: Macmillan, 1910.
Golden, Mark. *Greek Sport and Social Status*. Austin: University of Texas Press, 2008.
_____. *Sport and Society in Ancient Greece*. Cambridge: Cambridge University Press, 1998,
_____. *Sport in the Ancient World from A to Z*. London: Routledge, 2004.
Harris, H.A. *Greek Athletes and Athletics*. Westport, CT: Greenwood Press, 1964.
_____. *Greek Athletes and Athletics*. Bloomington: IN: University Press, 1966.
Harris, H.A. *Sport in Greece and Rome*. Ithaca, NY: Cornell University Press, 1972.
Jüthner, Julius. *Philostratus über Gymnastik*. Leipzig: Teubner, 1909.
Koursi, Maria, ed. *The Olympic Games in Ancient Greece*. Athens, Ekdotike Athenon, 2003.
Kyle, Donald G. *Athletics in Ancient Athens*. Leiden: E.J. Brill, 1987.
_____. *Sport and Spectacle in the Ancient World*. Malden, MA: Blackwell, 2007.
Merasham, Terrence, Elisabeth Spathari, and Paul Donnelly. *1000 Years of Olympic Games: Treasures of Ancient Greece*. Sydney: Powerhouse, 2000.
Miller, Stephen G. *Ancient Greek Athletics*. New Haven: Yale University Press, 2004.
_____. *Arete: Ancient Writers, Papyri, and Inscriptions on the History and Ideals of Greek Athletics and Games*. Chicago: Ares, 1979.
_____, ed. *Arete: Greek Sports from Ancient Sources*. Berkeley: University of California Press, 1991.
Newby, Zahra. *Athletics in the Ancient World*. London: Bristol Classical Press, 2006.
_____. *Greek Athletics in the Roman World*. New York: Oxford University Press, 2005.
Olivová, Věra. *Sports and Games in the Ancient World*. New York: St. Martin's Press, 1984.
O'Rielly, John Boyle. *Athletics and Manly Sport*. Boston: Pilot, 1890 (1888 edition had the title of *Ethics of Boxing and Manly Sport*).
Perrottet, Tony. *The Naked Olympics*. New York: Random House, 2004.
Raschke, Wendy J., ed. *The Archaeology of the Olympics: The Olympics and Other Festivals in Antiquity*. Madison: University of Wisconsin Press, 1988.
Romano, David Gilman. *Athletics and Mathematics in Archaic Corinth: The Origins of the Greek Stadion*. Philadelphia: American Philosophical Society, 1993.
Scanlon, Thomas. *Eros and Greek Athletics*. New York: Oxford University Press, 2002.
Schöbel, Heinz. *The Ancient Games*. Princeton: Van Nostrand, 1965.
Schuaus, Gerald P., and Stephen R. Wenn, eds. *Onward to the Olympics: Historical Perspectives on the Olympic Games*. Toronto: Laurier Press, 2007.
Sinn, Ulrich. Thomas Thornton, trans. *Olympia: Cult, Sport and Ancient Festival*. Princeton: Markus Wiener, 2000.
Swaddling, Judith. *The Ancient Olympic Games*. London: British Museum, 1980.
_____. *The Ancient Olympic Games*. Austin: University of Texas Press, 1999.
Sweet, Waldo E. *Sport and Recreation in Ancient Greece: A Sourcebook with Translations*. New York: Oxford University Press, 1987.
Tyrrell, William Blake. *The Smell of Sweat: Greek Athletics, Olympics and Culture*. Wauconda, IL: Bolchazy-Carducci, 2004.
Weeber, Karl-Wilhelm. *The Unholy Games: Ancient Olympia Between Legend and Reality*. Patmos Verlag, 2000.
Yalouris, Nicolaos. *The Eternal Olympics*. New Rochelle, NY: Karatzas Brothers, 1979.
Young, David C. *A Brief History of the Olympic Games*. Malden, MA: Blackwell, 2004.
_____. *The Olympic Myth of Greek Amateur Athletics*. Chicago: Ares, 1984.

Books on Specific Issues

Alexander, Christine. *Greek Athletics*. New York: Metropolitan Museum of Art, 1925.
Bowra, C.M. *Greek Lyric Poetry: From Alcam to Simonides*. Oxford: Oxford University Press, 1961.
Conway, Geoffrey C. (trans.). *The Odes of Pindar*. London: Dent, 1972.
Conway, G.S., and Richard Stoneman, eds. *Pindar: The Odes and Selected Fragments*. London: Everyman, 1998.
Davidson, James. *The Greeks and Greek Love*. New York: Random House, 2007.
Ebert, Joachim. *Zum Pentathlon Der Antike*. Berlin: Akademie-Verlag, 1963.

Fagles, Robert, trans. *Bacchylides: Complete Poems*. New Haven: Yale University Press, 1961.
Feeney, Dennis. *Caesar's Calendar: Ancient Time and the Beginning of History*. Berkeley: University of California Press, 2007.
Georgopoulos, Maria, et al., eds. *Following Pausinias: The Quest for Greek Antiquity*. Kotinos: Oak Knoll Press, 2007.
Hyde, Walter Woodburn. *Olympic Victor Monuments and Greek Athletic Art*. Washington, DC: Carnegie Institution of Washington, 1921.
Kennett, David. *Olympia: Warrior Athletes of Ancient Greece* (Illustrations). New York: Walker, 2002.
Klee, Theophil. *Zur Geschichte der Gymnischen Agone an Griechischen Festen*. Chicago: Ares, 1980 [reprint of 1918 Leipzig Berlin edition].
Knab, Rudolph. *Die Periodoniken*. Chicago: Ares, 1934.
Lefkowitz, Mary R. *The Victory Ode: An Introduction*. Park Ridge, NJ: Noyes, 1976.
Levi, Peter, trans. *Pausanias: Guide to Greece*. Vol. 2, *Southern Greece*. New York: Penguin, 1971.
Moon, Warren. *Polykleitos, the Doryphoros, and Tradition*. Madison: University of Wisconsin Press, 1995.
Pollard, Justin. *The Story of Archaeology: In 50 Great Discoveries*. London: Quercus, 2007.
Valavanis, Panos. David Hardy, trans. *Games and Sanctuaries in Ancient Greece*. Los Angeles: Getty, 2004.

Journal Articles

Pentathlon

Bean, George E. "Victory in the Pentathlon," *American Journal of Archaeology*, Vol. 60, No. 4 (October 1956), pp. 361–368.
Gardiner, E.N. "The Method of Deciding the Pentathlon," *The Journal of Hellenic Studies*, Vol. 23 (1903), pp. 54–70.
_____. "The System of the Pentathlon," *The Journal of Hellenic Studies*, Vol. 45, Part I (1925), pp. 132–134.
Gardner, P. "The Pentathlon of the Greeks," *Journal of Hellenic Studies*, Vol. 1 (1880), pp. 210–223.
Harris, H.A. "The Method of Deciding Victory in the Pentathlon," *Greece and Rome*, Vol. 19, Number 1 (April 1972), pp. 60–64.
Highmore, George. "The Victor of the Greek Pentathlon," *Folklore*, Vol. 67, No. 3 (September 1956), pp. 129–141.
Kyle, Donald G. "Winning and Watching the Greek Pentathlon," *Journal of Sport History*, Vol. 17, No. 3 (Winter 1990), pp. 291–305.
Langdon, Merle K. "Scoring the Ancient Pentathlon: The Final Solution," *Zeitschrift für Papyrologie und Epigraphik*, Vol. 78 (1989), pp. 117–118.
Lee, Hugh M. "Yet Another Scoring System for the Ancient Pentathlon," *Nikephoros*, Vol. 8 (1995), pp. 41–55.
Matthews, Victor. "The Greek Pentathlon Again," *Zeitschrift für Papyrologie und Epigraphik*, Vol. 100 (1994), pp. 129–138.
Myers, Ernest. "The Pentathlon," *Journal of Hellenic Studies*, Vol. 2 (1881), pp. 217–221.
Pihkala, L. "The System of the Pentathlon," in *Festshrift C. Diem* (Frankfurt-Vienna), 1962, pp. 82–87.
Sweet Waldo. "A New Proposal for Scoring the Greek Pentathlon," *Zeitschrift für Papyrologie und Epigraphik*, Vol. 50 (1983), pp. 287–290.

Discus

Gardiner, E.N. "Throwing the Diskos," *Journal of Hellenic Studies* 27 (1907), pp. 1–36.

Long Jump

Ackerman, A.S.E., et al., "The Long Jump in Ancient Greece," *Notes and Queries* 117 (1936), pp. 47–102.
Barney, R.K. "The Ancient Greek Pentathlon Jump: A Preliminary Reinterpretive Examination," in *Philosophy, Theology and History of Sport and of Physical Activity*, Book 8, published by Symposia Specialists, Miami, FL (1978), pp. 279–288.

200 Bibliography

Gardiner, E.N. "Further Notes on the Greek Jump," *The Journal of Hellenic Studies*, Vol. 24 (1904), pp. 179–194.

_____. "Phayllos and His Record Jump," *Journal of Hellenic Studies* 24 (1904), pp. 70–80.

Harris, H.A. "An Olympic Epigram: The Athletic Feats of Phaÿllos, *Greece and Rome*, Vol. 7, No. 1 (March 1960), pp. 3–8.

Hyde, W.W. "The Pentathlon Jump," *The American Journal of Philology*, Vol. 59, No. 4 (1938), pp. 405–417.

Lee, Hugh M. "The Halma: A Running or Standing Jump," pp. 153–165, in Gerald P. Schuaus and Stephen R. Wenn, eds., *Onward to the Olympics: Historical Perspectives on the Olympic Games*: Toronto: Laurier Press, 2007.

Javelin

Borthwick, E.K. "The Gymnasium of Bromius: A Note on Dionysius Chalcus, Fr. 3," *The Journal of Hellenic Studies*, Vol. 84, 1964, pp. 49–53.

Ellsworth, James D. "Pindar's Pythian 1.44: Agwnos Balien ecw, a New Suggestion," *The American Journal of Philology*, Vol. 94, No. 3 (Autumn 1973), pp. 293–296.

Gardiner, E.N. "Throwing the Javelin," *Journal of Hellenic Studies*, Vol. 27 (1907), pp. 249–270.

Harris, H.A. "Greek Javelin Throwing," *Greece and Rome*, 2nd series, Vol. 10, No. 1 (March 1963), pp. 26–36.

Lee, H.M. "The Tepma and the Javelin in Pindar, *Journal of Hellenic Studies*, Vol. 96 (1976), pp. 70–79.

Segal, C.P. "Two Agonistic Problems in Pindar, Nemean 7.70–4 and Pythian 1.42–45," *Greece, Rome and Byzantine Studies* 9 (1968), pp. 31–45.

Running

Crowther, Nigel B. "The Finish of the Greek Foot-Race," *Nikephoros*, Vol. 12 (1999), pp. 131–142.

_____. "Number of Contestants in Greek Athletic Contests," *Nikephoros*, Vol. 6 (1993), pp. 39–53.

Gardiner, E.N. "Notes on the Greek Foot Race," *The Journal of Hellenic Studies*, Vol. 23 (1903), pp. 261–291.

Kyle, Donald G. "Philostratus, Repêchage, Running and Wrestling: The Greek Pentathlon Again," *Journal of Sport History*, Vol. 22, No. 1 (Spring 1995), pp. 60–65.

Miller, Stephen G. "Turns and Lanes in the Ancient Stadium," *American Journal of Archaeology*, Vol. 84 (1980), pp. 159–167.

Romano, David G. "The Ancient Stadium: Athletics and Arete," *The Ancient World*, 7 Nos. 1 and 2 (1983), pp. 9–16.

Wrestling

Kyle, Donald G. "Philostratus, Repêchage, Running and Wrestling: The Greek Pentathlon Again," *Journal of Sport History*, Vol. 22, No. 1 (Spring 1995), pp. 60–65.

Lee, H.M. "Wrestling in the Repêchage of the Ancient Pentathlon," *Journal of Sport History*, Vol. 20 (1991), pp. 277–79.

Other Pentathlon Issues

Albanidis, Evangelos, and Sotirios Giatsis. "Athletic Games in Thrace During the Imperial Era," *Nikephoros*, Vol. 20 (2007), p. 183.

Barney, Robert Knight. "Criticisms of Segals's Interpretation of the Ancient Greek Pentathlon," in *The Third Canadian Symposium for the History of Sport and Physical Education*. Dalhousie (1974), 19.

Harris, H.A. "Notes on Three Athletic Inscriptions," *Journal of Hellenic Studies*, Vol. 82 (1962), pp.19–24.

Jackson, Donald F. "Philostratos and the Pentathlon," *Journal of Hellenic Studies*, Vol. 111 (1991), pp. 178–181.

Kyle, Donald G. "E. Norman Gardiner: Historian of Ancient Sport," *International Journal of the History of Sport*, Vol. 8, No. 1 (1991), pp. 28–55.

Maróti, Egon, and Maróti, György. "Zur Frage des Pentathlon-Sieges," *Nikephoros*, Vol. 6 (1993), pp. 53–59.

Merkelbach, Reinhold. "Der Fünfkämpfer Nikoladas," *Zeitschrift für Papyrologie und Epigraphik*, Bd. 67 (1987), pp. 293–295.

Miller, Stephen G. "The Pentathlon for Boys at Nemea," *California Studies in Classical Antiquity*, Vol. 8 (1975), pp. 199–201.

Paleologos Cleanthis. Legends of Olympia 6 (series), "Philombrotos of Sparta the Pentathlist," *Olympic Review* (1974), No. 74, pp. 39–43.
Paleologos Cleanthis. Legends of Olympia 9 (series), "Hysmon of Elis Pentathlist," *Olympic Review* No. 80 (1974), pp. 358–362.
Peiser, Benny. "The Crime of Hippias of Elis: Zur Kontroverse un die Olympionokenliste," *Stadion*, Vol. 16 (1990), pp. 37–65.
Schrodt, Barbara. "Sports in the Byzantine Empire," *Journal of Sport History*, Vol. 9, No. 3 (1981), pp. 40–59.
Tracy, Stephen V., and Christian Habicht. "New and Old Panathenaic Victor Lists," *Hesperia*, Vol. 60, No. 2 (April–June 1991), pp. 187–236.
Waddell, Gene. "The Greek Pentathlon," *Greek Vases in the J. Paul Getty Museum*, Santa Monica, CA, Vol. 5 (1990), pp. 99–106.
Young, David C. "First with the Most: Greek Athletic Records and 'Specialization,'" *Nikephoros* 9 (1996), pp. 175–197.

Journal Articles—General

Alexander, Christine. "Exhibition Illustrating Greek Athletics," *The Metropolitan Museum of Art Bulletin*, Vol. 20, No. 2, (February 1925), pp. 45–46.
Brothwick, E.K. "The Gymnasium of Bromius," *Journal of Hellenic Studies*, Vol. 84 (1968), pp. 49–53.
Casson, Lionel. "The Way Things Were at the First Olympics," *Smithsonian*, Vol. 15, No. 3 (June 1984), pp. 64–73.
Christesen, Paul. "The Transformation of Athletics in 6th Century Greece," pp. 59–68, in Gerald P. Schuaus and Stephen R. Wenn, eds., *Onward to the Olympics: Historical Perspectives on the Olympic Games*. Toronto: Laurier Press, 2007.
Crowther, Nigel B. "The Ancient Olympic Games Through the Centuries," pp. 3–13, in Gerald P. Schuaus and Stephen R Wenn, eds., *Onward to the Olympics: Historical Perspectives on the Olympic Games*. Toronto: Laurier Press, 2007.
_____. "Athlete and State: Qualifying for the Olympic Games in Ancient Greece," *Journal of Sport History*, Vol. 23, No. 1 (Spring 1996), pp. 34–43.
_____. "Number of Contestants in Greek Athletic Contests," *Nikephoros*, Vol. 6 (1993), pp. 39–53.
_____. "The Olympic Training Period," *Nikephoros*, Vol. 4 (1991), pp. 161–166.
_____. "Resolving an Impasse: Draws, Dead Heats and Similar Decisions in Greek Athletics," *Nikephoros*, Vol. 13 (2000), pp. 125–140.
_____. "Rounds and Byes in Greek Athletics," *Stadion*, Vol. 65, No. 1 (1992), pp. 68–74.
_____. "Victories Without Competition in the Greek Games," *Nikephoros*, Vol. 14 (2001), pp. 29–44.
Evjen, Harold D. "The Origins and Functions of Formal Athletic Competition in the Ancient World," *Proceedings of an International Symposium on the Olympic Games* (Coulson, William and Kyrieleis, Helmut, eds.), Athens, 1992.
Forbes, Clarence A. "Crime and Punishment in Greek Athletics," *The Classical Journal*, Vol. 47, No. 5 (February 1952), pp. 169–203.
Kyle, Donald G. "The First Hundred Olympiads: A Process of Decline or Democratization?" *Nikephoros*, Vol. 10 (1997), pp. 53–75.
Lee, Hugh M. "Some Changes in the Olympic Program and Schedule," *Proceedings of an International Symposium on the Olympic Games* (Coulson, William and Kyrieleis, Helmut eds.), Athens, 1992.
Mildner, Elizabeth S. "A Day in a Greek Gymnasium," *The American Journal of Nursing*, Vol. 30, No. 3 (March 1920), pp. 279–282.
Moretti, Luigi. "Nuova supplement al catalogo degli Olympionikai," *Proceedings of an International Symposium on the Olympic Games* (Coulson, William and Kyrieleis, Helmut eds.), Athens, 1992.
Papalas, Anthony J. "Boy Athletes in Ancient Greece," *Stadion*, Vol. 17, No. 2 (1991), pp. 165–192.
Pissanos, Paul. *448 BC Olympiad*, a Greek-English magazine with script to accompany DVD of same title, 2003.
Pleket, H.W. "Games, Prizes, Athletes and Ideology: Some Aspects of the History of Sport in the Greco–Roman World," *Stadion*, Vol. 1, No. 1 (1975), pp. 48–89.

_____. "Mass-sport and Local Infrastructure in the Greek Cities of Roman Asia Minor," *Stadion*, Vol. 24, No. 1 (1998), pp. 151–172.

_____. "The Participants in the Ancient Olympic Games: Social Background and Mentality," *Proceedings of an International Symposium on the Olympic Games* (Coulson, William and Kyrieleis, Helmut, eds.), Athens, 1992.

_____. "Some Aspects of the History of Athletic Guilds," *Zeitschrift für Papyrologie und Epigraphik*, Vol. 10 (1973), pp. 197–227.

Roller, Lynn E. "Funeral Games for Historical Persons," *Stadion*, Vol. 7, 1981, pp. 1–18.

Tod, M.N., "Greek Record Keeping and Record Breaking," *Classical Quarterly*, Vol. 43 (1949), pp. 105–112.

Tracy, Stephen V. "The Panathenaic Festival and Games: An Epigraphic Inquiry," *Nikephoros*, Vol. 4 (1991), pp. 133–53.

Young, David C. "Greece and the Origins of the Modern Olympic Games," *Proceedings of an International Symposium on the Olympic Games* (Coulson, William and Kyrieleis, Helmut, eds.), Athens, 1992.

Dissertation

Weir, R.G.A. "Roman Delphi and the Pythian Games," Ph.D. dissertation, Princeton University, 1998, pp. 465–492.

Modern Books on Track and Field

Doherty, J. Kenneth. *Track and Field Omnibook*. Los Altos, CA: Tafnews, 1975.

McNab, Tom. "The Ancient Pentathlon," *Decathlon*. London: British Amateur Athletic Board, 1972, p. 6.

Zarnowski, Frank. "The Ancient Greek Pentathlon," *The Decathlon: A Colorful History of Track and Field's Most Challenging Event*. Champaign, IL: Leisure Press, 1989.

_____. *How to Organize and Run a Decathlon*. Tucson: USTFF, 1972.

Index